Myth, Memory, and the Making of the American Landscape

Florida A&M University, Tallahassee
Florida Atlantic University, Boca Raton
Florida Gulf Coast University, Ft. Myers
Florida International University, Miami
Florida State University, Tallahassee
University of Central Florida, Orlando
University of Florida, Gainesville
University of North Florida, Jacksonville
University of South Florida, Tampa
University of West Florida, Pensacola

Myth, Memory, and the
Making of the American Landscape

Edited by Paul A. Shackel

University Press of Florida

Gainesville · Tallahassee · Tampa · Boca Raton

Pensacola · Orlando · Miami · Jacksonville · Ft. Myers

Library of Congress Cataloging-in-Publication Data
Myth, memory, and the making of the American landscape / edited
by Paul A. Shackel
p. cm.
Includes bibliographical references and index.
ISBN 0-8130-2104-9 (alk. paper)
1. Historic sites—United States. 2. Monuments—United States.
3. United States—Antiquities. 4. Memory—Social aspects—United
States. 5. Myth—Social aspects—United States. 6. National characteristics, American. 7. Archaeology and history—United States.
8. United States—History—Philosophy. I. Shackel, Paul A.
E159 .M97 2001
973—dc21   2001027596

The University Press of Florida is the scholarly publishing agency
for the State University System of Florida, comprising Florida A&M
University, Florida Atlantic University, Florida Gulf Coast University,
Florida International University, Florida State University, University of
Central Florida, University of Florida, University of North Florida,
University of South Florida, and University of West Florida.

University Press of Florida
15 Northwest 15th Street
Gainesville, FL 32611–2079
http://www.upf.com

For my Historical Archaeology classes

Contents

Figures

Foreword

Edward T. Linenthal

In his book *Rewriting the Soul: Multiple Personalities and the Sciences of Memory,* Ian Hacking (1995:5) observed that "we have learned how to replace the soul with knowledge, with science. Hence spiritual battles are fought, not on the explicit ground of the soul, but on the terrain of memory, where we suppose that there is such a thing as knowledge to be had." That various terrains of memory have become sites where spiritual battles are fought seems self-evident, but I suspect most of us do not characterize interpretive conflicts at historic sites in quite this fashion.

However, doesn't it make sense? Aren't the vigorous debates at the nation's battlefields over the meaning of sacrifice, or over the adequacy of representation of black Union troops in the Civil War, or over the transformation of shrines into historic sites—at the Little Bighorn Battlefield National Monument, for example—really debates about the spirit of the nation, the ineffable stuff that makes up who and what we were, have become, and want to be?

Museum exhibits, memorials, and historic sites are increasingly vibrant arenas for debates over issues of national identity, and the essays in this book offer a rich variety of case studies examining the contested landscape of American national memory. If there are readers who still think about the past as a storehouse of facts, as a fixed resource, with a single message to be retrieved by the historian, they will be quickly disabused of this notion. Rather, these essays make clear what the distinguished historian Carl Becker observed in his classic book *Everyman His Own Historian* (1935:253–54), that history is "an unstable pattern of remembered things redesigned and newly colored to suit the convenience of those who make use of it."

These essays reveal the many kinds of debates over the construction of a remembered past from this unstable pattern of remembered things. Comfortable and comforting mythic pasts are created at Jamestown and

Acadia; the heroic drama of battle conceals other stories and voices at Antietam, Arlington, and Camden Yards; shameful stories formerly consigned to oblivion at Manzanar and Wounded Knee are now excavated, and attempts to transform the national narrative to locate them appropriately are underway. The politics of location and authenticity are apparent in the fascinating stories of *The Woman Movement* Memorial, George Washington's birthplace, and the Lincoln log cabin; the evolution of the meaning of a monument is evident in the story of the Robert Gould Shaw memorial, now more popularly known as the Fifty-Fourth Massachusetts memorial.

Notice that these processes of construction, of concealment, of excavation, of contestation, of evolution, reveal the dynamism of these terrains of memory. The meaning of such places is often a variable one, never frozen for long. Their lives move in two directions. Like memorials to World War I, some will become part of what Jay Winter (1995:98) calls a "trajectory of decomposition, a passage from the active to the inert," while others will emerge from the buried past to challenge us with their messages.

Ultimately, the vibrant activity at our nation's memory terrains reveals more about our own labors of shaping cultural identity than about getting the past "just right." These essays are part of an important literature examining the history of interpretation and the biography of historic sites. We should be thankful for their contribution.

References

Becker, Carl
 1935   *Everyman His Own Historian.* F. S. Crofts, New York.
Hacking, Ian
 1995   *Rewriting the Soul: Multiple Personalities and the Sciences of Memory.* Princeton University Press, Princeton, New Jersey.
Winter, Jay
 1995   *Sites of Memory, Sites of Mourning: The Great War in European Cultural History.* Cambridge University Press, Cambridge, England.

Acknowledgments

I teach historical archaeology at the graduate and undergraduate levels at the University of Maryland in an Applied Anthropology Program, and my classes inspired me to compile this volume. In my historical archaeology course we examine the dynamic meanings and uses of materials culture; one of the class assignments consists of doing a contextual analysis of a nationally significant object or landscape. Students explore how meanings change through time, and they observe how different groups may have contrasting meanings for the same object. The ideas and research that came out of these evening seminars were fascinating and profound. The students' investigations generated an excitement that could not be contained within the confines of Woods Hall.

I thought it would be a fascinating project to use this same theme, providing a contextual analysis of nationally significant sites and/or objects and exploring their changing and various meanings. The authors of the essays in the volume have spent considerable time examining the issues that they present, and I appreciate their willingness to participate here. Their conclusions have important social and political relevance to our contemporary society and allow us to examine the way we view myth and memory on the American landscape. I appreciate the authors for contributing to this volume. I hope their impressive work inspires other professionals and students in anthropology, public history, and American studies who are addressing these same issues.

I am delighted and relieved that compiling this book was a rather painless process. There are several people whom I would like to thank for their help and guidance along the way. I appreciate the encouragement and enthusiasm provided to me by Meredith Morris-Babb. She skillfully helped to shepherd this volume through the publication process. I also appreciate the hard work and in-depth reviews provided to me from Paul Mullins and James Delle. Their helpful insights have improved the quality of this volume, and I am grateful for their input. I am also indebted to Edward Linenthal for providing review comments on the volume and for writing the foreword. He used precious time to help with the manuscript while he was also writing a very important book on the Oklahoma City bombing. I also appreciate the suggestions and comments made by Paul Mullins, James Delle, Edward Linenthal, Erika K. Martin Seibert, and Matthew Palus to help improve the introduction to this book. Matthew Palus helped to compile the selected bibliography. I also appreciate the support of and love from Barbara Little throughout the production of this book.

Introduction: The Making of the American Landscape

Paul A. Shackel

Introduction

The goal of this collection of essays is to show the dynamic nature of creating meanings—past and present—of nationally significant sites and symbols on the American landscape. Whether internally coherent, or contradictory to the dominant view, memories validate the holders' version of the past by sanitizing an event or glamorizing a group. Memories can be about a moment in time, such as a protest or a riot, or they can be about a longer-term event, such as a war or a social movement. Memories may serve individual or collective experiences. Sometimes there are competing interests that struggle to create a specific memory of national heritage. Other times people simply ignore dominant histories altogether and do not contest them on any tangible level. Understanding how and why some groups tend to remember a particular past, while others forget or ignore a past, is an important issue for critically evaluating and understanding the development and meaning of the American landscape.

The systematic study of collective memory was first introduced by Maurice Halbwachs in 1925 when he "maintained that individuals required testimony and evidence of other people to validate their interpretations of their own experiences, to provide independent confirmation (or refutation) of the content of their memories and thus confidence in their accuracy" (Thelen 1989:1122). He noted that people need other people as a second reference in order to establish subjectivity and create recollection. As a group, people decide which experiences to collectively remember and which ones to forget, as well as how to interpret these experiences.

People develop a collective memory by molding, shaping, and agreeing upon what to remember.

Since the 1980s, scholars have increasingly explored the interrelationship between history and memory and its use in Western culture. In archaeology some of the important scholarship that critically evaluates the production of history includes that written by Trigger (1989), Leone et al. (1987), and Shanks and Tilley (1987). These works evaluate the management and use of prehistoric and historic resources. They view the production of historical consciousness as an outcome of the struggle between groups.

In much the same way, the authors in this book—public historians and archaeologists—rely on some of the more influential works in public history. For instance, the *Journal of American History* in 1989 dedicated an entire issue to the topic of memory. The subject has also appeared with increasing frequency in *Public Historian* (see for instance, Glassberg 1996:7–23; and the comments by Lowenthal 1997:31–39; Frisch 1997: 41–43; Linenthal 1997:45–47; Kammen 1997b:49–52; Shopes 1997:53–56; Blatti 1997:57–60; Archibald 1997:61–64; Franco 1997:65–67). In cultural anthropology Handler and Gable's *The New History in an Old Museum* (1997) serves as an excellent example of deconstructing the production of history in a museum like Williamsburg's.

While the study of memory is not new, there is a difference between the scholarship a half century ago (see for instance Smith 1950; Miller 1953), and the recent work that has been influenced by the writings of David Lowenthal (1985), Michael Frisch (1990), David Glassberg (1990), Michael Kammen (1991), John Bodner (1992), and Edward Linenthal (1993). No longer can we assume that all groups, and all members of the same group, understand the past in the same way. The same historical and material representation may have divergent meanings to different audiences (Glassberg 1996:9–10; Lowenthal 1985). For some groups, history may be important to justify a particular agenda, while others do not care to create their own history.

The essays in this book focus on how individual and collective memories develop through dialogue. The individual memory is closely linked to a community's collective memory, and there is sometimes a struggle to create or subvert a past by various competing interest groups (see, for instance, Peterson 1994; Neustadt and May 1986). Different versions of the past are communicated through various institutions, including schools, amusements, art and literature, government ceremonies, families and friends, and landscape features that are designated as historical.

Therefore, collective memory does not rely solely on professional historical scholarship, but it also takes into account the various individuals and institutions that affect and influence the versions of histories that have become part of the collective memory.

The authors in this book show how groups create and control the collective national memory of revered sacred sites and objects. Different group agendas may clash, causing the established collective memories to be continuously in flux. While some subordinate groups can subvert the dominant memory, other groups compromise and become part of a multivocal history. Others fail to have their story remembered, while others do not care to have their history recognized. The tension between and within groups who struggle for control over the collective public memory is ongoing, since the political stakes are high. Those who control the past have the ability to command social and political events in the present and the future.

Control over the uses and meanings of material culture can be accomplished in several ways. Memory can be about forgetting a past, creating and reinforcing patriotism, and developing a sense of nostalgia to legitimize a heritage. These categories, although not complete, serve as an organizational point for this book, although many of the chapters can easily fit into more than one section. While we recognize that objects and landscapes have different meanings to different people at different times, the essays demonstrate how the memories associated with highly visible objects are always being constructed, changed, challenged, or ignored.

An Exclusionary Past

Memories can be public as well as private, and they serve to legitimize the past and the present. Public history exhibits, monuments, statues, artifacts, national historic parks, commemorations, and celebrations can foster the myths that create a common history that allows for divergent groups to find a common bond. Therefore, a shared history and the creation of community become a very complex set of interactions. Elements of the past remembered in common, as well as elements of the past forgotten in common, are essential for group cohesion (Glassberg 1996:13).

While collective memory can be about forgetting a past, it often comes at the expense of a subordinate group. Those who are excluded may try to subvert the meaning of the past, or they may strive for more representation in the form of a more pluralistic past. Sometimes they may not even call attention to their absence in the collective memory. When we reflect on the traditional meanings associated with a collective national memory, it has focused on elites and traditional heroes. The perception is that American history is linear and straightforward. This uncomplicated story occurs only when we leave "others" out of the picture. This "sacred story with strong nationalist overtones . . . derived much of its coherence from the groups it ignored or dismissed" (Leff 1995:833; also see Nash et al. 1998:100). Those who disagree with a multicultural history have claimed that "it is difficult . . . to see how the subjects of the new [social] history can be accommodated in any single framework, let alone a national and political one. . . . How can all these groups, each cherishing its uniqueness and its claim to sovereign attention, be mainstreamed into a single, coherent, integrated history?" (quoted in Nash et al. 1998:100–1).

We often find that while accounts of ordinary people and subaltern groups do not necessarily find their way into official accounts, they do become part of the private memory (see, for instance, Wachtel 1986:2–11). While many federally funded museums extol the glories of economic and social progress as a result of industry, many members of the working class view the preservation of old buildings and ruins as an attempt to save a degrading phase of human history. Robert Vogel of the Smithsonian Institution notes: "The dirt, noise, bad smell, hard labor and other forms of exploitation associated with these kinds of places make preservation [of industrial sites] ludicrous. 'Preserve a steel mill?' people say, 'It killed my father. Who wants to preserve that?'" (Lowenthal 1985:403). Therefore, while there are individual dissenting views on the true benefits of industrialization, the federal government remains strong in propping up the idea of the glories of industrial progress at national parks such as Lowell and Saugus in Massachusetts, Hopewell and Steam Town in Pennsylvania, and Harpers Ferry in West Virginia.

Collective memory can be challenged, as competing groups celebrate contrasting values. Whether the challenge to the collective memory succeeds depends upon the political strength and perseverance of the subordinate group. Sometimes challenging the entrenched views of powerful institutions such as the federal government can be an overwhelming task. Such is the case of the Lakota's struggle to take control of their history at Wounded Knee (see Gail Brown's essay on Wounded Knee, chapter 5). Their history of the event has been overlooked, because it serves Euro-American needs to dehumanize the Lakota and justify conquest. Recently, the site became a symbol for American Indian sovereignty and rebirth, while Euro-Americans view it as a place of rebellion and unlawfulness.

Many local Lakotas fear losing control of their past if the site is commemorated as a National Historic Site.

Understanding the constructed nature of landscapes is important for understanding how we remember our past. At sacred American sites like Jamestown, the story often focuses on the wealthy, and alternative histories are often forgotten. In another example, the views and histories of the Appalachian people living in the Shenandoah Valley have also been intentionally forgotten by the federal government (see "Of Saints and Sinners," chapter 1, by Audrey Horning). In the 1930s the federal government condemned lands and displaced many communities to make Shenandoah National Park. The government created a history that described these lands as historically pristine and claimed that destiny dictated that the lands should be used as a recreational area for those living in urban areas like Washington, D.C. By contrast, historical and archaeological surveys identify displaced people proud of their early heritage and trying to reestablish their voice in the history of the area.

Creating a linear history and excluding others is also evident at Manassas National Battlefield Park. There, the National Park Service (NPS) commemorates two Confederate victories but has selectively ignored the histories associated with some of the people who once lived within the current park boundaries (see Erika Martin Seibert's "The Third Battle of Manassas," chapter 3). In particular, not only have the stories of agriculturalists and African-Americans been ignored, but also any traces of their existence after the Civil War have been removed from the landscape by the NPS. Archaeology at these sites is beginning to promote these previously ignored histories.

In many cases the subaltern group has a choice. It can subscribe to the dominant interpretation, ignore the dominant view, or fight for representation in the public memory. In the case of *The Woman Movement,* women fought to have representation in the Capitol by honoring three prominent advocates of the women's movement (see Courtney Workman's "*The Woman Movement,*" chapter 2 herein). While the statue was presented and displayed in the U.S. Capitol in the early 1920s, the Capitol architect soon moved it to a basement closet and later to the crypt. From the 1920s, many women fought to have the statue again displayed in the Capitol. They finally won the right in the 1990s to have it on display, although this move appears to be temporary.

In the case of Manzanar National Historic Site, Japanese-Americans continue to fight for the official memory to recognize the atrocities practiced against them by the U.S. government (see "Remembering a Japanese-American Concentration Camp," chapter 4, by Janice L. Dubel). During World War II the federal government placed Japanese-Americans living on the West Coast in concentration camps. At the same time that Japanese-Americans insist on making this event part of the national collective memory, some American groups are fighting to suppress the commemoration of this site. The patriotic groups argue that since the Japanese were our enemy during the war, the federal government was justified in imprisoning them and placing them under surveillance. Although a National Historic Site exists, the federal government provides virtually no money for upkeep and interpretation.

Commemoration and the Making of a Patriotic Past

Another way to control the past is to create a public memory that commemorates a patriotic past. The official expression, sponsored by the federal government, is concerned with promoting and preserving the ideals of cultural leaders and authorities, developing social unity, and maintaining the status quo. This view interprets the past and present reality in a way that helps to reduce competing interests (Bodner 1992:13). Government agencies often advance the notion of "community of the nation while suppressing authentic local group memories and collective identities" (Glassberg 1996:12). John Bodner (1992:15) notes:

> Adherents to official and vernacular interests demonstrate conflicting obsessions. Cultural leaders orchestrate commemorative events to calm anxiety about change or political events, eliminate citizens' indifference toward official concerns, promote exemplary patterns of citizen behavior, and stress citizen duties over rights. They feel the need to do this because of the existence of social contradictions, alternative views, and indifference that perpetuate fears of societal dissolution and unregulated political behavior.

While groups may strive to change the official meanings of the past, they do not always succeed, as the notions of patriotism and commemoration can supercede any ideas about a pluralistic past. For instance, the *Enola Gay* exhibit at the Smithsonian Institution is an excellent example of how the government suppressed an alternative view on the grounds that it was not patriotic. The original plans for the exhibit ran counter to the collective memory of powerful lobby groups, and reactions to it showed the strain of our country's political culture (see Neil Harris et al., "History and the Public" 1995:1029–1144).

In January 1994, the Smithsonian made public a draft of the institution's *Enola Gay* exhibit. The exhibit plans showed the effects of the bomb, displaying pictures of the victims at "ground zero," and questioned the use of the bomb (Cornell 1994). Veteran groups like the Veterans of Foreign Wars and the American Legion, and a lobbying organization for the Air Force, the Air Force Association, felt that the Smithsonian Institution had bowed to political correctness; they felt the exhibit was pro-Japanese (Harwit 1996:245).

These lobby groups successfully got the attention of politicians. Congressman Sam Johnson stated that the Smithsonian was "disregarding history in order to promote their own agenda." He also noted that it was important to teach our children what was "good about America . . . and reflect the values on which this great country is based" (Johnson 1995). Political pressure from Congress, the president, the vice president, the Senate majority leader, the speaker of the House, the chief justice of the Supreme Court, and the Smithsonian Board of Regents reduced the exhibit to a story about the crew of the *Enola Gay* and the necessity of dropping the bomb in order to save numerous lives (Noble 1995:xiii; Lifton and Mitchell 1995:296). The Smithsonian omitted the story of the horrors associated with the event.

As implied by Congressman Johnson's statement, American history produces obedient, patriotic citizens. "The argument," notes Michael Frisch (1989:1153), "has traveled a long way from its humanistic origins, arriving at a point where education and indoctrination—cultural and political—seem almost indistinguishable." The *Enola Gay* exhibit heightens our awareness of how histories are remembered, forgotten, and created. The exhibit makes explicit the role of public history and the function interest groups play in creating collective memories in a very contentious arena.

While collective memories can be challenged by subordinate groups, the ideas of the dominant group must be supported through ceremonies and commemorations if its ideas and histories are to last. One of the most popular commemorative events in American history is the creation and reinterpretation of American Civil War battlefields and landscapes. The struggle over which memory the nation should celebrate was being settled by the end of Reconstruction, and it solidified through the early and mid–twentieth century. As David Blight (1989:1159) writes: "Historical memory . . . was not merely an entity altered by the passage of time; it was the prize in a struggle between rival versions of the past, a question of will, of power, of persuasion. The historical memory of any transforming or controversial event emerges from cultural and political competition, from the choice to confront the past and to debate and manipulate its meaning."

From the late nineteenth century through most of the twentieth century, African-American representation in the war became rather limited in American literature. Southern whites gained tremendous political and social power after Reconstruction, and they developed a Southern patriotic past that could overcome historical humiliation. They created a glorious past of honor and dedication to a cause, excluding African-Americans from the story. African-Americans' participation in the Civil War vanished from the American consciousness (Aaron 1973:332–33). "Slavery, the war's deepest cause, and black freedom, the war's most fundamental result, remain the most conspicuous missing elements in the American literature inspired by the Civil War" (Blight 1989:1176).

Memorialization helped to create the idea of a patriotic past. Both the North and the South constructed monuments after the Civil War that commemorate the courage and valor of their heroes. In the case of the post-Reconstruction South, Southerners increasingly memorialized their participation in the war. With the aim of rewriting the histories of the Reconstruction era, the United Daughters of the Confederacy along with the Sons of the Confederacy constructed a faithful-slave monument in Harpers Ferry. In fact, the metaphor of the slave fighting for the South persists today. For instance, a new exhibit at the Tennessee Civil War Museum in Chattanooga claims that more than 35,000 African-Americans fought in the Confederate Army. It's an estimate that James McPherson (1999), a Civil War historian and Pulitzer Prize winner, calls absurd.

Since there are many views of the past, the decision to commemorate a particular patriotic moment in America's history can be highly contentious. The NPS decision to freeze or restore a battlefield landscape is a major part of this memorialization process. For instance, the NPS agreement to restore the landscape at Antietam National Battlefield to the eve of this Civil War battle is highly controversial (see Martha Temkin, "Freeze-Frame, September 17, 1862," chapter 6). Freezing can effectively silence the histories that came before and after the battle. The process can also damage significant cultural resources belonging to other eras and to other cultural groups if they are removed to make the landscape conform to the plan. Perhaps time-freezing the battlefield to the day before the Battle of Antietam is a way for the NPS to quell sectional strife by not overtly creating a landscape that memorializes a Union victory.

The creation of the Robert Gould Shaw Memorial on the Boston Common is another effort to reinforce a patriotic heritage, but in a very different way (see Paul A. Shackel, chapter 7, "The Robert Gould Shaw Memorial"). Unveiled in 1897, the monument shows Colonel Shaw riding above his African-American troops of the Fifty-Fourth Massachusetts. While the monument explicitly conveys the social Darwinian ideals of racial hierarchy popular during the era, its meaning became coopted by the African-American community in the late twentieth century. In 1997, during the 100th anniversary of its unveiling, the statue was praised by many African-American national figures. It was used to highlight and commemorate the deeds of the Fifty-Fourth Massachusetts Volunteer Infantry. The memory of Robert Gould Shaw played a significantly diminished role, compared to a century earlier. The monument has become a statue that celebrates African-American honor, glory, and participation in the Civil War.

Some monuments and landscapes do allow for the various voices to be heard, and so the space can anchor multiple identities. Such is the case at the Arlington National Cemetery and the Robert E. Lee Memorial (see "Buried in the Rose Garden" by Laurie Burgess, chapter 8). The grounds surrounding Robert E. Lee's mansion became the burying ground for the Union dead beginning in 1864. It is now a burial ground for all "patriotic" Americans, although the degree of its inclusiveness has been contested over the years. The NPS continues to interpret the Arlington House as Lee's family residence. Here divergent histories of the North and South create two very different patriotic pasts at this single spot.

Nostalgia and the Legitimation of American Heritage

Another way to create memory is to develop a sense of heritage, a phenomenon that took a long time in America. Citizens of the early American Republic resisted the development of an American collective memory and frowned upon the commemoration of a sacred past. Adherence to republican values in the early nineteenth century produced tensions between democracy and tradition. John Quincy Adams noted: "Democracy has no monuments. It strikes no medals. It bears the head of no man on a coin" (Everett 1879:38). In the antebellum era, Americans saw the United States as a country with a future rather than a glorious past worth commemoration. They believed in the value of succeeding without patronage or family influence. Emerson (Lowenthal 1997:35) wrote that Americans were "emancipated from history, happily bereft of ancestry, untouched and undefiled by the usual inheritances of family and race."

Because of the resistance to creating an American heritage, large-scale commemoration activities began slowly, and only after the middle of the nineteenth century. Women became the primary custodians of American heritage, and they took pride in demonstrating their patriotism for America's past. The Mount Vernon's Ladies Association (1856) and the Ladies' Hermitage Association (1889) are important early preservation groups involved in the American historic preservation movement. Those who did not have strict ancestral roots could join other groups, like the Patriotic League of the Revolution formed in 1894. The League's goal was to "create and promote interest in all matters pertaining to American history, to collect and preserve relics of the period of the American Revolution, and to foster patriotism" (Kammen 1991:267).

Until the 1890s the U.S. government did little to assist historic preservation or to create a national collective memory. From 1880 through 1886, legislators introduced eight bills to Congress to preserve historic lands, but none were enacted. In the 1890s Congress finally authorized the establishment of five Civil War battlefields as national military parks to be administered by the Defense Department—Chickamauga, Antietam, Shiloh, Gettysburg, and Vicksburg. Several Revolutionary War sites were also added. By 1906, protection became available for prehistoric ruins, with the establishment of the Antiquities Act.

This national movement helped to develop and foster a collective memory and national heritage. Heritage creates a useable past, and it generates a precedent that serves our present needs. We know that people have used heritage to control the past and the present for at least as long as there has been writing. More recently the political uses of heritage have been made very explicit within Western culture. We live in a society that has an unquenchable thirst for nostalgia. Kammen (1997a:214–19) calls the creation of Americans' consciousness for historic preservation since the 1950s the "heritage phenomenon." Heritage connotes integrity, authenticity, venerability, and stability. "History explores and explains pasts grown ever more opaque over time; heritage clarifies pasts so as to infuse them with present purposes" (Lowenthal 1996:xv).

Heritage is essential for creating community and cultural continuity. A nation uses heritage to create collective memory, to look for more innocent and carefree days. We remember what we perceive as good and forget the rest. Heritage can create a national mythology based on even the smallest kernel of truth. False notions of the past may be upheld in order to create and sustain national mythology. For instance, David Lowenthal elaborates on the myth behind the founding of Londonderry. Contrary to local belief, the city was not founded by St. Columba, and the famed siege of 1689 was only a blockade. "But Derry folk dote on these founding fables all the more because they are fabulous" (Lowenthal 1996:129). The same can be seen in the creation of myth surrounding Lincoln's cabin (see chapter 12, "Abraham Lincoln's Birthplace Cabin," by Dwight Pitcaithley). In the late nineteenth century, at the beginning of the American heritage and commemoration movement, people used Lincoln's cabin as a national symbol to reinforce the Horatio Alger myth, and to commemorate a patriotic past. Although the NPS has the Lincoln cabin on display, the structure is an invention, and none of the logs have been shown to have any connection with Lincoln's home. Lincoln never lived in the cabin on display, and some of the logs may be from Jefferson Davis's cabin. Americans and many patriotic groups hold on to that symbol as authentic since it conveys the story of the humble beginnings of one of the country's most heralded leaders.

The use of heritage is also important for the creation of George Washington's birthplace home (see Joy Beasley's "Birthplace of a Chief," chapter 10). In 1930 the National Park Service created the George Washington Birthplace National Monument, but few people could agree to the exact location of the Washington home. While early archaeological excavations indicated that the area designated for commemoration was not the location of the birthplace home, the National Park Service and committee members for the commemoration ignored this information. They built a Memorial House on early outbuilding foundations. The reconstructed building bore no resemblance to a 1730s house.

Closely linked with the idea of heritage is nostalgia. Nostalgia for things that are a reminder of earlier days has replaced the early American Republic's ideals of progress and development. Nostalgia is about nurturance and stewardship. Beleaguered by loss and change, Americans remember a bygone day of economic power. They have angst about the loss of community. In a throwaway society, people are looking for something lasting (Lowenthal 1996:6). Massive migrations of the last two hundred years have also sharpened feelings of nostalgia. Tens of millions of people have sought refuge outside their native lands, fleeing hunger, violence, and hatred. Rural people have increasingly migrated to urban areas. People have been cut off from their own past, and they are increasingly seeking out their roots (Lowenthal 1996:9). Nostalgia is a way to veil disharmony and the angst of progress. In the case of the development of Baltimore's waterfront, Camden Yards, a new state-of-the-art sports facility recollects the pastoral days often associated with baseball (see Erin Donovan, "Nostalgia and Tourism," chapter 11). This nostalgic feeling ignores the fact that one of the Baltimore & Ohio Railroad's most violent strikes occurred on the same grounds as the stadium. Nostalgia takes precedence over labor history.

The development of nostalgia is also very evident in John D. Rockefeller, Jr.'s development of carriage roads on Mount Desert Island (see "Authenticity, Legitimation, and Twentieth-Century Tourism," by Matthew M. Palus, chapter 9). Rockefeller developed an extensive network of carriage roads in Acadia National Park during an era when automobiles became increasingly popular among middle-class Americans. While controlling the construction and care of the carriage roads from the 1930s, he insisted that the roads remain free of automobiles. The increasing numbers of middle-class vacationers to the island via the automobile could not access the carriage roads in secluded parts of Acadia National Park. Only Rockefeller and his wealthy neighbors could use them. The roads provided positive public relations for Rockefeller, and they created a facility for genteel recreation. The national park at Acadia has reinforced a positive image associated with John D. Rockefeller, Jr.'s construction and donation of the roads to the park.

Conclusion

Material culture in the form of statues, monuments, museums, artifacts, or landscapes may have some ascribed meanings—past and present—associated with it, and these meanings vary between individuals and interest groups. This material culture can be transformed into a sacred object when serving the goals and needs of any group.

John Gillis (1994) and Charles Maier (1993) propose that in our postnationalist era, there is a general disillusionment with the nation-state. This phenomenon has led to an emerging interest in local and family history. Glassberg (1996:16) also notes the importance of the power of agency in determining the role of individual memory. How an individual or a locale creates its own meaning of the past can reshape perceptions of national collective meaning. "Individuals and groups can envision themselves as members of a collective with a common present—and future"

(Glassberg 1998:5). Various individuals and groups can transcend barriers to be part of a collective memory with a common past, present, and future.

This point is made explicit in Timothy Breen's (1989) study of East Hampton, Long Island; he demonstrates how a community actively created its own history. He shows how individuals and groups made decisions about what history to create about their past, decisions influenced by economic development choices. Therefore, the creation of collective memories on the personal and local levels does not necessarily exclude larger issues.

Although individuals were active in creating a past in East Hampton, Kammen (1997a:51) downplays the role of agency in most situations, claiming that larger influences in a culture dominated by mass media shape the perception of ordinary folks. The battle over how collective memories develop on the national level shows some of the more visible conflicts over how we define and redefine ourselves as a nation. Many scholars (see, for instance, Nash et al. 1998:103) have noted the explicit role the government played in creating a conservative agenda in public history during the 1980s and 1990s. William Bennett and Lynne Cheney served as chairs of the National Endowment for the Humanities from the early 1980s through 1992. They discouraged funding projects that encouraged a pluralistic view of the past. They sharply curtailed any projects dealing with women, labor, or racial groups, or any project that might conflict with the national collective memory. Cheney packed the advisory council "with critics of multiculturalism and women's studies," and they rejected any proposal that seemed "vaguely left wing" (quoted in Nash et al. 1998:103).

While there was a strong movement to remove subordinate memories from our national collective memory, some minority groups struggled to have their histories remembered. The clash over the control of public history occurs at some of the most visible places on the landscape, like national monuments and national parks. They are the arenas for negotiating meanings of the past (see, for instance, Linenthal 1993; Linenthal and Engelhardt 1996; Lowenthal 1996). The making of heroic symbols on the American landscape is never static, as they are continually being negotiated and reconstructed.

References

Aaron, Daniel
1973   *The Unwritten War: American Writers and the Civil War.* Knopf, New York.

Archibald, Robert R.
1997   Memory and the Process of Public History. *Public Historian* 19(2): 61–64.

Blatti, Jo
1997   Public History as Contested Terrain: A Museum Perspective. *Public Historian* 19(2): 57–60.

Blight, David W.
1989   "For Something beyond the Battlefield": Frederick Douglass and the Struggle for the Memory of the Civil War. *Journal of American History* 75(4): 1156–78.

Bodner, John
1992   *Remaking America: Public Memory, Commemoration, and Patriotism in the Twentieth Century.* Princeton University Press, Princeton, New Jersey.

Breene, Timothy H.
1989   *Imagining the Past: East Hampton Histories.* Addison-Wesley, Reading, Massachusetts.

Cornell, J. T.
1994   War Stories at Air and Space: At Smithsonian, History Grapples with Cultural Angst. *Air Force Magazine,* April 24.

Everett, Edward
1879   *Orations and Speeches on Various Occasions.* Little, Brown, Boston.

Franco, Barbara
1997   Public History and Memory: A Museum Perspective. *Public Historian* 19(2): 65–67.

Frisch, Michael
1989   American History and the Structure of Collective Memory: A Modest Exercise in Empirical Iconography. *Journal of American History* 75(4): 1131–55.

1990   *A Shared Authority: Essays on the Craft and Meaning of Oral and Public History.* State University of New York Press, Albany.

1997   What Public History Offers, and Why It Matters. *Public Historian* 19(2): 41–43.

Gillis, John
1994   Introduction to *Commemorations: The Politics of National Identity,* edited by John Gillis, 3–24. Princeton University Press, Princeton, New Jersey.

Glassberg, David
1990 *American Historical Pageantry: The Uses of Tradition in the Early Twentieth Century.* University of North Carolina Press, Chapel Hill.
1996 Public History and the Study of Memory. *Public Historian* 18(2): 7–23.
1998 Presenting History to the Public: The Study of Memory and the Uses of the Past. Understanding the Past. *CRM* 21(11): 4–8.
Handler, Richard, and Eric Gable
1997 *The New History in an Old Museum: Creating the Past at Colonial Williamsburg.* Duke University Press, Durham, North Carolina.
Harris, Neil, Martin Harwit, Richard H. Kohn, Edward T. Linenthal, Martin J. Sherwin, David Thelen, and Thomas A. Woods
1995 History and the Public: What Can We Handle? A Round Table about History after the *Enola Gay* Controversy. *Journal of American History* 82 (3):1029–1114.
Harwit, M..
1996 *An Exhibit Denied: Lobbying the History of the* Enola Gay. Copernicus, New York.
Johnson, Sam
1995 Prepared Statement of Congressman Sam Johnson before the Senate Committee on Rules and Administration Hearing on the Smithsonian Institution: Management Guidelines for the Future. Federal News Service: Federal Information System Corp. May 18, In the News.
Kammen, Michael
1991 *Mystic Chords of Memory: The Transformation of Tradition in American Culture.* Knopf, New York.
1997a *In the Past Lane: Historical Perspectives on American Culture.* Oxford University Press, New York.
1997b Public History and the Uses of Memory. *Public Historian* 19(2): 49–52.
Leff, Mark H.
1995 Revisioning United States Political History. *American Historical Review* 100:833.
Leone, Mark P., Parker B. Potter, Jr., and Paul A. Shackel
1987 Toward a Critical Archaeology. *Current Anthropology* 28(3): 283–302.
Lifton, R. J., and G. Mitchell
1995 *Hiroshima in America: Fifty Years of Denial.* Putnam, New York.
Linenthal, Edward
1993 *Sacred Ground: Americans and Their Battlefields.* University of Illinois Press, Urbana.
1997 Problems and Promises in Public History. *Public Historian* 19(2): 45–47.
Linenthal, Edward, and Tom Engelhardt
1996 *History Wars: The* Enola Gay *and Other Battles for the American Past.* Holt, New York.

Lowenthal, David
   1985   *The Past Is a Foreign Country.* Cambridge University Press, Cambridge, England.
   1996   *Possessed by the Past: The Heritage Crusade and the Spoils of History.* Free Press, New York.
   1997   History and Memory. *Public Historian* 19(2): 31–39.
Maier, Charles
   1993   A Surfeit of Memory? Reflections on History, Melancholy, and Denial. *History and Memory* 5 (Fall/Winter): 136–52.
McPherson, James
   1999   A Debatable Picture of the Confederacy: Tenn. Museum Says Many Blacks Fought for South; Scholars Call Claim Bogus. *Washington Post,* December 27: A16.
Miller, Perry
   1953   *The New England Mind: From Colony to Province.* Harvard University Press, Cambridge.
Nash, Gary B., Charlotte Crabtree, and Ross E. Dunn
   1998   *History on Trial: Culture Wars and the Teaching of the Past.* Knopf, New York.
Neustadt, Richard, and Ernst May
   1986   *Thinking in Time: The Uses of History for Decision-makers.* Free Press, New York.
Noble, P.
   1995   *Judgement at the Smithsonian.* Marlowe, New York.
Peterson, Merrill
   1994   *Lincoln in American Memory.* Oxford University Press, New York.
Shanks, Michael, and Christopher Tilley
   1987   *Re-Constructing Archaeology.* Cambridge University Press, Cambridge.
Shopes, Linda
   1997   Building Bridges between Academic and Public History. *Public Historian* 19(2): 53–56.
Smith, Henry Nash
   1950   *Virgin Land: The American West as Symbol and Myth.* Harvard University Press, Cambridge.
Thelen, David
   1989   Memory and American History. *Journal of American History* 75(4): 1117–29.
Trigger, Bruce
   1989   *A History of Archaeological Thought.* Cambridge University Press, Cambridge.
Wachtel, Nathan
   1986   Memory and History, Introduction. *History and Anthropology* 2 (October): 2–11.

Part I

An Exclusionary Past

An Exclusionary Past

Remembering a particular past often means that there are those in subordinate groups who must either find strategies to exist within the dominant interpretation of the past, or struggle to get their views assimilated into the collective memory. An important concept for understanding the struggle for the control of meaning among members of subordinate groups comes from W.E.B. Du Bois. Writing during the Jim Crow era, a time when laws increasingly segregated African-Americans from white America, Du Bois (1994 [1903]:5) introduced the notion of double consciousness. He noted that African-Americans saw themselves through the eyes of others. "One ever feels his two-ness—an American, a negro; two souls, two thoughts, two unreconciled strivings; two warring ideals in one dark body, whose dogged strength alone keeps it from being torn asunder." The history of the African-American, according to Du Bois, lies in this conflict of operating in two worlds. The concept of double consciousness creates a more dynamic understanding of public memory within the context of a muted group (see also Mullins 1996, 1999; Shackel 2000). It allows us to develop frameworks for understanding material culture expressions of a subordinate group.

This section of *Myth, Memory, and the Making of the American Landscape* is about how subaltern groups survive in a state of "two-ness." They exist along with the dominant meaning, sometimes in order to seek a more pluralistic history; at other times their history is successfully subverted. For instance, how the federal government uses or ignores subaltern histories to justify their claims has varied, depending upon the public and social circumstances. In one case, the National Park Service has denigrated many of the achievements of Appalachian Americans in order to justify the government's control over the local, traditional, ancestral lands in an area now called Shenandoah National Park, as Audrey Horning discusses in chapter 1. Erika Martin Seibert in chapter 3 looks at Manassas National Battlefield Park, where African-Americans have disappeared from the battlefield landscape. The park, which commemorates two Confederate victories, has intentionally erased landscape features related to African-Americans. Interpreted is only a narrow segment of time, the Confederate victories. In this case the African-American community has been quiet and has not raised objections with the park about their lack of historical representation on the battlefield.

In another case, which Janice L. Dubel explains in chapter 4, Japanese-Americans are fighting to keep in the American consciousness their inhuman treatment in America during World War II. Even though they were American citizens, the federal government placed many West Coast Japanese-Americans in concentration camps. While some Americans feel that this action was immoral, others believe that we should never create a national historic site to remember Japanese-Americans because they are descendents of our World War II enemy.

In another public forum, American Indians have actively sought to have their story told at Wounded Knee. They fear losing control of their history if the site is made into a national park controlled by the federal government, a circumstance Gail Brown explores in chapter 5. They have been very active in expressing themselves through American Indian organizations to communicate their concerns.

The federal government is also very explicit in how it views women's achievements in a male-dominated society. As Courtney Workman explains in chapter 2, the statue commemorating the Woman Movement was presented to Congress in the 1920s. The statue, to be displayed in the Capitol, was almost immediately removed to the basement. It has taken over a half century to display it again, although its resurrection appears to be only temporary.

In all of the case studies presented in this section, Asian-Americans, women, African-Americans, displaced Appalachians, and Native Americans are seen as subordinate groups who must live in a state of "twoness." They must exist within the dominant culture, where the meaning of the landscape is controlled by a dominant group. In some cases they are reasserting the right to give their own meaning and history to sacred objects and landscapes, and in other cases they are ignoring their lack of representation.

References

Du Bois, W.E.B.
 1994 [1903] *The Souls of Black Folk*. Gramercy Books, New York.
Mullins, Paul Raymond
 1996 The Contradictions of Consumption: An Archaeology of African America and Consumer Culture, 1850–1930. Ph.D. dissertation, University of Massachusetts, Amherst.
 1999 *Race and Affluence: An Archeology of African America and Consumer Culture*. Kluwer Academic/Plenum, New York.
Shackel, Paul A.
 2000 Craft to Wage Labor: Agency and Resistance in American Historical Archaeology. In *Agency Theory in Archaeology*, edited by John Robb and Marcia-Anne Dobres, 232–46. Routledge Press, London.

Of Saints and Sinners: Mythic Landscapes of the Old and New South

Audrey J. Horning

The 1930s found many young American men gratefully toiling away at various federal relief projects throughout the nation, part of the New Deal's Civilian Conservation Corps, or CCC. In Virginia, camps of CCC "boys" labored at two new national parks—one in the Tidewater at Jamestown, where the first permanent English New World settlement was established in 1607, and the other at Shenandoah National Park in the Blue Ridge mountains. The work performed by recruits in the two parks was vastly different. At Jamestown, CCC recruits became archaeologists, spending their days wielding shovels, unearthing the physical traces of Jamestown's seventeenth-century glory (fig. 1.1). The foundations they uncovered were soon enshrined as monuments to America's English heritage, monuments long held dear by native Virginians as proof that the true roots of America lie squarely in the South. Today, the landscape on Jamestown Island remains celebratory, shadowed by the 1907 Tercentenary Monument and replete with statuary, its carefully mown fields dotted with whitewashed bricks outlining buried archaeological features—all concealing a much more complex history below ground.

While the CCC boys at Jamestown were busy unearthing the bricks, nails, and broken bottles discarded by Virginia's forefathers, their compatriots in the Blue Ridge were hastily destroying evidence of historic occupation. Recruits were tasked with eradicating the physical traces of European settlement, aiding in the creation of a "natural" park through the purchase and condemnation of more than three thousand individually owned tracts of land. Many of the five hundred or so families compelled to leave their homes in the nearly 200,000-acre Shenandoah National Park relied upon the fresh-faced CCC boys to truck away their worldly

Figure 1.1. CCC recruits excavating at Jamestown's Structure 17, a row of three brick houses constructed in the 1660s. 1935–36. (Courtesy Colonial National Historical Park.)

goods. Some witnessed the young recruits dismantle and burn their homes, while one family was forcibly evicted by CCCrs.

Although some of the newly abandoned houses in the park dated back to Virginia's golden years as the political hub of a post-Revolution nation, they too were put to the torch or consigned to decay, stripped of their useful fittings just as they had been of their human occupants. Trees—including exotic species—were planted in their place, nature to be restored from the ravages of human activity and safely viewed from the 105-mile-long Skyline Drive, wending its way along the peaks in the service of a mobile society so recently democratized by the automobile (Engle 1997, 1998; Horning 1998a, McClelland 1998). "Where else," asks one chronicler, "has the supposedly inevitable trend of civilization, toward more and more consumption of earth's resources, been so completely reversed by democratic decision on so large an area?" (Lambert 1971).

The activities of the CCC in Jamestown and in Shenandoah National Park created two equally mythic landscapes that reflect not only the perceived adversarial relationship between culture and nature, but also the dichotomy of two remembered Virginias, of two remembered Souths—the white-wigged and flower-sprigged colonial glory days versus the pellagra-ridden, barefooted, post–Civil War rural anti-idyll—particularly as encapsulated in a notional "Appalachia." Today's manicured Jamestown serves as a metaphor for the conquest and subjugation of wilderness, the wild unfamiliar New World, the American frontier, while the reforested Blue Ridge celebrates the nation's capacity to reform through civilizing the uncivilized mountaineer, through ushering a landscape back to its "natural" state—a state decreed and defined by society (fig. 1.2).

Beyond presuming a curious separation of human life from the natural world, landscape manipulation in both parks—wrought through a process of selective cultural memory—has impeded historical research and continues to affect visitor perceptions. Unremitting emphasis upon the

Figure 1.2. CCC recruits "restoring" nature in Shenandoah National Park by importing exotic trees from western national parks. 1936. (Courtesy Shenandoah National Park Archives.)

proto-American nature of Jamestown has threatened our ability to understand the actualities of its seventeenth-century past, the daily experiences of its occupants and visitors, who were far more English or Irish or Dutch or African in outlook than American, let alone Southern American. Even in the heyday of planning for the 350th anniversary, this oversimplification of the past left a sour taste in the mouth of Jamestown archaeologist John Cotter, as he lamented the way Jamestown's past had been "obscured by upwards of two hundred years of neglect and romantic musings" (Cotter 1956:1).

Emphasis upon the salvation of the "wilderness" has necessarily downplayed the cultural past in Shenandoah National Park. But is it reasonable, let alone feasible, to return a region to its "natural" state? How exactly does one define a "natural" state? The expressed aim was to return the land to its (presumably static) condition before the environmental depredations wreaked by Europeans and exacerbated by the poor farming technique of the twentieth-century mountaineer. The pasts to be forgotten were those of the hardscrabble eighteenth-century frontier settler—the antithesis of the cultured Tidewater planter—as well as the generalized poverty of the post–Civil War South. Beyond the environmentally questionable decision to "restore" nature, the notion that the land was pristine wilderness until the 1730s also implied that Native American activity was not really "cultural." Today's "natural" landscape is as much a cultural creation as were the farms of the 1930s and the stone quarries of eight thousand years ago (Horning 1998a).

Recent archaeological research in Colonial National Historical Park and Shenandoah National Park, sponsored by the National Park Service and carried out via a cooperative agreement with the Colonial Williamsburg Foundation, has confronted the issue of mythic landscapes and the false culture-nature dichotomy specifically to inform future management and interpretation of cultural resources. In a broader context, the environmental and interpretive issues raised by both projects speak to the debate over the role of national parks in a multicultural, increasingly urbanized society. What pasts do we choose to remember, and why? The research has also contributed to the ever present, yet ever changing, debate over the cultural and historical meaning of "the South." The combination of material evidence with documentary, ethnographic, and ethnohistoric sources exposes the accepted past commemorated at Jamestown and the presumed past condemned at Shenandoah National Park as cultural constructions without any firm basis in reality.

Specifically, the Jamestown Archaeological Assessment was charged with assessing cultural resources on the fifteen-hundred-acre portion of Jamestown Island maintained by the National Park Service. The project employed an interdisciplinary approach, emphasizing the relationship between human activity and environmental change. The Assessment included a reevaluation of all previously excavated materials (excavations took place in the seventeenth-century townsite from 1934 to 1941, in 1948, and between 1954 and 1956), new historical research, limited excavation in the townsite, extensive survey of the entire island, geophysical prospecting, and environmental study (Brown 1993; Edwards and Brown 1994; Horning 1998b). The Survey of Rural Mountain Settlement in Shenandoah National Park centered on locating, recording, and evaluating cultural resources in three former historic communities—Nicholson, Corbin, and Weakley Hollows—encompassing twenty-five hundred acres on the eastern slopes of the Blue Ridge in Madison County. By 1937, 460 persons had vacated their homes in these hollows to make way for the national park. One impetus for the survey of these hollows is the continued existence of dilapidated buildings that were exempted from CCC destruction. The study was designed to inventory these rapidly disappearing historic structures, while compiling a revised understanding of the park's human past (Horning 1998a).

The history of Jamestown and the history of European settlement in the Blue Ridge mountains, as "remembered" and presented, appear to be diametrically opposed. Yet their histories are inextricably linked, two ends on the spectrum of Southern history, tied together by the realities of their shared past, tied together through their twentieth-century construction. As with all good Virginia stories, the divergent tales of these two places begin their twisting paths together—aboard the storm-tossed *Sea Venture* that carried the energetic Englishman John Rolfe to the three-year-old Jamestown settlement in 1610, bearing the seeds of the West Indian *Nicotiana Tabacum*. The entrepreneurial Rolfe *should* be forever remembered for introducing the tobacco crop that answered Virginia's commodity-seeking prayers, yet he is better known for besting the virile Captain John Smith in attaining the matrimonial hand of Pocahontas. A bronze statue of this tamed daughter of Powhatan paramount chief Wahunsonacock remains a prominent component of the symbolic Jamestown landscape, forever commemorating the subjugation of the native population. According to the recent archaeological survey, European activity represents less than one-half of 1 percent of a ten-thousand-year continuum of human activity on Jamestown Island (Blanton and Kandle 1997). As in the Blue Ridge, however, the complexity and longevity of Jamestown's prehistoric past has been brushed into the natural landscape, a mere backdrop to English arrival.

By the time John Rolfe lost his young wife to an English disease in 1617, reliance on his "stinking weed" was already enveloping the Atlantic world. As the Chesapeake colonies expanded upon the cultivation and export of tobacco, so too did towns in England upon its import and processing. One such town, Whitehaven, was no more than a small fishing village on the windswept Cumbrian coast when landowner Sir Christopher Lowther began importing Virginia tobacco. By the time his son, Sir John, took control in 1663, Whitehaven had expanded on the back of the Atlantic trade to incorporate eighty-four households. By 1702, nearly three thousand Whitehaven residents relied upon a fleet of seventy-seven ships taking coal to Ireland and exporting locally produced commodities to Virginia in exchange for tobacco. Lowther grew wealthy by controlling shipping, encouraging manufactures, and directing the establishment of the physical town (Collier 1991; Hay 1997; Tyson 1986).

Lowther's reliance on the tobacco trade stimulated a lively interest in the New World. A 1699 inventory of his estate noted maps of Virginia in his two dining rooms (Hainsworth 1983:687–90), while his letters indicate a fascination with New World plants. Steward John Gale, whose son sailed to Virginia, wrote regretfully to Lowther in October of 1697 that his son "was not well provided of what my lord desired, (a collection of noveltyes, seeds, plants, and the like); in which case it behooveth that a person were there in the propper season" (Hainsworth 1983:445). Whitehaven, despite the handicap of a small, artificial harbor, soon took its place as one of England's six largest ports outside of London (Collier 1991).

While Jamestown may now be remembered as an isolated outpost where the nascent seeds of Americanness were sown, its seventeenth-century occupants remained blissfully unaware of their future, maintaining constant contact with England. Impressed by the model of Lowther and entrepreneurs of his ilk, developers in Jamestown attempted to replicate the success of the British towns. Although Jamestown would be abandoned in 1699, throughout the seventeenth century the town experienced sporadic development episodes that are directly linked to speculative efforts by wealthy landowners, spurred on by official town acts in the 1630s, 1660s, and 1680s. This relationship was noted through the spatial analysis of artifact dates from structures and features across the fourteen-acre townsite, which highlight periods of activity followed by abandonment (Edwards and Brown 1994; Horning and Brown 1995; Horning 1995; Horning and Edwards 1997; Horning 2000c).

Early speculation centered around manufacturing. In the northwestern part of town, immediately adjacent to the present visitor center where visitors learn about "the village where Western civilization took root" (Cotter 1957b:44), a series of manufacturing features were excavated in the 1950s. Reexamined from 1993 to 1996, the brick, tile, lime, and pottery kilns, brewhouse and apothecary, and traces of tanning and metalworking have now been attributed to 1630s governor John Harvey (McCartney and Kiddle 1998). Harvey was obsessed with economic diversification and town growth, passing laws that designated Jamestown sole port of entry and required artisans to settle in town. The governor's personal investments suggest a desire to reap the same profits from speculation as his English counterparts. Harvey was wrong—and unpopular. Ejected from office in 1639 for his tyrannical tendencies, he went bankrupt. Artifact, seed, pollen, and microstratigraphic analysis from the features on Harvey's forfeited property show all craft activities ceasing by the early 1640s. While the visitor center remembers Jamestown as "the place where many American industries were born in the New World" (Hudson 1957b:iii–iv), the archaeological record is clear—manufacturing at Jamestown was a dismal failure (Horning 1995; Horning and Edwards 1997; Kelso et al. 1995; McCartney 1998; McCartney and Kiddle 1998).

Just as the mere presence of manufacturing at Jamestown inspires celebratory rhetoric, so does the unusual presence of brick buildings in a timber-rich land replete with earth-fast dwellings. One inspired architectural historian waxed eloquent over how Jamestown's brick row houses emulated "Oxford or Chipping Camden or even the great London herself" (Forman 1957:50), their traces now gracing a "buried city of romance" (Forman 1938). Reconstruction paintings of uniform and neatly trimmed brick edifices commissioned in the 1950s adorn signs posted near the foundations, suspiciously echoing the architecture common in twentieth-century subdivisions and clearly hinting at the domestic civility of the occupants. Investigation in 1993 of one row house, Structure 17, revealed how (just as in many suburban homes) the brash façade barely hid an ugly truth. Next to one of the three twenty-by-forty-foot units was an abandoned, garbage-filled cellar hole for an addition left incomplete in the 1670s, dovetailing neatly with new documentary research indicating that Jamestown's brick houses were seldom occupied (Horning 1995). By the 1690s, two of the three completed houses at Structure 17 were described as decayed and ruinous, while the third was occupied by an unlucky tenant of owner Micajah Perry, a tobacco merchant with strong ties to the Whitehaven fleet (McCartney and Kiddle 1998; McCartney 1998). The dereliction of the buildings reflects another failed attempt to replicate the town-building success of English entrepreneurs. Jamestown's investors waited in vain for the flood of job-seeking migrants that had populated towns such as Whitehaven. Migrants to the Chesapeake flooded the fields, not the towns.

While the remembered past of Jamestown focuses upon the wealthy politicos who once squelched through its muddy lanes, Jamestown also sheltered the unremarkable. Legislation to channel the flow of settlers away from tobacco lands succeeded in attracting a few artisans and ordinary people to the struggling town. Catering to the administrative functions of the capital, some operated taverns for visitors "at extraordinary rates" while others plied their trades. Recent reanalysis of artifact collections coupled with new property research pinpointed a discrete domestic complex in the eastern end of the townsite centering around a dwelling, well, and refuse pit (McCartney and Kiddle 1998; McCartney 1998; Brannon and Horning 1999; Horning and Wehner, in prep.). Nearly obliterated in the 1930s by overzealous excavators who employed augers in their search for brick foundations, all that remains of Structure 24 is the crimson ghost of a brick footing. Here dwelt the family of gunsmith John Jackson in the 1620s. Judging from the quantities of lead shot and gun parts excavated in the vicinity of their home during the summers of 1998 and 1999, Jackson the gunsmith enjoyed regular employment, capitalizing upon the shortage of artisans in the colony. Goods recovered from the well, refuse pit, and house area included a variety of imported ceramics and glassware that suggest the Jamestown lifestyle was far more comfortable than it would have been had the Jacksons turned to farming tobacco on Virginia's fertile, if fickle, fields. Yet the lure of tobacco and land was never counterbalanced by the apparent advantages of Jamestown—the relative success of artisans and the availability of cheap rental housing.

Although the use of brick at Jamestown reflected the same fire-preventive building regulations imposed in the busy streets of Whitehaven, it was a fire in 1698 that precipitated the shift of the capital to Middle Plantation, renamed Williamsburg. Celebration of Jamestown settlement—described by British ambassador James Bryce in 1957 as "one of the great events in the history of the world"—began as soon as the fires cooled, with Lieutenant Governor Francis Nicholson planning a 1707 centennial jubilee. A bicentennial celebration in 1807 found "an immense assembly . . .

convened on the plains of Jamestown" (McCartney 1994:90; Tyler 1899–1900:222), while later in the century steamboats ran daily excursions from Richmond and Norfolk.

The townsite that had once been the colonial capital soon sprouted the tobacco for a slave-dependent plantation. Tobacco had won, and the die was cast for that defining element in the history of the South—rural agrarianism. Another two centuries would pass before the South recovered enough from this first urban-planning disaster to see its scattered cities flourish and grow. Jamestown, however, will never be remembered as the seat of yet another eighteenth-century plantation, despite the brick ruins of the three-story Ambler house that loom over the barely perceptible traces of the seventeenth-century town. Despite its commanding presence, the eighteenth-century Ambler house has no place in the remembered past of America's first permanent English settlement, and it is conspicuously absent from site interpretation.

Also absent from site interpretation is the simple truth that Jamestown's most American hallmark lies in its failure. On the wrong side of the tobacco trade, Virginians never could replicate a British port, but they possessed a commodity far more appealing (and more defining of "Americanness") than thriving towns—*land*. The opening of western lands by the eighteenth century attracted a vast flow of discontented and displaced Europeans, who soon teemed into northern ports and streamed south into Virginia's fertile Shenandoah Valley. There, settlers from England, Ireland, Scotland, the Palatinate, and France, as well as West Africa, jostled and struggled with one another and with a confusion of native inhabitants and native invaders.

The ethnic and religious diversity of the eighteenth-century Southern backcountry was familiar beyond the American frontier. The extensive trade ties of Whitehaven ensured that residents were keenly aware of the religious upheavals taking place throughout Europe. During the turmoil in Ireland caused by the Williamite wars of 1688–1691, many fleeing Protestants found safety in Whitehaven (Collier 1991; Hay 1977). A consummate businessman, Sir John Lowther had no qualms about favoring wealthy dissenters. In 1694, a group of Nonconformists, including mariners William and Timothy Nicholson, successfully petitioned Lowther for land to build a chapel (Collier 1991; Hainsworth 1983; Lowther Papers, Whitehaven). Timothy Nicholson and Clement Nicholson, another mariner, were frequent travelers to Virginia, trading with Jamestown landlord Micajah Perry (Ince 1998).

Another seagoing Nicholson, Thomas, joined the tide of migration to the Virginia backcountry. Like Timothy and William Nicholson's, Thomas Nicholson's name does not appear on any Anglican church registry in Whitehaven (parish registries, Cumbria Archives, Whitehaven). The year 1732 found Nicholson (seeking religious freedom?) patenting one thousand acres of land just outside the present boundary of Shenandoah National Park (Culpeper County Deed Book A). Nicholson did not abandon the sea for the plow, however. Shipping records indicate that he continued to sail between Virginia and Whitehaven, ferrying cargoes of tobacco, barrel staves, timber planks, and animal skins to the bustling Cumbrian port (Ince 1998). On his trips from the Blue Ridge to the Tidewater, Nicholson must have been familiar with the streets of Virginia's new colonial capital, Williamsburg. As ill-fated as Jamestown, Williamsburg was destined to relinquish the reins of government to the Piedmont town of Richmond in 1799, a locale better situated to serve the needs of the newcomers who had "tamed" the expanse of western Virginia.

While Nicholson maintained his ties with Whitehaven, some of his progeny were won over by the lure of the Blue Ridge. In the 1790s, the mariner's grandson John and his wife, Anne, purchased a tract near the original Nicholson grant in a mountain hollow now known as Nicholson Hollow.[1] There they built a home with the aid of at least four grown sons (Madison County Deed Book 2:294). Archaeological survey of their holdings located the traces of a small log structure with an external fieldstone chimney and a loosely coursed fieldstone foundation that John and Anne may once have called home. Artifacts from within and around the modest structure support a late-eighteenth-century construction date, while documents suggest that the dwelling was converted into a slave quarter in the 1810s, to serve a more substantial, newly built log-and-stone dwelling a few feet away (Madison County Deed Book 5:452). Virginia slavery, a legacy of the tobacco economy, not only reached far into the Blue Ridge but also stretched back to England, with Whitehaven ships trading in slaves as well as tobacco. Meanwhile, back at Jamestown, enslaved Africans living on the plantation of the Ambler family in the midst of the former "cradle of our Republican liberties and values" (Tylor 1906) would pay dearly for their participation in a local revolt.

The descendants of John and Anne Nicholson remained in the broad, sheltered hollow, forever altering the local landscape by clearing fields, terracing hillsides, shoring up rivers, digging channels to serve gristmills, sawmills, and distilleries, and exchanging forest for fields, farm buildings, schools, and churches. Yet something went terribly wrong. In the 1930s, when plans for Shenandoah National Park were in motion, a journalist visiting the Nicholson Hollow region "made the journey . . . back to an era and a mode of living only slightly changed from that of Colonial days" (Hampton 1932), while a colleague found only "ragged hungry families housed in windowless, tumble-down shanties" (Henry 1936). What had happened to radically change—or halt—the course of life since the time of Thomas Nicholson?

The answer to that question lies squarely in the role that the Southern mountain region—Appalachia—played in the early-twentieth-century American mindset, a contradictory mindset that both extolled the modern and industrial and lamented the loss of the rural and traditional. The creation of "Appalachia" as a foil or justification for post–Civil War modernization has long been recognized by scholars (e.g., Shapiro 1966, 1978; Batteau 1990). The developing urban middle class in the North eagerly devoured the products of a new literary genre, the monthly magazine that specialized in short stories. Fiction writers zeroed in upon the insecurities of their rising middle-class readers and sagely (if cynically) chose subjects that emphasized the contrast between their local-color characters—generally Southern agriculturists—and the virtues of the "modern" industrial world. Following Will Wallace Harney's 1873 publication of "A Strange Land and Peculiar People," a parade of writers flocked to the mountains in search of "Our Contemporary Ancestors" (Frost 1899) existing in a "Rip van Winkle sleep" on their "retarded frontier." That these odd mountaineers, as presented, were white and at least vaguely Protestant served as their only saving grace, rendering them worthy of paternalistic ministrations at a time of political isolationism, rampant racism, and celebration of America's Anglo-Saxon roots at sacred sites like Jamestown.

The commodification of Jamestown as a sacred site is rooted in the same patronizing attitude of Northern writers toward the South that imposed "Dogpatch" history on Appalachia. Preservationist societies such as the Association for the Preservation of Virginia Antiquities (APVA) were hastily created to combat Northern history, which "remembered" only the Plymouth Colony and the Philadelphia Congress. In their battle to wrest American history from the hands of New Englanders, the APVA venerated Virginia and the Old South as the most appropriate model for the nation, reflecting—according to cultural historian James Lindgren—a reactionary impulse to prove that "the old Dominion had founded the nation, established representative government, instituted racial order through slavery, and stood for civility and grace" (Lindgren 1993:9). In 1893 the APVA acquired 22.5 acres of Jamestown Island. Rapidly gearing up for the 1907 celebrations, the ladies of the APVA dug up foundations, planted gardens, erected statues of Pocahontas and John Smith, reconstructed the church to symbolize the (Southern) Protestant roots of America, and created a commemorative landscape that remains virtually unchanged. A similar desire to reverence the colonial golden era *in illo tempore* soon inspired the Rockefellers to resurrect the dilapidated eighteenth-century Virginia capital of Williamsburg; then followed the creation of a national park at Jamestown. As Jean C. Harrington prepared to serve as chief archaeologist at Jamestown, Nicholson Hollow residents prepared to leave lands first chosen by Whitehaven mariner Thomas Nicholson.

While Thomas Nicholson could lay claim to participating in Virginia's golden era, geography saddled his twentieth-century descendants with the burden of an unwelcome past and an unsavory present, as the fictional creation of Appalachia evolved into the received history of the Southern mountains. Writing in 1884 of Tennessee mountaineers, novelist Mary Nailles Murfree endowed her subjects with a "habitual mental atmosphere" that was "a vague hazy reverie" (Murphree 1884). Amusing as fiction, perhaps, but eerily echoed in the 1933 Blue Ridge study *Hollow Folk* by sociologist Mandel Sherman and journalist Thomas Henry. Manipulating images of landscape, the authors intoned: "The deep silence and drowsiness of the mountains are fascinating, . . . an ideal bedchamber designed by nature." Lulled to sleep, inhabitants "were almost completely cut off from the current of American life . . . [they were] not of the twentieth century" (Sherman and Henry 1933:1–2). Sherman and Henry were describing Nicholson, Corbin, and Weakley Hollows, and thus the descendants of Thomas Nicholson. These lurid descriptions of mountain isolation garnered public support for the removal of residents to create Shenandoah National Park (Perdue and Martin-Perdue 1979–80; Horning 1999b, 2000a).

Amongst the journalists and park promoters who roamed the hollows to document "eighteenth-century lifeways" was Farm Security Administration photographer Arthur Rothstein, a recent Columbia University graduate. Rothstein traversed Nicholson and Corbin Hollows, photographing picturesque log cabins and their inhabitants (Johnson 1985; Campbell 1987). One of his compositions focuses upon an unsmiling Mrs. Bailey Nicholson, squinting into the sun on her front porch, clad in an old dress and a homespun apron, and sporting an oversized sunbonnet—the very picture of a sturdy Appalachian matron (fig. 1.3). Rothstein's image is well composed but is clearly one-dimensional. Turning into the house from her flower-bedecked porch, Mrs. Nicholson would have reentered

Figure 1.3. Arthur Rothstein's 1935 portrait of Mrs. Bailey Nicholson, titled "A Blue Ridge Matron." (Courtesy Farm Security Administration Virginia Collection.)

the private domain where, among other activities, she joined her family in dining on a matched set of Japanese porcelain. Fragments of several plates, tea bowls, and an oversized serving platter were found in the charred soils within the foundation of Mrs. Nicholson's former home. The association of the sherds with hardware from a brass trunk chronicles a hasty, fraught departure from the slopes of Corbin Mountain.

Just as the materials unearthed at the Bailey Nicholson site counterbalance the Rothstein portrayal, so too do artifacts recovered from the other eighty-eight sites surveyed in Nicholson, Corbin, and Weakley Hollows.

An array of kitchen and dining wares, pharmaceutical items, liquor bottles, mail order toys, specialized agricultural tools, store-bought shoes, costume jewelry, 78 RPM record fragments, and even dry-cell batteries and automobiles, all indicate that mountain residents were as bombarded by mass consumer culture as any other early-twentieth-century American, and that they exercised their ability to participate in that consumer culture according to their own interest and means (fig. 1.4). Furthermore, park land records and extant building traces reveal that no one lived in "window-less shanties" (Henry 1936). Housing in the hollows ranged from nine-room frame-and-stone dwellings to two-room log cabins, situated on farms that varied from one to more than four hundred acres. Hollow residents had clearly not stagnated in splendid isolation from the days of Thomas Nicholson (tract maps and land acquisition records).

Settlement in the hollows from the time of Thomas Nicholson to the removal of the last resident has been traced through the analysis of documents, oral historical evidence, and archaeological data, revealing how inhabitants balanced the creation of a local community with their involvement in wider political and social systems, and the demands of the mountainous environment. Weakley Hollow, a long, broad valley situated between the jagged, granite-topped Ragged Mountain and the worn, forested peaks of the Blue Ridge proper, was the first of the hollows to be settled. Survey turned up two sites with eighteenth-century components, and documents note that a road traversed the hollow as early as the 1750s (Horning 1998a, 2000b, 1999b; Lillard and Vernon 1992). The level terrain and ease of accessibility encouraged settlement and aided in the growth of small-scale enterprises such as gristmills, sawmills, and smithies. By the 1930s, the hollow had its own post office and two general stores, and several residents owned automobiles—proof that inhabitants *were* "of the twentieth century" (Sizer 1932b).

Nearby Nicholson Hollow, not blessed with a through road, remained reliant on farming, but not mere subsistence farming. Surplus crops were consistently produced, according to census data, and actively marketed. Following the dedication of the park, "restoration" of nature began in earnest, with Nicholson Hollow set aside as the singular cultural history exhibit. In a blatant manipulation of landscape, only small log buildings were permitted to remain. Visitors now see only one restored cabin in a forested wilderness instead of fields and farmhouses. This landscape perpetuates notions of isolation and ultimately denies the complexity of the region's history (Horning 1998a).

Figure 1.4. Range of items found in Nicholson, Corbin, and Weakley Hollows, including a toy truck, Coke bottle, 78 rpm record fragments, a World War I military utensil set, decorated ceramics, and pharmaceutical glassware. (Photo: Andrew C. Edwards, Colonial Williamsburg Foundation Department of Archaeological Research.)

Conversely, the steep, rocky slopes of Corbin Hollow discouraged intensive farming. Archaeological, documentary, and oral historical evidence has demonstrated that settlement hinged directly upon the 1880s establishment of the nearby Skyland resort. Residents of Corbin Hollow capitalized upon their proximity to Skyland, relying upon employment there for their subsistence. Corbin Hollow sites lack the extensive outbuildings common on farms in the adjacent hollows, and there is little physical evidence of field clearance. Thus when the Depression hit, hollow residents found themselves out of work and unable to farm the uninviting slopes. Their resultant poverty was exploited by the park promoters, one of whom—George Freeman Pollock—was the proprietor of Skyland (Pollock 1960). Most of the popularized images of park-area poverty were taken from Corbin Hollow. While some photographs were clearly contrived, there is no denying the existence of poverty. Corbin Hollow sites are mainly evidenced by hastily built, randomly laid stone foundations or piers, which once supported log homes far smaller on average than the log, frame, and stone houses common in Nicholson and Weakley Hollows. In a clear inversion of the "hollow folk" logic, the decision to engage in modern wage labor rather than to continue small-scale traditional farming caused the economic downfall of Corbin Hollow—not the reverse (Horning 1998a, 1999b, 2000b).

In the end, what the archaeological study revealed about the historic occupation of the hollows is a story of complexity and variety. While a clear sense of community existed within the hollows, it was in no sense predicated upon isolation, nor was it dependent upon equality. Inhabitants were clearly involved in regional economic and social networks, and within the hollows there were widely varying household economies. Initially, there were slaveholders shoulder to shoulder with struggling tenant farmers. Later, some inhabitants countered shrinking farm sizes, due in part to the practice of partible inheritance (Vernon 1976), by developing businesses such as distilleries. Farmers in Nicholson Hollow experimented with cash crops and with raising sheep and poultry, while in the early twentieth century the upper slopes in Weakley Hollow were covered in apple orchards, the business venture of two entrepreneurial Nicholson brothers. In the twentieth century there was serious poverty in Corbin Hollow, yet Model Ts tooled down the road from Weakley Hollow to the cinema at the county seat. (One inspired theatergoer from the Dyer family carved "TARZAN" into a poplar tree near the family farmhouse. The house is gone, but the graffiti survives.)

Despite all of the evidence to the contrary, displaced park dwellers were still perceived as living carriers of colonial traditions thirty years after the 1936 park dedication, when an invitation was extended to mountaineers William Cody Cook and Lucy Cook to journey to the Colonial Williamsburg museum to teach costumed interpreters how to recreate "authentic" eighteenth-century baskets. Descendants of Whitehaven emigrant Thomas Nicholson, who long before had tramped the streets of Williamsburg, the couple was described as "looking as much at home as if they had been there since the days of George Wythe himself" (Humelsine 1968). The Cooks stayed in residence at the restored town from 1968 to 1971 (Horning 1997).

The Cooks' basketry skills, developed during the Depression, did not result from an "isolated" lifestyle but were a function of the burgeoning tourism that provided a market for mountain crafts, crafts that had continually evolved and changed with demand (Suter 1996; Martin-Perdue 1983). Demand increased owing to the national handicraft movement, which eschewed mass production and venerated individually crafted pieces as a "protest against the conditions of modern factory production, with its minute divisions of labor and mechanical processes" (West 1904:1597). Alteration and innovation are always integral to handicrafts, ensuring their continued economic viability. In a recent interview, basket maker Elmer Price related how his father, Sam, brother of William Cody Cook, had developed a popular "running board basket" to accommodate his motoring customers (Suter 1996). Still, the handicraft movement, like the local colorists, had found its poster child in Southern Appalachia.

At present, the National Park Service has declared its intention to reverse the policy of ignoring cultural resources within Shenandoah National Park, and of presenting the past inhabitants as "poor, destitute, and unintelligent people" (Michaud 1998:11). "Given the considerable benefit of hindsight and retrospection," the park superintendent recently stated, "we are today actively involved in many long-needed programs that help us better understand and tell the story of human use inside the park boundaries" (Morris 1998:3). The reversal in park policy evolved in part because of strong agitation by a descendants' advocacy group calling itself the Children of Shenandoah, composed primarily of the children and grandchildren of the displaced, who never knew life "on the mountain." The group's purpose is to raise awareness of the removals and to promote their own version of the past, one that emphasizes traditional mountain values of community, egalitarianism, and connection to the land.

The complex Blue Ridge past revealed by the archaeological study is at odds now with two received histories, that of the 1930s with its roots in nineteenth-century fiction, and the idealized version promoted by the descendant community. The latter is a valid past, insofar as it has been constructed by its recipients, but it is as inaccurate as that of Sherman and Henry. To publicly admit that yes, there was poverty in the Blue Ridge, and yes, there were wealthy individuals who didn't help their neighbors, and yes, life in the mountains may have looked a lot like life elsewhere in rural America would not only undermine the cause—that of gaining recognition—but also suggest that there was nothing unique or special about mountain life. Modern-day "Appalachians" are trapped in a paradox, needing to prove their civilized nature and modern ways yet desperate to retain a sense of otherness—an internalized otherness that was imposed from outside that now reifies a community.

Which remembered past will win out at Shenandoah? Can we do anything more than make all pasts available, allowing the visitor to weigh the choices and balance the facts? In the end, visitors to places like Jamestown and Shenandoah will find only the pasts they personally choose to remember. Hikers in Shenandoah National Park crave an isolation that never existed in the past and long for evidence of a kinder, gentler time when humans and nature lived in harmony. For them, the truth that the Blue Ridge was once home to mines, mills, and large-scale farming enterprises is as unsavory as the tales of poverty are to the descendants. At Jamestown, despite Herculean efforts to interpret the complex history of the site, visitors have only to step onto the property of the APVA to rub the bronze hands of the 1907 Pocahontas statue. Interpretation of the excavations sponsored by the APVA on the site of the original James Fort continues to emphasize the sanctity of the site because of its "early" nature (Kelso 1994, 1995, 1996; Kelso, Luccketti, and Straube 1997, 1998). Even preeminent historical archaeologist Ivor Noël-Hume waxed poetic over the opportunity to dig the First Fort: "Few archaeologists are privileged to excavate ground so close to the heart of a nation. But the thrill of discovery inevitably is tempered with awe by the magnitude of the responsibility" (Noël-Hume 1994). Noël-Hume's reduction of Jamestown and the role of archaeologists to the sentimental denigrates the complex history of the settlement by pandering to the received history.

What is the point of excavating at Jamestown, or anywhere else, if it is not to add to our knowledge and provide alternative histories? As emphasized by the overtly ideological public education program sponsored by archaeologists in Annapolis (e.g., Leone et al. 1987), today's public is capable of understanding and appreciating archaeological discoveries beyond their transparent symbolic importance as the first, oldest, or rarest of their kind—even if, in the end, they choose to remember just that. Michael Shanks is correct in asserting that if archaeologists "have nothing positive to do or say to people, if we cannot stimulate them with our ideas, we should stop what we are doing" (Shanks 1990:308).

Stimulating, balanced interpretations will never wholly replace the remembered pasts of emotive landscapes such as those of Jamestown and the Blue Ridge. Remembered histories are as much a part of the past as they are reflective of the time of their construction, and they will continue to reverberate in the present, and into the future. "However much a construct, the archaeological record has an infinite capacity to surprise—the past can be as much discovered as the land. Any adequate account of archaeological practice must make this fact as central as the recognition that the past as we know it will always have mythic dimensions"(Wylie 1993:15). So too will landscapes of the past—and the present. Accepting and understanding the constructed nature of our landscapes and our understanding of the past should not, cannot, and does not cripple our ability to learn about—discover—the past. Furthermore, addressing the construction of landscape in our national parks in particular can only enhance interpretation of resources to visitors. Jamestown will always be a potent American symbol, particularly now as the 2007 anniversary draws near. Similarly, the beauty of Shenandoah National Park will always beckon to the world-weary while (one hopes) providing safe haven to threatened animal and plant species. It is our job to intertwine understandings of myth, memory, and landscape with presentations of the complex pasts we "discover" through sound interdisciplinary archaeological, documentary, and ethno- and oral historical research.

Note

1. I accept the reasoning put forth by genealogist Julia Ince that the John Nicholson who patented land in the Shenandoah National Park area was the grandson of Thomas Nicholson rather than the son, as assumed by researchers Nancy Martin-Perdue and Charles Perdue. However, I do not yet know of any direct link between John Nicholson of Madison County and the earlier Thomas, so all relationships are postulated, albeit on strong circumstantial evidence. See Perdue and Martin-Perdue 1979–1980; Ince 1998.

References

Batteau, A. W.
  1990   *The Invention of Appalachia*. University of Arizona Press, Tucson.
Blanton, Dennis
  1994a   The Archaeological Survey of Jamestown Island: Preliminary Results. Paper presented at the Middle Atlantic Archaeology Conference, Ocean City, Maryland, April 8–10.
  1994b   Preliminary Investigations beyond the Town Site. *Jamestown Archaeological Assessment Newsletter* 1(2–3): 19–21.
Blanton, Dennis, and Patricia Kandle
  1997   *The Archaeological Survey of Jamestown Island*. Jamestown Archaeological Assessment Technical Report Series 2, submitted to and on file at Colonial National Historical Park, Jamestown, Virginia.
Brannon, Nick, and Audrey J. Horning
  1999   English Towns in Unfamiliar Landscapes: Seventeenth-Century Coleraine and Jamestown. Paper presented at the Society for Historical Archaeology Conference, Salt Lake City, January 8.
Brown, Marley R., III
  1993   National Park Service Archaeological Assessment of Jamestown, Virginia: Research Plan, 1992–1994. *Jamestown Archaeological Assessment Newsletter* 1(1): 1–5.

Campbell, Edward D. C., ed.
1987   Shadows of an Era. *Virginia Cavalcade* 36(3): 128–43.

Collier, Sylvia
1991   *Whitehaven 1660–1800*. Royal Commission on the Historical Monuments of England, London.

Cotter, John L.
1956   Completion Report: Jamestown Archaeological Explorations, 1954–1956. National Park Service files, Colonial National Historical Park, Jamestown, Virginia.
1957a   Excavations at Jamestown, Virginia, Site of the First Permanent English Settlement in America. *Antiquity*, March, 19–24.
1957b   Jamestown: Treasure in the Earth. *Antiques* (46)1: 44–46.
1957c   Rediscovering Jamestown. *Archaeology* 10 (1): 25–30.
1958   *Archaeological Excavations at Jamestown, Virginia*. No. 4, National Park Service Archaeological Research Series. United States Department of the Interior, Washington, D.C.

Cotter, John L., and Edward B. Jelks
1957   Historic Site Archaeology at Jamestown. *American Antiquity* 22(4): 25–30.

Culpeper County Deed Books
1749–   Office of the Culpeper County Clerk, Culpeper Courthouse, Culpeper,
1793   Virginia.

Edwards, Andrew C., and Marley R. Brown III
1994   The Archaeological Assessment of Jamestown Island, Project Overview. Paper presented at the Middle Atlantic Archaeology Conference, Ocean City, Maryland, April 8–10.

Engle, R.
1997   The Creation of Shenandoah National Park. Lecture presented October 10, 1997, at the Rappahannock County Library, Washington, Virginia.
1998   Shenandoah National Park: Historical Overview. *CRM* 21(1): 7–10.

Forman, H. Chandlee
1938   *Jamestown and St. Mary's: Buried Cities of Romance*. Johns Hopkins University Press, Baltimore.
1957   *Virginia Architecture in the Seventeenth Century*. 350th Anniversary Celebration Corporation, Richmond.

Fox, J., Jr.
1901   The Southern Mountaineer. *Scribner's Magazine* 29:387–99, 556–70 (April–May).

Frost, W. G.
1899   Our Contemporary Ancestors in the Southern Mountains. *Atlantic Monthly* 83:311 (March).

Hainsworth, D. R.
1983   *The Correspondence of Sir John Lowther of Whitehaven, 1693–1698*. British Academy, London.

Hampton, Joan
1932   The Primitive Life in Modern Virginia: A Crisis for the Hill Folk. *Baltimore Sun,* May 1, magazine section.

Harney, Will Wallace
1873   A Strange Land and a Peculiar People. *Lippincott's Magazine,* October: 429–38.

Harrington, J. C.
1943   *Historic Site Archaeology in the United States.* University of Chicago Press, Chicago.

1954   Dating Stem Fragments of Seventeenth and Eighteenth Century Clay Tobacco Pipes. *Quarterly Bulletin of the Archaeological Society of Virginia* 9(1): 10–14.

1984   Jamestown Archaeology in Retrospect. In *The Scope of Historical Archaeology,* edited by David Orr and Daniel G. Crozier, 294–310. Temple University Press, Philadelphia.

Hay, D.
1977   *Whitehaven: An Illustrated History.* Michael Moon's Book Shop, Whitehaven, Cumbria, England.

Henry, Thomas D.
1936   200 Years of Calm in Blue Ridge Hollow Broken as Resettlement Workmen Erect New Village. *Washington Times.* (Clipping on file in Shenandoah National Park archives, Luray, Virginia. n.d.)

Hitch, M.
1931   Life in a Blue Ridge Hollow. *Journal of Geography* 30(8): 309–22.

Horning, Audrey J.
1995   "A Verie Fit Place for the Erecting of a Great Cittie": Comparative Contextual Analysis of Archaeological Jamesown. Ph.D. dissertation, University of Pennsylvania.

1996   Myth Versus Reality: Agricultural Adaptation and Innovation in the Nicholson Hollow District, Shenandoah National Park. In *Upland Archaeology in the East,* compiled by Michael B. Barber, Eugene B. Barfield, Harry A. Jaeger, and William Jack Hranicky, 17–115. U.S. Department of Agriculture, Forest Service Special Publication (38)5, Archaeological Society of Virginia, Richmond.

1997   Connections: An Archaeological Perspective on Becoming Americans. *Colonial Williamsburg Research Review* 7(1): 25–29.

1998a   "Almost Untouched": Recognizing, Recording, and Preserving the Archeological Heritage of a Natural Park. *CRM* 21(1): 31–33.

1998b   Journey to Jamestown. *Archaeology,* March–April.

1999a   Finding the Town in Jamestown: Archaeology of the Seventeenth-Century Capitol *CRM* (22)1:7–9.

1999b   In Search of a "Hollow Ethnicity": Archaeological Explorations of Rural Mountain Settlement. In *Current Perspectives on Ethnicity in Historical Archaeology,* edited by M. Franklin and G. Fesler, 121–38. Research

Publications Series, Colonial Williamsburg Foundation, Williamsburg, Virginia.

2000a Archaeological Considerations of Appalachian Identity: Community-Based Archaeology in the Blue Ridge Mountains. In *The Archaeology of Communities: A New World Perspective*, edited by Marcello Canuto and Jason Yaeger, 210–30. Routledge Press, London and New York.

2000b Beyond the Valley: Interaction, Image, and Identity in the Virginia Blue Ridge. In *After the Backcountry: Nineteenth-Century Life in the Valley of Virginia*, edited by W. Hofstra and K. Koons. University of Tennessee Press, Knoxville.

2000c Urbanism in the Colonial South: The Development of Seventeenth-Century Jamestown. In *Archaeology of Southern Urban Landscapes*, edited by Amy Young, 52–68. University of Alabama Press, Tuscaloosa.

Horning, Audrey J., and Andrew C. Edwards
1997 *The Jamestown Archaeological Assessment: Archaeology in New Towne, 1993–1995*. Jamestown Archaeological Assessment Technical Report Series 3, submitted to and on file at the Colonial National Historical Park, Jamestown, Virginia.

Horning, Audrey J., Andrew C. Edwards, and Gregory J. Brown
1993 Archaeological Investigations in New Towne. *Jamestown Archaeological Assessment Newsletter* 1(1): 8–12.

Horning, Audrey J., and Karen B. Wehner
In Investigations at Jamestown's Structure 24. Report to be submitted to
prep. Colonial National Park by the Colonial Williamsburg Foundation, Williamsburg, Virginia.

Horning, Audrey J., and Marley R. Brown
1995 Return to Jamestown: The Problem of Permanency and Urbanity in the Early Chesapeake. Paper presented at the annual conference of the Society for Historical Archaeology, Washington, D.C. January.

Hudson, J. Paul
1957a Jamestown Artisans and Craftsmen. *Antiques* 46(1): 47–50.

1957b A Pictorial Booklet on Early Jamestown Commodities and Industries. Virginia 350th Anniversary Celebration Corporation, Richmond.

Humelsine, Carlisle H.
1968 *Preserving Our Handicrafts: The President's Report*. The Colonial Williamsburg Foundation, Williamsburg, Virginia.

Ince, Julia
1998 Nicholson Family Records. Genealogical research on the Nicholson family. Copies in the possession of the author.

Johnson, Brooks
1985 *Mountaineers to Main Streets*. Catalogue of exhibition of Farm Security Administration photographs. Chrysler Museum, Norfolk, Virginia.

Kelso, Gerald K., Stephen Mrozowski, Andrew C. Edwards, Marley R. Brown III, Audrey J. Horning, Gregory J. Brown, and Jeremiah Dandoy

1995   Differential Pollen Preservation in a Seventeenth-Century Refuse Pit, Jamestown Island, Virginia. *Historical Archaeology* 29(2): 43–54.

Kelso, William M.

1994   New World Order: Life in Early Jamestown. Paper presented at the annual conference of the Council for Northeastern Historical Archaeology, Williamsburg, Virginia, October 21–23.

1995   *Jamestown Rediscovery I: The Search for James Fort.* Association for the Preservation of Virginia Antiquities, Richmond.

1996   *Jamestown Rediscovery II.* Association for the Preservation of Virginia Antiquities, Richmond.

Kelso, William M., Nicholas M. Luccketti, and Beverley A. Straube

1997   *Jamestown Rediscovery III.* Association for the Preservation of Virginia Antiquities, Richmond.

1998   *Jamestown Rediscovery IV.* Association for the Preservation of Virginia Antiquities, Richmond.

Lambert, Darwin

1971   *The Earth-Man Story: Parks, Man, and His Environment.* Bulletin No. 6, Shenandoah Natural History Association, Luray, Virginia.

Leone, Mark P., Parker B. Potter, Jr., and Paul A. Shackel

1987   Toward a Critical Archaeology. *Current Anthropology* 28(3): 283–302.

Lewis, Kenneth E., Jr.

1975   The Jamestown Frontier: An Archaeological Study of Colonization. Ph.D. dissertation, University of Oklahoma, Norman.

Lillard, D., and R. Vernon

1992   Surveys and Land Grants of Madison County, Virginia. Manuscript draft, February 19. On file at the Department of Archeological Research, Colonial Williamsburg Foundation, Williamsburg, Virginia.

Lindgren, James M.

1993   *Preserving the Old Dominion: Historic Preservation and Virginia Traditionalism.* University Press of Virginia, Charlottesville.

Lowther, Sir John

        Family papers, Cumbria Archives, Whitehaven, Cumbria, England.

Madison County Deed Books

1794–   Madison County Courthouse, Madison, Virginia.
1936

Martin-Perdue, N.

1983   Case Study—On Eaton's Trail: A Genealogical Study of Virginia Basketmakers. In *Traditional Craftsmanship in America: A Diagnostic Report,* edited by J. C. Camp, 79–101. National Council for the Traditional Arts, Washington, D.C.

McCartney, Martha W.
  1994   Preliminary History of Jamestown Island. Draft report on file at Colonial
          National Historical Park, Jamestown, Virginia.
  1998   *Biographical Sketches: People of Jamestown Island.* Jamestown Ar-
          chaeological Assessment Technical Report Series 5(3), submitted to and
          on file at Colonial National Historical Park, Jamestown, Virginia.
McCartney, Martha W., and Christina A. Kiddle
  1998   *Jamestown Island Land Ownership Patterns.* Jamestown Archaeologi-
          cal Assessment Technical Report Series 5(2), submitted to and on file at
          Colonial National Historical Park, Jamestown, Virginia.
McClelland, L. F.
  1998   Skyline Drive Historic District: A Meeting Place of Culture and Nature.
          CRM 21(1): 13–15.
Michaud, K.
  1998   Shenandoah National Park: Laboratory for Change. *CRM* 21(1): 11–
          12.
Morris, Douglas K.
  1998   Foreword: Shenandoah—Managing Cultural Resources in a Natural
          Park. *CRM* 21(1): 3.
Murfree, Mary Noailles [Charles Egbert Craddock]
  1884   *In the Tennessee Mountains.* Houghton, Mifflin, Boston.
Noel-Hume, Ivor
  1994   Jamestown Rediscovery. Fundraising pamphlet, Association for the Pres-
          ervation of Virginia Antiquities, Richmond.
Perdue, C., and N. J. Martin-Perdue
  1979–   Appalachian Fables and Facts: A Case Study of the Shenandoah National
  1980   Park Removals. *Appalachian Journal* 7:84–104.
  1991   To Build a Wall around These Mountains. *Magazine of Albemarle County
          History* 49:49–71.
Pollock, G. F.
  1960   *Skyland.* Chesapeake Book Company, Berryville, Virginia.
Reeder, J., and C. Reeder
  1991   *Shenandoah Secrets: The Story of the Park's Hidden Past.* Potomac Ap-
          palachian Trail Club, Washington, D.C.
Shanks, Michael
  1990   Reading the Signs: Responses to Archaeology after Structuralism. In
          Archaeology after Structuralism, edited by Ian Bapty and Tim Yates,
          294–310. Routledge Press, London.
Shapiro, H.
  1966   A Strange Land and Peculiar People: The Discovery of Appalachia,

1870–1920. Ph.D. dissertation, Rutgers University, New Brunswick, New Jersey.

1978   *Appalachia on Our Mind.* University of North Carolina Press, Chapel Hill.

Sherman, M., and T. R. Henry

1933   *Hollow Folk.* Virginia Book Company, Berryville, Virginia.

Sizer, M.

1932a A Brief Comparison of Psychological and Educational Data. Report for the Resettlement Administration. On file, National Archives, College Park, Maryland.

1932b Tabulations: Five Mountain Hollows. Report for the Resettlement Administration. On file, National Archives, College Park, Maryland.

Suter, S. H.

1996   Basketry and Invisible Skills: Gaps in the Archaeological Record. In *Upland Archaeology in the East,* compiled by Michael B. Barber, Eugene B. Barfield, Harry A. Jaeger, and William Jack Hranicky, 126–34. U.S. Department of Agriculture, Forest Service—Southern Division, Special Publication 38(5). Archaeological Society of Virginia, Richmond.

Tanner, D.

1978   *Madison County Place Names.* Virginia Place Name Society, Occasional Publications No. 21, Charlottesville, Virginia.

Tract Maps and Land Acquisition Records

1926– Surveyed by the Commonwealth of Virginia Commission on Conserva-
1928   tion and Development. Shenandoah National Park Archives, Luray, Virginia.

Tyler, Lyon G.

1899– Glimpses of Old College Life *William and Mary Quarterly* (1st series)
1900   8:213–27.

1906   *The Cradle of the Republic, Jamestown and James River.* The Hermitage Press, Richmond.

Tyson, B.

1986   Some Aspects of Whitehaven's Development before 1700. *Ancient Monuments Society Transactions* NS 30:149–85.

U.S. Bureau of the Census

1880– U.S. Census, Agriculture, Madison County, Virginia.
1950

Vernon, R. W.

1976   Historical Demography in Shenandoah National Park: A Study of Cultural Adaptation in Upland Madison County. M.A. thesis, University of Virginia, Charlottesville, Virginia.

West, Max
  1904   The Revival of Handicrafts in America. U.S. Bureau of Labor *Bulletin* 9
          (55): 1573–1622.
Wylie, A.
  1993   Invented Lands/Discovered Pasts: The Westward Expansion of Myth
          and History. *Historical Archaeology* 27(4): 1–19.
Yonge, Samuel H.
  1903   *The Site of Old Jamestown.* Association for the Preservation of Virginia
          Antiquities, Richmond.
Yowell, C. L.
  1926   *A History of Madison County, Virginia.* Virginia Publishing House,
          Strasburg, Virginia.

2

The Woman Movement: Memorial to Women's Rights Leaders and the Perceived Images of the Women's Movement

Courtney Workman

Introduction

The statue formally known as *The Portrait Monument* was designed by Adelaide Johnson in 1920 to commemorate the passage of the Nineteenth Amendment, which enfranchised women on August 26, 1920. The monument portrays Elizabeth Cady Stanton, Susan Brownwall Anthony, and Lucretia Mott, prominent leaders of the suffrage movement. Over the years the statue has been known by several other names. Records indicate that the statue was originally entitled *The Woman Movement;* however, the architect of the Capitol, when unable to verify this title in 1963, created interpretive signage for the statue and formally designated it as *The Portrait Monument*—which does little to explain the political impact the women's actions had on the nation (Maloney 1997a, vol. 1:1, 1997b, vol. 1:2; National Woman's Party 1995:1). Another name, *Three Ladies in a Bathtub,* refers to what detractors see as an unusual and cumbersome design. More recently, the statue has become known by some as *The Suffrage Statue,* because of the three women's involvement in and leadership of the national suffrage campaign. The lack of consensus for the name of the statue is the first obstacle in defining the purpose and meaning of the monument and its relationship to women. As a result, the magnitude of the work the three women accomplished and the statue's contribution to national history remain unsettled in the national public memory.

Since its creation in 1920, and its unveiling before the Capitol building, the statue has never been fully recognized or sanctioned by Congress. Reeling already from the embarrassment of having given women the vote, members of the Joint Committee on the Library (of Congress), which is responsible for the placement of artwork in the Capitol, declared they would not accept the statue (Capitol Surrendered, 1921:7). After the National Woman's Party forced Congress to take the monument, Congress quickly relocated it from the Rotunda to the Capitol basement, where it remained hidden for seventy-five years. Three separate times, in 1928, 1932, and 1950, women's groups lobbied for legislation that would have returned the statue to the Rotunda. Not until the fourth attempt in 1995 did such lobbying bring success (Sparks 1995).

As legislation traveled through the House and Senate in 1995 and 1996 calling for the statue to be moved to another prominent place, it encountered an enormous amount of opposition. The monument's validity was attacked on the basis of its appearance, the monument was cited as being racially oppressive, and the monument became an object of contest for two successful political action committees and their perceptions of what a woman pioneer is. The sentiments for and against the statue's display—and the contested meanings surrounding the statue—continue today. Several diverging groups claim authoritative knowledge of what the monument represents and compete in a public forum to promote their views (fig. 2.1). (I have selected brief phrases from the statue's inscription to introduce the sections that follow; each such heading appears in quotation marks.)

"The Three Great Destiny Characters of the World"

The various titles that the statue has been given are indicative of the value that groups have placed on the monument. The title that I support and will use to refer to the statue is *The Woman Movement*. The sculptor of the statue, Adelaide Johnson, chose this title to represent "the movement's past, present, and future" (Mayo 1980:381; Mayo 1996:2). In addition, this title encompasses the many elements of the women's movement, instead of being restricted to the issue of suffrage.

Throughout the nineteenth century American democracy was largely based on English common law, which denied that women were autonomous beings. Because of this limited definition, women were not considered U.S. citizens, and while they did have to pay taxes, they could not own property or businesses, divorce their husbands, attend institutions of

Figure 2.1. *The Woman Movement* displayed in the Capitol rotunda. 1998. (Photo: Aaron Tark.)

higher education, or vote (Evans 1997:22). Supporters of the women's movement in the 1800s and 1900s fought against this state of affairs. They asserted "that women were full human beings who should be legal persons as much as men, exercising the same rights as men in society in legal, political, and economic transactions, as well as having access to education and employment" (Radford-Ruether 1996). In order to achieve political, social, civil, and economic rights for women, Elizabeth Cady Stanton, Susan B. Anthony, and Lucretia Mott worked to redefine the concept of womanhood.

Stanton, Anthony, and Mott used organizational tactics that they had learned from the temperance and abolitionist movements to organize women and demand the right to vote. Stanton and Mott, a Quaker preacher, had met in London at the Anti-Slavery Convention of 1840, where female delegates were barred from the meeting's proceedings. This event convinced Stanton and Mott that they needed to work together to improve the lot of women (Evans 1997:81; Schneir 1992:76). In 1848 they orchestrated the Women's Rights Convention, held in Seneca Falls,

New York, from which the guidelines, the principles, and the tone of the women's rights movement would emerge (Griffith 1984:50–54). For the convention, Stanton wrote the Declaration of Sentiments, premised on the Declaration of Independence, which stated: "The history of mankind is a history of repeated injuries and usurpations on the part of man toward woman, having in direct object the establishment of an absolute tyranny over her" (Stanton 1848:78). One of the declaration's resolutions called for women to receive the voting franchise—a notion so radical that it garnered the bare minimum of votes needed to be adopted as a resolution by the gathering (Schneir 1992:77).

Three years later, in 1851, Stanton and Anthony met at the home of a mutual friend. They immediately formed a unique friendship with a strong and compatible division of labor and in 1869 cofounded the National Woman Suffrage Association (Evans 1997:124). Stanton wrote about their teamwork: "She [Anthony] supplied the facts and statistics, I the philosophy and rhetoric, and, together, we have made arguments that stood unshaken through the storms of long years; arguments that no one has answered. Our speeches may be considered the united product of our two brains" (Schneir 1992:117).

"Women, Their Rights, and Nothing Less"

The sculptor of *The Woman Movement,* Adelaide Johnson (1859–1955), completed the statue in 1920 at her studio in Italy (Dunford 1989:151). Johnson constructed the heads and torsos of Anthony, Stanton, and Mott from an eight-ton piece of Italian Carrara marble, working from individual busts she had previously displayed at the 1893 Chicago Exposition (Mayo 1980:380). Johnson left unfinished marble as the base of the statue and rising behind the heads of the three pioneers in order to represent the ongoing nature of the women's movement (Faragasso and Stover 1997: 54; Mayo 1996:1).

In September 1920, the National Woman's Party submitted a request to Congress to display the statue of the three suffragists in the Capitol rotunda. The request was not given a high priority by the all-male Sixty-Sixth Congress, and the issue was not addressed during the legislative session. When Congress reconvened on December 6, 1920, they continued to ignore the issue of the statue's placement until its arrival at the steps of the Capitol on February 5, 1921. The Congress hurriedly met to discuss the issue, and on February 10, 1921, the Joint Committee on the Library

Figure 2.2. Left, Adelaide Johnson, sculptor of *The Woman Movement*, and Alice Paul, president of the National Woman's Party, in front of *The Woman Movement*. February 15, 1921. (Courtesy Library of Congress.)

agreed to accept the monument with the understanding that the National Woman's Party would withdraw its demand that the statue be displayed in the Rotunda. Alice Paul, president of the National Woman's Party, agreed to the stipulation, which caused great discontent on both sides (Guthrie 1998:3) (fig. 2.2).

Just three weeks before the statue's acceptance by Congress, the vice president of the United States had declared "that the statues of the three pioneer suffrage leaders would never go into the Capitol with his permission" (Capitol Surrendered 1921:7). Much of the U.S. population was at the time still opposed to women's enfranchisement, as illustrated by a 1921 editorial stating that Congress could not "hide the humiliation of its own sheepish surrender to a handful of militant Amazons" (Loose 1995; Capitol Surrendered 1921:7).

The statue was formally presented to Congress on February 15, 1921, which would have been Susan B. Anthony's 101st birthday, at a dedication ceremony featuring Sara Bard Field and F. H. Gillett, Speaker of the House (Faragasso and Stover 1997:55; Field 1921:1; Mayo 1980:381; U.S. Capitol 1995a:1; Perusek 1997:10). Sara Field, offering the statue to the House Speaker, declared: "Mr. Speaker, we women who are uniting in this presentation do not feel we are so much honoring these three rebel leaders as we are honoring Congress itself by committing these busts to its keeping" (Field 1921:3). Gillett replied that the statue was indeed "symbolic of a change of tremendous significance—the admission of women into our electorate as equal partners in the great business of government" (Guthrie 1998:5).

Following the dedication ceremony, *The Woman Movement* was displayed in the Rotunda for two days before being removed and sent to a broom closet in the Capitol basement (Maloney 1997b:1; Radford-Ruether 1996:22). Although the National Woman's Party had agreed to the stipulation that the statue could not be displayed in the Rotunda, the group objected to the willful mistreatment of the statue and made numerous complaints about its storage (National Museum of Women's History 1997a:3). In 1922, women's groups actually visited the Capitol to personally clean the faces of the three women, an act headlined in a 1922 article, "Angry Women Invade the Capitol" (Loose 1995). Also in 1922 the gold-leaf inscription, discreetly placed on the back of the statue so as not to detract from the women's images, was blotted out with paint. Congress ordered the paint job because they believed the message in the inscription was "fulsome" and "blasphemous" (Loose 1995; Brooke 1996). Included in the inscription were the words: "Woman, first denied a soul, then called mindless, now arisen declared herself an entity to be reckoned." The inscription also referred to Stanton, Anthony, and Mott as "the three great destiny characters of the world, who guided the only fundamental universal uprising on our planet" (U.S. Capitol 1995b:1).

Women's groups for more than twenty-five years lobbied Congress to approve a bill that would remove the statue from the broom closet (Brooke 1996; Sparks 1995). In 1963, the monument was moved into the Capitol crypt—the temporary holding place for the bodies of deceased presidents (Radford-Ruether 1996). It was at this time that the monument's formal name, *The Woman Movement,* was changed to *The Group Portrait Monument* (Brooke 1996; Maloney 1996; Mayo 1996:2). Later that year, the crypt opened to visitors, and the statue, just a few feet from a concession stand, was still displayed without any interpretation. In fact, the statue faced a wall. This was the "esthetic and historic integrity" of the statue that George White, architect of the Capitol, would later convey to House Speaker Newt Gingrich as he recommended not to relocate the statue (Love 1996:6).

In 1995, the United States celebrated the seventy-fifth anniversary of the Nineteenth Amendment, and there were renewed public efforts to relocate the statue for display at a more prominent site. Women's rights activists Joan Meacham and Karen Staser, founders of the National Museum of Women's History, created the Women's Suffrage Statue Campaign in order to raise funds and public awareness about the statue, and to lobby Congress to relocate it (Radford-Ruether 1996). On July 17, 1995, the Senate unanimously voted to raise the statue back into the Capitol rotunda. The resolution was temporarily stalled, however, when Representative Sue Myrick objected to using federal funds ($75,000) to move the statue (Love 1995; Maloney 1997a:1). To quell concern, the Women's Suffrage Statue Campaign mobilized seventy-eight other women's organizations and mounted an aggressive campaign to raise the necessary funds. On May 12, 1997, the statue was lifted into the Rotunda; a rededication ceremony, reception, and open house took place on June 26, 1997 (Maloney 1997d:1).

"Justice, Not Favor"

For some individuals *The Woman Movement* is simply a work of art, and they do not take into account the intentions of the artist or the purpose for commissioning the statue. The statue's relocation was hindered several times on account of its appearance. When Sue Myrick delayed the Senate's resolution to move the statue, she stated to the press: "I only deep-sixed moving it with public money. I don't think it's very attractive either" (Brooke 1996). George Will, columnist for the *Washington Post,* wrote in 1997: "The answer to Freud's famous question—'What does a woman want?'—is an unattractive statue in the Capitol Rotunda" (Will 1997).

Congresswoman Carolyn Maloney replied to Will's jibe: "Dismissing the statue's importance by calling it 'unattractive' belittles the accomplishments of the women who are depicted. Mr. Lincoln is not in the Rotunda because of his beauty. He is there because of his contributions to the nation. Leading the battle to enfranchise half the population of the United States is no minor feat. It is one of the most significant accomplishments in our nation's history" (Maloney 1997c:1).

Referring to the statue as ugly diminishes the accomplishments of the women it honors. The "ugliness" of the statue refers both to the individual women—Elizabeth Cady Stanton, Susan B. Anthony, and Lucretia Mott—and the cumbersome design of the statue. The purpose of the Capitol rotunda is not to present sculptures on the basis of their aesthetics; it is to commemorate the achievements of Americans and to recognize important moments in the nation's history. The argument that the statue is unattractive has been used so often, however, that it is necessary to question why the attractiveness of the statue is so pertinent to its acceptance.

A fellow visitor I spoke with at the Capitol one day remarked that *The Woman Movement* seemed very austere when compared to the many other statues, all of them male, in the Rotunda. He interpreted those remaining male statues as appearing proud and determined. After questioning other visitors, I realized that his interpretation was similar to that of many other people who saw the statue. The facial expression of every statue in the Rotunda is very similar and could best be interpreted as grim. The main difference in the appearance of the statues is that the male statues are life-size and the men are standing on pedestals raised several feet from the floor. In some cases their faces and eyes are focused downward—a posture that seems imposing and domineering. Their stance and stature contribute to a feeling of superiority, but not necessarily of pride. *The Woman Movement* shows only the torsos and heads of the three women pioneers. Their faces do not look upward in idealization, nor downward in a dominating posture like the male statues. Their gazes are focused straight ahead, as though they are concentrated on the task at hand—a position and posture that can certainly be recognized as determination.

The posture of the male statues attaches them to a history of American individuality and strength; they are portrayed as leaders and conquerors, and their form implies that they have accomplished great things. Because we expect powerful men to have stern expressions, the statues comply with our notion of what great men are, and we associate this notion with pride. In contrast, great women are stereotyped as being moderate in personality, poised, and confident. A successful woman must be able to navigate socially, and this is not congruent with someone who is grim-faced. It is difficult to separate the purpose of the statue from the appearance of the women it portrays. The women cannot be viewed as successful because they are grim, and they are regulated to a subordinate position among the powerful male figures that surround them. This image is compounded by the fact that the women are sculpted as a bust. The only other personage in the Rotunda who is represented by a bust is Dr. Martin Luther King, Jr. The King statue and *The Woman Movement* are the only two statues that represent minorities in the Rotunda, as well.

"*The Woman Movement* Is the All-Enfolding One"

Just a few months before *The Woman Movement* was moved to the Capitol rotunda in 1997, the National Political Congress of Black Women mounted an aggressive drive to block its relocation. Led by C. DeLores Tucker, the group demanded that a likeness of Sojourner Truth be sculpted into a portion of the unfinished marble at the back of the statue (Merida 1997; Mondics 1997:424–25). Truth (1795–1883), a friend of Elizabeth Cady Stanton's, was freed from slavery in 1827 and devoted her life to the abolitionist movement. Although she never learned to read or write, she became widely known in scholarly and activist circles (Schneir 1992:93–94). Sojourner Truth was an influential and perceptive leader of the women's movement. The controversy over whether she should be a part of *The Woman Movement* concerns more than honoring her memory; it is an attempt to rewrite a shameful part of the feminist struggle. Because the statue depicts three middle-class white women, it is interpreted by many African-Americans as a testament to racist conflict in the suffrage movement (Mungen 1997; Tucker 1997:2).

Antislavery actions and abolitionist sentiments spurred the feminist movement of the nineteenth century. Working in organizations to promote the abolishment of slavery accomplished two things for white women—it gave them the tools and experience with which to organize around an issue, and it broadened their perception of oppression and how it applied to various groups. While many white women fought to end slavery, they formed connections between the subjugation of women and the practice of slavery. John Stuart Mill defined this connection as the only two occupations (besides royalty) that a person was born into that resulted in a complete lack of choice for the individuals (Mill 1869). Following the Civil War and emancipation, white women utilized the organizational tactics that they had learned as abolitionists to advocate for their own liberation. Although they had decried the use of slavery, they were not prepared to accept an African-American woman as one of themselves.

In many cases, "black suffragists sometimes felt that white feminists, for the sake of expediency, disenfranchised and excluded black women if they felt it would help politically" (Mungen 1997). Today, members of the National Political Congress of Black Women led by C. Delores Tucker and their supporters—the NAACP, the Congressional Black Caucus, and many others—see *The Woman Movement* as outdated and a biased reconstruction of the suffrage movement (Merida 1997). The statue represents an oppressive era for African-Americans in general, and black women in particular. Addressing the issue of the statue, Tucker said: "We are tired of our contributions to this nation being ignored and passed over. If they insist on putting it [the statue] in the Rotunda, it will be a monument of feminine racism" (Mondics 1997:424). The National Museum of Women's History, responsible for raising the necessary funds to relocate the statue, maintains that the museum fully intends to honor Sojourner Truth's life and accomplishments (as well as those of other suffrage and women's rights leaders, black and white), but that this statue "was intended to honor only the first three women to organize at a national level" (National Museum of Women's History 1997b:1). Tucker argues that "the fact that so few remember the past in which African-American women did march for suffrage, not twice, but three times is telling evidence of the need to provide an accurate symbol for the twenty-first century generations to come" (Tucker 1997:4).

"The Emancipation of Womanhood"

The Woman Movement is also at the center of one of the nation's most controversial issues—abortion. Two groups claim to know which side the women pioneers would choose to support. On one side of the debate is EMILY's List. EMILY's List was founded in 1995 (Women Are Gaining 1997) by activist Ellen Malcolm to help female candidates who were seeking political office. The acronym EMILY stands for Early Money Is Like Yeast and is meant to provide an early and large supply of funds to campaigning women so that political candidacy can become a viable option for more women (McCarthy 1997:9). In 1995, EMILY's List raised $5.8 million for women, which made it the number one fund-raiser among all political action committees (Cohen 1996:834). In 1996, the group raised $6.7 million (Women Are Gaining 1997). In order to be eligible for the financial support EMILY's List offers, a candidate must meet four requirements: she must be a woman, she must be a Democrat, she must have a realistic chance of winning, and she must be pro-choice (Cohen 1996:834).

In response to EMILY's List, the Susan B. Anthony List was created. Anthony's List has only one political requirement—that a candidate be pro-life. Founded in 1993, Anthony's List claims to have already helped elect seven women (all Republican), and to have taken office seats from two officeholders financially backed by EMILY's List (Malcolm 1997:8; McCarthy 1997:9).

Both organizations supported the relocation of *The Woman Movement*, and EMILY's List was a strong financial backer in the statue's relocation. Each organization advertises that the statue reflects its political beliefs. Anthony's List claims to use Anthony's name because they believe Anthony condemned the practice of abortion. To validate their argument the group points to writings authored by Anthony in *The Revolution*, a liberal newspaper Anthony and Stanton coproduced from 1868 to 1870 (Schneir 1992:137). Anthony's List has interpreted several of Anthony's comments in *The Revolution* as being antiabortion although the comments are vague and never explicitly state "abortion." One Anthony's List candidate, Congresswoman Helen B. Chenoweth, praised Anthony publicly for her early writings on the "sin of abortion." Chenoweth quoted Anthony from the July 8, 1869, issue of *The Revolution*: "We want prevention, not merely punishment. We must reach the root of the evil. . . . It is practiced by those whose inmost souls revolt from the dreadful deed" (McCarthy 1997:8). Jennifer Bingham, executive director and national fund-raiser for the Susan B. Anthony List, added that Anthony described abortion as "the horrible crime of child murder" and that she denounced men's reaction to the issue, claiming: "All the articles on the subject that I have read have been from men. They denounce women alone as guilty, and never include man in any plans proposed for the remedy of evil" (Malcolm 1997:8). Bingham noted that Anthony's List believes that if Anthony were alive today, she "would have been appalled to find that feminism today is often linked to support for abortion" (Malcolm 1997:8).

Although EMILY's List and Anthony's List illustrate the pervading belief that the physical materials left by these women lend themselves to definitive knowledge of the women's beliefs and personality, it is contentious to label pioneers like Stanton, Anthony, and Mott as "feminist" or to describe them as pro-choice or pro-life, because these terms were absent from their lexicon and because the meaning of theses terms is contested today. However, as pioneers of the women's movement, Stanton, Anthony, and Mott are referred to as feminists today. Extending from the concept of feminism and the women's work in the ninteenth century, Stanton, Anthony, and Mott are considered to be liberal women. Feminism is closely tied to the issue of abortion, and while certainly not all feminists consider themselves pro-choice, it is generally accepted that feminists have pro-choice and reproductive rights agendas. This acceptance can sometimes prove problematic. As Abigail McCarthy writes in *Commonweal,* a Catholic and pro-life journal, "EMILY's List was intended to support women with a liberal agenda, but it was hung up on the belief that has paralyzed the women's movement generally—that the right to abortion is liberating and must be upheld by any women seeking office" (McCarthy 1997:9). It might be time to redefine feminism to encompass a wider range of liberal beliefs and practices including a continuum of pro-choice to pro-life beliefs. Still, liberal feminists have become very angry over pro-life Republican women's appropriation of Susan B. Anthony's name. They feel that Republicans are co-opting an agenda contrary to feminism under a misleading feminist title; Republicans believe that liberals never owned this title.

"Principle, Not Policy"

Today, alongside each monument in the Capitol rotunda is a plaque posted in a solid wooden casing, enclosed in glass, with an explanation of the statue beside it. *The Woman Movement* sits in the Rotunda without the original 1920 inscription restored to the statue or displayed nearby. Its plaque fails to recognize Stanton, Anthony, and Mott's accomplishments; it merely offers their names and dates (fig. 2.3). The plaque appears out of place because it is plastic and temporary looking. If this is an attempt to create a national meaning, then it is one that says women do not have a permanent place in history nor should they.

Whether the statue's display is temporary is still unknown. The original legislation, House Resolution 216, adopted in 1996, allowed for the relocation of the monument and specified a one-year time limit for display. At the conclusion of one year, a commission of eleven interested parties, including congressional members and the architect of the Capitol, would convene to determine a permanent home for the statue. Why this one-year period was designated is unclear. Representative Maloney suggested that "if this congress was 90 percent female and 10 percent male—not 90 percent male and 10 percent female as it is today—I believe that there would not be a 1–year clause and that the women's suffrage statue would become a permanent fixture in the Rotunda" (Maloney 1996:2). Karen

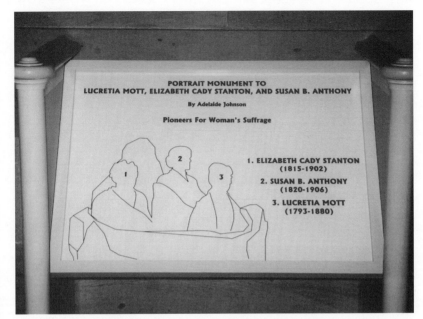

Figure 2.3. Placard for *The Woman Movement,* beside the monument in the Capitol rotunda. 1998. (Photo: Aaron Tark.)

Staser of the National Museum of Women's History believes that the clause was inserted solely to annoy the activist groups who had been bothering the House committee for the past seventy-six years. In addition, she noted that while no one could give her an explanation for the one-year time period, this rule had also been stipulated for the display of the Dr. Martin Luther King, Jr., bust, moved to the Rotunda in 1986 by Senate Resolution 84 and House Bill 153 (Staser 1999). Both *The Woman Movement* and the Dr. King monument have been on display for more than a year.

Part of the reason that *The Woman Movement* is still exhibited may have to do with funding. When House Resolution 216 was passed, it determined that funds to raise and lower the statue had to be raised by private groups. The $75,000 needed to raise the statue was quickly gathered, but the groups who collected it have not begun to raise funds to remove the statue. If Congress chooses to proceed in removing the monument from the Rotunda, public funds would have to be used. The public outcry that would result from removing the only woman's monument or the bust of Dr. Martin Luther King, Jr., from the Rotunda makes removal highly unlikely.

The work that remains is to approve and create the monument's interpretive signage. The placard proposed by the National Museum of Women's History included the text originally inscribed on the monument, acknowledgment of the 1848 Women's Rights Convention at Seneca Falls and its influence in the passage of the Nineteenth Amendment, and an explanation of why the statue appears unfinished. The Joint Committee on the Library, charged with the task of developing a plaque, has decided not to reinstate or even display the original inscription. What they have approved is:

PORTRAIT MONUMENT TO LUCRETIA MOTT, ELIZABETH CADY STANTON, AND SUSAN B. ANTHONY
BY ADELAIDE JOHNSON

A democracy's greatest benefit is the right to vote. The women suffrage movement was initiated in 1848 at Seneca Falls, New York. The efforts of the three women featured in this Portrait Monument statue were directed toward the passage of the 19th Amendment to the Constitution, which was adopted in 1920, and granted women the right to vote. Based on the artist's intent the unfinished portion of the Portrait Monument was to symbolize the future generations who would be concerned about women's rights. The monument was donated to the Capitol by the National Woman's Party and accepted for Congress by the Joint Committee on the Library on February 10, 1921.

DEDICATED FEBRUARY 15, 1921, PLACED IN THE CAPITOL ROTUNDA BY RESOLUTION OF CONGRESS FOR THE PERIOD MAY 1997–MAY 1998

This notice is inadequate for several reasons. First of all, it does not mention Stanton's and Mott's involvement in creating the Seneca Falls Convention. Second, this plaque does not express the enormity of what Mott, Stanton, and Anthony accomplished, their central role in the women's movement, and their relationships to the organizations that secured the vote for women. The statement "Based on the artist's intent, the unfinished portion of the *Portrait Monument* was to symbolize the future generations who would be concerned about women's rights" is insulting to women who incorporate activism into their lives. Adelaide Johnson intended the unfinished portion to be a testament to the women who would continue to fight for their equal rights. The use of the word "concern" diminishes women's actions in this context and construes the women's movement as less important and less active in contemporary society.

Finally, this placard formalizes the name of the monument as *The Portrait Monument,* which implies that the statue is nothing more than portraits of women. Similarly, when the statue is called *The Suffrage Statue,* it restricts the accomplishments of the women to a single event, instead of the more widespread reevaluation of women's roles and capacities, encompassing "civil, social, political and economic equality for women," that these three women introduced (Mayo 1996:2). The sculptor, Adelaide Johnson, noted: "This crusade was made with but one weapon—a Righteous Idea—the right of the human unit to freedom. Suffrage, the struggle which was so prolonged and made so spectacular by the opposition, was but one item, and became impinged upon the mass mind but will pass, as mere processes pass, as the mightiest thing, Equal Rights, freedom of the human unit becomes established" (Johnson 1934).

Displaying the monument in the Rotunda allows it to represent important American women in a national theater. Simone de Beauvoir wrote that language was socially constructed so that "man represents both the positive and the neutral, as is indicated by the common use of man to designate human beings in general; whereas woman represents only the negative, defined by limiting criteria (de Beauvoir 1953:13). Because "history" does not refer explicitly to a particular gender, it has become a neutral term and implicitly male. "Women's history" is a limiting term that regulates women's activities only to the realm of woman-ness and denies their relevance to that which is of the public domain. With women currently comprising 53 percent of the nation's population, their activities can no longer be confined to women alone and must be accorded and welcomed into their rightful place in national history.

Exhibiting *The Woman Movement* in the Capitol rotunda is an important step in honoring real women and their achievements rather than allegorical women. The female statues that Congress has traditionally supported are not historically based; they are fictional people that symbolize abstract meanings. In 1993 Congress allocated funds from the Capitol Preservation Committee—which oversees a private fund that is controlled by Congress and has a revenue of $23 million—to renovate the Statue of Freedom that adorns the top of the Capitol building (Love 1996:6). The renovation cost $750,000—ten times the cost to relocate *The Woman Movement.* As Karen Staser, cochair of the Women's Suffrage Statue Campaign, points out, "The Statue of Freedom, the Statue of Liberty, these are icons, not real women that girls and women can look up to." However, when seventy House members petitioned Newt Gingrich, chairman of the Preservation Committee, to use the Capitol Preservation funds for the relocation of *The Woman's Movement,* their pleas were rejected (Brooke 1996).

The Capitol is an internationally known symbol; in the Capitol brochure it is described as "the most recognized symbol of democratic government in the world." The description goes on to say that "the Capitol has grown along with the Nation," and that its "ceilings are decorated with historic images, and its halls are lined with statuary and paintings representing great events and people in the nation's history" (U.S. Congress 1997:1). Displaying *The Woman Movement* in the Capitol defines the women portrayed in the monument as "great people" and acknowledges that the statue must have real historic value. Furthermore, Adelaide Johnson saw the statue's exhibition as the "breakthrough of the spirit of feminism into the stronghold of its antithesis—the United States Capitol" (Mayo 1996:2). Displaying *The Woman Movement* in a nationally significant building is the first step toward promoting a national meaning for the statue.

Conclusion

Statistics clearly show that women are not equally commemorated on the American landscape. A National Park Service survey recently estimated that of the 2,200 National Historic Landmarks across the country, only 5 percent are dedicated to women (Brooke 1996). Inside the Capitol are approximately 200 statues; 11 of these statues portray women (*The Woman Movement* counts as three). Few of these statues succeed in showing women as positive role models; instead they feature women by their relationship and sometimes subordination to men. For example, there is a statue of Pocahontas kneeling before a man as she is baptized outside of her faith. There is also a statue of an anonymous woman with an inscription thanking her for giving the greatest gift possible to the United States— her sons and husband. The Rotunda is filled with male statues, and women are virtually invisible—the implicit message is that "women don't count" (Loose 1995).

By displaying *The Woman Movement* in a national context, Congress is taking a step toward addressing the gender inequality that exists in contemporary U.S. society. Denying the importance of the statue by refusing to exhibit it in a nationally significant site and to inform visitors of its history permits Congress to create policies against women and reinforces the notion of democracy as a glorified patriarchy. Eugenia Lopez of International Alert stated: "It is not individuals that perpetuate patriarchy and gender hierarchies. It is institutions and their embedded politics, practices and ideologies that are central in the continuation of women's marginal decision making role" (Glass Ceilings 1997). Former Representative Patricia Schroeder drew a parallel between the statue's history and issues relevant to women as they proceed through the legislative services, saying that like the statue, these issues are not allowed to come to the first floor of Congress and that she hopes "people watch what happens to that statue of those three women, and wake up and find out what is happening to the statutes that so many women have cared about" (Schroeder 1995: H9745–9746). Displaying memorials of women would continue to bring women back into the center of history and become a tool of empowerment for females. The prominent display of the statue offers an avenue for women and girls to reconnect with the achievements of their foremothers and sisters and encourages them to explore the range of opportunities before them. Congress is aware of the positive ramifications of the statue's display; Senate Concurrent Resolution 21 states that "the relocation of the Portrait Monument to a place of prominence and esteem in the Capitol rotunda would serve to honor and reserve the contribution of thousands of women" (U.S. Congress 1995).

It took seventy-six years to return *The Woman Movement* to the Rotunda; in comparison, it took women seventy-two years to gain the right to vote (National Museum of Women's History 1997a:4). "The fate of this statue is significant because it tells us a lot about how to tell the American story and create a public memory. Women's history and the struggle for women have been typically unimportant and forgettable, as is graphically illustrated by the saga of the statue of the three leaders of the women's suffrage movement" (Radford-Ruether 1996). The journey of this statue is one filled with obstacles and triumphs, which makes it an appropriate statue to represent women's contributions to national history.

References

Brooke, James
  1996   3 Suffragists (in Marble) to Move Up in the Capitol. *New York Times,*
          September 27, A18.

The Capitol Surrendered to Militants

1921   *Woman Patriot* 5(8/9): 7–13. Library of Congress, Washington, D.C. Call No. JK1903.A2.W6.

Cohen, Richard E.

1996   Plenty of Dough, but Little to Show. *National Journal* 28:15, 833–35.

de Beauvoir, Simone

1953   Introduction to *The Second Sex*. In *The Second Wave,* edited by Linda Nicholson, 11–18. Routledge Press, New York.

Dunford, Penny

1989   *A Biographical Dictionary of Women Artists in Europe and America since 1850*. University of Pennsylvania Press, Philadelphia.

Evans, Sara M.

1997   *Born for Liberty.* Free Press, New York.

Faragasso, Frank, and Doug Stover

1997   Adelaide Johnson: A Marriage of Art and Politics: Placing Women in the Past. *CRM* 20(3): 54–55.

Field, Sara Bard

1921   Speech to Congress at the presentation of the marble busts of three suffrage pioneers. Library of Congress, Washington, D.C. Call No. HQ1412.F53. Nine-page booklet.

Glass Ceilings and Sticky Floors

1997   *Women Envision* 44:4. [Found at http://www.jca.apc.org/aworc.]

Griffith, Elizabeth

1984   *In Her Own Right: The Life of Elizabeth Cady Stanton*. Oxford University Press, New York.

Guthrie, Gayle E.

1998   Susie, Lucy, and Liz. January 19. Unpublished paper. On file, National Museum of Women's History, Alexandria, Virginia.

Johnson, Adelaide

1934   Speech Delivered in the Capitol at the Monument to the Founders of the Woman Movement of the World February 15. On file, National Museum of Women's History, Alexandria, Virginia.

Loose, Cindy

1995   They Got the Vote, but Not the Rotunda. *Washington Post,* August 19.

Love, Alice A.

1995   Latest Round in War of the Statue Pits Warner against GOP Women. *Roll Call,* October 5, 3.

1996   Women's Groups to Raise $75,000 to Move the Statue. *Roll Call,* February 19, 6.

Malcolm, Teresa

1997   List Helps Women Candidates. *National Catholic Reporter* 33:17, 1997 [cited October 15, 1997]. [Found at http://www.umi.com.]

Maloney, Carolyn B.

1996   Providing for Relocation of Portrait Monument. Testimony before the

U.S. House of Representatives, September 26, E1869. On file, National Museum of Women's History, Alexandria, Virginia.

1997a State of the Statue. Volume 1. On file, office of Carolyn B. Maloney, Washington, D.C. January 17.

1997b State of the Statue. Volume 1. On file, office of Carolyn B. Maloney, Washington, D.C. February 4.

1997c State of the Statue. Volume 1. On file, office of Carolyn B. Maloney, Washington, D.C. February 24.

1997d State of the Statue. Volume 1. On file, office of Carolyn B. Maloney, Washington, D.C. June 17.

May, Nina

1997 A Renaissance of Womanhood: The Founding Mothers Fought for More Than Equality. *Paradigm,* Spring: 4–7.

Mayo, Edith

1980 Adelaide Johnson. In *Notable American Women,* vol. 4, *The Modern Period,* edited by Carol Hurd Green and Barbara Sicherman, 380–81. Harvard University Press, Cambridge.

1996 History of the Suffrage Pioneers Monument. On file, National Museum of Women's History, Alexandria, Virginia.

McCarthy, Abigail

1997 Women and Money and Politics. *Commonweal* 124:14.

Merida, Kevin

1997 A Vote against Suffrage Statue. *Washington Post,* April 4, A1.

Mill, John Stuart

1869 The Subjection of Women. In *Feminism, the Essential Historical Writings,* edited by Miriam Schneir, 163–78. Vintage Books, New York.

Mondics, Chris

1997 Black Women's Groups Fight Plan for Prominent Placement of Suffragist Statue Depicting Only White Women. Knight-Ridder/Tribune News Service, April 24, 424–25.

Mungen, Donna

1997 Let's Get the History and Our Statue Right. *USA Today,* April 25, A15.

National Museum of Women's History

1997a Fact Sheet, 3–4. On file, National Museum of Women's History, Alexandria, Virginia.

1997b Myths and Facts about the Group Portrait Monument to the Pioneers of the Woman Suffrage Movement, 1–2. On file, National Museum of Women's History, Alexandria, Virginia.

National Woman's Party

1995 The Woman Movement's History and Current Status. On file, National Museum of Women's History, Alexandria, Virginia. April.

Perusek, Anne M.

1997 Ground Swell of Support Raises Monument from Crypt to Rotunda. *Magazine of the Society of Women Engineers,* July/August, 10–12.

Radford-Ruether, Rosemary
  1996   Fight for Women's Vote Key to Nation's Identity. *National Catholic Reporter* 33(4): 22.
Schneir, Miriam, ed.
  1992   *Feminism, the Essential Historical Writings*. Vintage Books, New York.
Schroeder, Patricia
  1995   This Congress Is Antieverything the Congressional Caucus on Women's Issues Has Worked For. Testimony before the U.S. House of Representatives, October 10, H9745–9746.
Sparks, Caroline H.
  1995   Remarks (testimony before the U.S. Senate). July 24, S10563. On file, National Museum of Women's History, Alexandria, Virginia.
Stanton, Elizabeth Cady
  1848   Declaration of Sentiments. In *Feminism: The Essential Historical Writings*, edited by Miriam Schneir, 77–82. Vintage Books, New York.
Staser, Karen
  1999   Personal interview. March 19.
Tucker, C. DeLores
  1997   An Open Letter to the Council of Presidents. June 19. On file, National Museum of Women's History, Alexandria, Virginia.
U.S. Capitol
  1995a   Office of the Curator. Brief Chronology of the Portrait Monument to Lucretia Mott, Elizabeth Cady Stanton, and Susan B. Anthony. On file, National Museum of Women's History, Alexandria, Virginia.
  1995b   Office of the Curator. Original Inscription on the Portrait Monument. August. On file, National Museum of Women's History, Alexandria, Virginia.
U.S. Congress. House of Representatives.
  1996   Concurrent Resolution 216, September 26, H. Doc. 11359. 104th Congress, 2nd Session.
U.S. Congress. Senate.
  1995   Concurrent Resolution 21, July 14, S. Doc. 10011. 104th Congress, 1st Session.
  1997   Sergeant at Arms. Capitol brochure. U.S. Senate Sergeant at Arms, Washington, D.C.
Will, George F.
  1997   Ladies in the Rotunda. *Washington Post*, March 23, C6.
Women Are Gaining and Exercising Power in All Facets of Their Lives
  1997   About Women and Marketing 10:9, 1997 [cited November 13, 1997]. Contemporary Women's Issues from Responsive Database Services. [Found at http://www.silverplatter.com.]

3

The Third Battle of Manassas: Power, Identity, and the Forgotten African-American Past

Erika K. Martin Seibert

Introduction

The National Park Service (NPS), with its commitment to the preservation of our nation's past, has made an effort to interpret history through various methods. Museums, monuments, and statues in our national parks all attest to this ongoing preservation effort. Since the 1960s however, various groups who have been left out of traditional presentations have lobbied to be represented as an integral part of this history. The effort to develop more inclusive histories at Civil War national battlefields has been such a struggle.

Many national battlefield parks are almost exclusively about commemorating the event. Increasingly, Civil War battlefield park managers are recognizing that the land set aside for preservation and interpretation of this event often includes communities who were affected by the Civil War. They existed on this land long before and after this event, and their stories and material past can contribute a new dimension to the park's interpretation.

Manassas National Battlefield Park in Manassas, Virginia, is an example of a place where the area's diverse social history has not made its way into the park's everyday interpretation. Since its creation as a Confederate Park in the 1920s, the presentation of history at Manassas has been influenced by both its geography and memories of the "Lost Cause." There have been many chances to incorporate social history into the park, although at present little of this can be seen. In fact, over the past fifteen years new research has uncovered information about a large and diverse community consisting of wealthy, middling, and poor European-American and African-American agriculturalists who lived in the area. Documentary research and oral history paint a picture of life in this Southern community from many different perspectives and can enrich park history by broadening the scope of information about life before, during, and after the two battles of Manassas. Much of this information has been ignored in the construction of new interpretive displays in the park's visitor center, and park managers and interpreters continue to focus on the battles themselves at the expense of other time periods and histories.

Manassas National Battlefield Park: Confederates in the Attic?

In the past, community members and park staff in Manassas have been concerned with the preservation of a particular perspective of the Civil War that emphasizes the two battles of Manassas (Bull Run) and the Civil War period over other time periods and histories. In addition, since the park's inception, the NPS, the local community, and several Civil War groups including the United Daughters of Confederate Veterans (UDC) and Sons of Confederate Veterans (SCV) have participated in the preservation of cultural resources at the park. These groups have also been instrumental in restoring and preserving the landscape of the park to its 1861–1862 appearance at the expense of other time periods and histories.

Manassas is located approximately twenty-six miles southwest of Washington, D.C. This area of the Virginia Piedmont has been used by several different cultural groups for at least the last ten thousand years. Native Americans hunted buffalo in the area and regularly burned the forests, creating plains (Zenzen 1995:60). During the middle to late seventeenth century, English colonial settlers moved there from the Tidewater area, displacing the Native American population, and established small farms. By the 1720s Robert "King" Carter had amassed approximately 100,000 acres and divided it into leased tracts. Carter formed a network of large plantations worked by African slaves (Zenzen 1995:60). Enslaved Africans provided labor for the grain crops produced in this area and also held a wide variety of other labor roles, such as personal servant and artisan (Reeves 1998:2.2). Eventually, free African-Americans and freed African slaves represented a significant portion of the population in the area.

During the latter half of the eighteenth century the rise in agricultural production spurred a network of roads and small towns in the area (Reeves 1998:2.2). By the nineteenth century, the Warrenton Turnpike and the Orange and Alexandria Railroad facilitated occupation in this area and westward (Zenzen 1995:60). The location of the railroad line and its junction at Manassas proved an important strategic position and drew Union and Confederate troops here in July 1861 for the Civil War's first major land battle, which lasted approximately ten hours (Zenzen 1995:60). Less than two months after the Confederate victory at Manassas, Southern soldiers erected a historic marker in honor of Col. Francis S. Bartow of the Eighth Georgia Infantry. While these lands were still privately owned, the landscape began to take on a different meaning, particularly for the soldiers who fought there and the Southern community that recognized this area as a memorial of a Southern victory.

The Union and Confederate armies met for a second time in the Manassas area in August 1862, this time for three days. Again, the Confederacy won the battle; however, it wasn't until June 1865 that another memorial was erected on the Manassas battlefield. This time, under orders from the U.S. Army, two memorials were erected, under the direction of Lieut. James M. McCallum of the Sixteenth Massachusetts Battery. Lieutenant McCallum oversaw soldiers from the Fifth Pennsylvania Heavy Artillery as they constructed the monuments. One monument was placed on Henry Hill, an area that had seen heavy fighting during First Manassas, and one at Groveton, an area that had seen action during Second Manassas. Both memorials display the inscription, "In memory of the patriots who fell" (Zenzen 1995:23; Sarles 1955:5–7, 10). In 1867 a group of women from the local community established the Groveton Cemetery "for the purpose of reinterring Confederate remains" (Zenzen 1995:24), and in 1904 the Bull Run Chapter of the United Daughters of the Confederacy erected a Confederate monument in this cemetery. Only a few years later, in 1906, the State of New York added three granite monuments to commemorate the Fifth New York Volunteers, the Tenth New York Volunteers, and the Fourteenth Brooklyn (Eighty-Fourth New York).

During the postwar period it seemed that Manassas represented a memorial for both North and South, a place where veterans could come together from both sides and shake hands on the battlefield where their fellow soldiers had once killed each other. In July 1911 the Manassas National Jubilee of Peace was held in observance of the fiftieth anniversary of the first battle. Both Union and Confederate veterans displayed their support of the jubilee and joined in the festivities. However, the continued erection of monuments and memorial rituals by both the South and Confederate organizations, and the North or U.S. government, represents the struggle for control of the memory of the Civil War in Manassas.

In 1921 the SCV established a Confederate Park on Henry Hill. With help from the UDC, funds were raised and the Manassas Battlefield Corporation was created. E.W.R. Ewing, the historian-in-chief of the SCV, served as the president of the corporation and saw as its mission an opportunity to give voice to the South's "distinct, wonderful, equally thrilling, all-important story": "The corporation saw the Confederate park as a way to 'offer the *full truth*,' in the hopes that the 'truth shall make our children free.' . . . The corporate directors intended the Manassas National Battlefield Confederate Park to serve as the 'supreme battlefield memorial' to all Confederate soldiers" (Zenzen 1995:42–43).

To show their support for the park and its mission, several organizations donated money, including the UDC, the Southern Confederated Memorial Association, the Confederate Veterans, and the SCV, as did individuals throughout the South. The Virginia state legislature donated $10,000. Each Southern state had a representative on the corporation's audit board and contributed to the organization for the park (Zenzen 1995: 44). Despite these contributions, the Confederate Park suffered financially, and by the 1930s the corporation began negotiations with the National Park Service.

By 1935 the Roosevelt administration had already designated 1,476 acres of the Manassas battlefields as the Bull Run Recreational Demonstration Area. Recreational demonstration projects by the Roosevelt administration helped to provide recreational facilities for low-income families (Roosevelt 1938:146–47). Negotiations between the corporation and the National Park Service were intense. When members of the SCV learned that the Park Service wanted to incorporate the lands of the Manassas Battlefield Confederate Park into a national park, they were opposed because they "held reservations about having the federal government take a park that Southern money and dedication had created" (Zenzen 1995:47). Despite these hesitations, in June 1935, after a "bitter all day debate," the SCV voted to donate their lands to the NPS; however, the SCV placed restrictions on their gift (Zenzen 1995:58). The SCV received a promise that the Park Service would erect a museum at the park and stipulated that historic markers and monuments had to display the "strictest accuracy and fairness" and not detract from the "glory due the Confederate heroes" (Zenzen 1995:66).

The park focused more on troop movements than on social and economic aspects of the war in order to remain "fair" to opposing views for the impetus of the Civil War. "Causes of the Civil War also did not find expression in the [original] museum plan. While contemporary historiography has addressed issues such as the polarization of North and South over slavery, states' rights, economic considerations and international relations, the Park Service chose to focus on military maneuvers. In this way, the federal government did not antagonize its northern and southern visitors by discussing contentious issues" (Zenzen 1995:72–73).

Not straying from its focus on military maneuvers, the Park Service remained dedicated to restoring the landscape of the park to its 1861–1862 appearance. As a result, the interpretive focus outside the museum on the land itself has ignored the social history of the community. In addition, historic structures have been destroyed or left to crumble, monuments have been moved from their original locations, and land use within and around the park has been limited so as not to impinge on the visitor's view. For instance, in the 1960s the park acquired the Stone Bridge, a prominent landmark during both battles. While the park wanted the bridge, a monument erected by the UDC on the bridge represented an intrusion to the historic scene. Superintendent Francis Wilshin convinced UDC president Isabel Hutchison that the monument should be destroyed, arguing that the removal of the monument to restore the landscape to its 1861–62 appearance would "further the cause of her dear Confederacy" (Zenzen 1995:121).

In several instances, developers have planned to intrude on the historic scene by building adjacent to the park. Two theme parks have been dissuaded to use land adjacent to the park, the Great America theme park (1973) and Disney's America (1994). The developer Hazel/Peterson proposed a corporate office park in the 1980s adjacent to the park. This too was halted. Also, in the 1980s the SCV donated $7,000 for a new audiovisual program in the park's visitor center. Local residents and other individuals have rallied to recreate the 1861 landscape and rekindle memories of the "Lost Cause."

The cost of placing one particular history over another has been loss of diversity for Manassas National Battlefield. Since the park's creation, questions of the history of the community itself, its European-American and African-American residents, and the effects of the Civil War on slave populations and women and children have not been addressed. These subjects have gained increased public attention as a result of social and civil rights movements since the 1960s; however, this was not reflected in the park's interpretative focus. Manassas continued to focus its interpretation on the troop movements and soldier life of the Civil War.

Archaeological and historical investigations on the battlefield have uncovered a diverse African-American community consisting of African slaves and free African-American landowners, farmers, and tenant farmers, blacksmiths, teachers, laborers, and others. The exclusion of social history and, in particular, of African-American history in the interpretive focus is also a loss to Manassas National Battlefield and the NPS. The two African-American archaeological sites described here show that this history is an important part of the story of the Manassas community.

The Robinson House Site

The Robinson House site was in the midst of the fighting during the First Battle of Manassas and was used as a headquarters, as well as a field hospital, during the Second Battle of Manassas. The house stood as a symbol of African-American heritage, representing the struggles and continuity of this community.

The original Robinson House, built by James Robinson, also known as Gentleman Jim, was constructed in the 1840s and went through a series of structural additions in the late 1800s (fig. 3.1). The original house is believed to have been completely removed in 1926 when a section of the house was rebuilt. "The 1926 era Robinson House stood until 1993 when arsonists burned the structure" (Parsons, in press:4). The National Park Service dismantled the house, contending that more could be learned about the site by dismantling the house and examining architectural evidence and by archaeological excavations. The east chimney and stone foundations were left on the battlefield, and these became a symbol of the African-American presence on the battlefield.

Little is known about the early life of James Robinson other than the fact that he was born in 1799. Oral tradition contends that his father was Landon Carter, grandson of Robert "King" Carter (Parsons 1996:1), and his mother was a slave on the plantation Pittsylvania, also located on Manassas National Battlefield. Court records have confirmed that James was born free, although he was indentured for a period of time as a young man.

James Robinson was married to a slave named Susan Gaskins and had six children, all born into slavery. The Robinson papers show that Robinson bought one of his sons, Tasco, out of slavery, and at one point "bound out," or indentured his daughter. The documents also show that Robinson came to own his own farm and was a trusted and respected member of his community who conducted business with many prominent families. James Robinson died on October 16, 1875, and his property was divided among his wife and children. Members of the family continued to

Figure 3.1. Photo of the late-nineteenth-century Robinson House, showing structural additions. (Courtesy Manassas National Battlefield Park.)

live at the site until 1936, when the Robinsons sold the house and surrounding property to the U.S. government, which soon turned it into Manassas National Battlefield Park.

Archaeological excavations were performed in 1995 and 1996. Several significant features were located during these excavations, including the base and portion of a hearth of the 1840s Robinson House chimney, a Civil War–era barn, a possible root cellar or privy, foundations to an unidentified outbuilding, and the remains of an icehouse, later used as a trash pit by the family. Material culture recovered during the excavations reflects the technological development during the nineteenth century, as well as the ability of the Robinsons to recover financially and emotionally from the war. For instance, various farm implements were recovered from the site. A horse-drawn plow was eventually replaced by a tractor. An early form of butter churn was eventually replaced by a later one (Martin and Parsons 1998).

The trash-pit feature is believed to have been the original icehouse used by the family. The move from using this type of food storage to an indoor icebox provided the family with indoor refrigeration and the use of the outdoor space, previously occupied by the icehouse, as a trash pit. The material evidence shows the success of this family as they faced changing racial ideologies in this area of Virginia.

Despite the years of adversity the Robinsons survived and remain a strong voice in the Manassas community (Martin Seibert 1999).

The Nash Site and Other African-American Households on the Battlefield

The Nash site was discovered during an archaeological survey in 1990 and was excavated during the summer of 1991 by NPS employees and volunteers (Galke 1992b:8). The site was occupied by an African-American family, Philip Nash and his wife and children, during the mid to late nineteenth century.

Although census records for 1860 and 1870 do not mention the Nash family or the structure, artifacts suggest the family began living at the site sometime during the mid–nineteenth century. Prince William County census records from 1880 list the Nash household, which included Philip Nash, a 42-year-old black farmer, his 44-year-old wife, Sarah, and five children—Frances (age 12), Henry (age 10), Hallie (age 8), Lucy (age 6), and Sallie (age 2)—living near the community of Groveton (McCartney 1992:123).

Archaeological evidence proves intriguing in that it may be indicative of the Nash family's African heritage. Material culture—including colonoware ceramics (a low-fired, locally made earthenware indicative of the traditional potting techniques of Native American and African potters), tobacco pipes, blue beads, mancala gaming pieces, and marine shells—has been found within several African-American contexts on Manassas National Battlefield Park, including the sites of Portici, Brownsville, Nash, and the Robinson House (Hernigle 1991; Galke 1992a,b; Parsons 1999). (Mancala games originated in Africa and Asia and are still played today.) The recurrence of these items on African-American sites in the Chesapeake region and Virginia Piedmont suggests that they represent the continuity of an African identity (see Brown and Cooper 1990; Cabek 1990; Epperson 1991; Kelso 1986; Ryder 1991a, 1991b).

Artifacts, such as quartz crystals and blue beads, found at the Nash site suggest that the site may have been a location for African-Americans to meet in order to practice traditional religions out of the sight of their owners or others in the Euro-American community. "Its location would have been ideal, situated along a major transportation route, and central to several nearby plantations" (Galke 1992a:10). As archaeologist Laura Galke explains:

[A] . . . more covert form of resistance available to African-Americans was the development and maintenance of ethnic identity. Through the development and maintenance of a unique subculture, . . . [African-Americans] were able to promote group cohesion without directly confronting [white society]. The sharing of culture amongst African-Americans developed unity, pride, and courage for the daily struggle which they endured. (Galke 1992a:10)

A cache of six quartz crystals recovered at the Nash site, which included the mineral galena and a quartz projectile point, as well as crystals found in other contexts at the site suggest that they may have been used as part of traditional African divination or conjuring practices (Galke 1992a:10; Jones 1999:1). Quartz crystals have also been found in African-American contexts in Virginia and Maryland, at Thomas Jefferson's Poplar Forest (Patten 1992) and at the Charles Carroll House (Logan et al. 1992; Jones 1999).

Some ceramic sherds recovered at the site may also be indicative of the continuity of an African belief system. The broken ceramics are geometrically shaped smooth pieces that are thought to have been used in the game of mancala. Similar game pieces have been found at African-American sites throughout Virginia, Maryland, and the Caribbean, including Drax Hall in Jamaica (Armstrong 1990), Monticello (see Parker and Hernigle 1990:207), Garrison Plantation (Klingelhofer 1987), on Montserrat, at Galways Plantation (see Patten 1992), at Thomas Jefferson's Poplar Forest (Patten 1992), and at Manassas National Battlefield at Portici Plantation (Parker and Hernigle 1990:207–8), Brownsville (Galke 1992b), and the Robinson House (Parsons 1999).

Several other African-American sites have been identified on the Manassas battlefield. These include the Davis household at the Sudley Post Office site (Reeves 1998). Artifacts and other information recovered during archaeological investigations at this site have provided insight into the consumer behavior and use of the landscape by the Davis family during the early twentieth century. Archaeology shows us that the Davis's use of yard space may be explained by both functional and social factors. They confined their activities to the rear yard, a behavior unlike that of the former white occupants (Reeves 1998).

Excavations at the Brownsville site also produced information about African-Americans. Since the time of its creation in the late eighteenth century, Brownsville had been the home of up to forty-six African slaves. Archaeological investigations uncovered three structures that may have been dwellings for these slaves. In addition, artifacts recovered at this site include blue beads, which Singleton has noted as being worn to protect the wearer and ward off the evil eye (Cabak 1990; Singleton 1991:164).

Of the sites at the park that have had some archaeological investigation, Portici, a middling plantation, was the home of up to twenty enslaved Africans in the mid–nineteenth century. Excavations of both field and domestic slave quarters in 1986 and 1987 uncovered artifacts brought from Africa to America, such as an ebony ring. A ring of carved horn was also recovered, as well as mancala gaming pieces and fragments of colonoware (Galke 1998:4).

Although several African-American sites on the battlefield have been excavated, there are many that remain unexplored. These sites include slave occupations at Pittsylvania, the home of Landon Carter; the Andrew Redman Household; the Tasco Robinson house site; and the Jennie Dean family household. In 1893 Dean persuaded Susan B. Anthony to give $12,000 for the education of African-Americans in the northeast areas of Virginia. As a result, the Manassas Industrial School opened its doors. The school continued to educate African-American students in grades one through twelve until Virginia's schools were desegregated in the 1960s (Katz 1969:270–71; Lewis 1994).

A preliminary survey of the battlefield has also identified the home of the Peters family. Oral history contends that James Peters was an enslaved field laborer at Woodland, a local plantation owned by Landon Carter. In 1860 James learned from his brother John, an enslaved house servant, that he was to be sold away from his family. To avoid being sold and perhaps to escape the horrors of slavery, James ran away to Alexandria, Virginia, which was occupied at that time by the Union army (Montgomery Peters interview, March 1982, quoted in Johnson et al. 1982:29). James Peters's service records indicate that he enlisted in the Union army in June1863 (NPS 1979). His regiment, the First U.S. Colored Infantry, experienced considerable action during the final year of the Civil War.

U.S. Census records indicate that James returned to the Manassas area in 1865, where he "used timbers from an abandoned schoolhouse that had been damaged during the War to build a home" (Reeves, in press). The census also indicates that during the 1870s he was employed as a plasterer's helper and later as a farm laborer (USBC 1880). By 1880 James had married, and he and his wife, Josephine, had children. In 1883 the family purchased two acres of land near the crossroads of the community of Groveton, where James had built his home in 1865 (Prince William County Deed Book). "While the land they bought was large enough for their home and garden plot, the Peters likely farmed additional land on a tenant basis" (Reeves, in press).

Oral histories indicate that James and Josephine eventually had ten children (Johnson et al. 1982:30). By the 1930s the Peters family had acquired approximately 100 acres, and in 1970 the family sold their land to the National Park Service, which incorporated it into Manassas National Battlefield Park (Reeves, in press).

Information from these sites about African-American life presents exceptional research and interpretive opportunities at Manassas National Battlefield Park to investigate diversity in the Manassas area and in the African-American community. The information adds additional context for understanding the complex historical forces that shaped the war (Foner 1998: 17); understanding the effects of emancipation on the African-American community and changing racial ideologies; confronting the past neo-Confederate sentiments associated with the park; and tackling one of the most controversial topics that has been discussed recently at battlefields: the role of slavery in the Civil War.

Defining and Interpreting Place

Inscribing meaning, including a particular perspective of history, upon a place yields the power to define and interpret that place according to one's own will or ideology. The exploration of this process provides insight into power relations that may reflect a larger ideology, social situation, or culture. In the case of Manassas National Battlefield, certain groups have had the power to influence history and the landscape. The Southern heritage groups who had a hand in the creation of the park and have remained active in the park's interpretation and activities have helped to create a public memory of the Civil War and have perpetuated the ideas behind the "Lost Cause" and helped to develop an identity for the South as a cultural region. In turn, the history of Manassas becomes not just the story of Manassas, but the story of the South as a collective. The collective heritage is rooted in group ownership. "[W]e exalt our own heritage not because it is demonstrably true but because it *ought* to be" (Lowenthal 1998:128).

At Manassas National Battlefield we have a version of history that stems from a heritage, forsaking other versions of history in order to control a public memory. This phenomenon also occurs at other parks, museums, towns, and schools. It is the nature of history to be presented as fact, when history is, rather, a story told from the point of view of the person or group telling it, who manipulates the "facts" for their own purposes. Chris Wilson comments on history and heritage as fact, calling it the "invention of tradition." Wilson argues that like history, heritage is also continually reinvented to serve the purposes of modern groups. He says, "Paradoxically, invented traditions frequently are clothed in historical garb; they deny their modern origins, while claiming historical authenticity." In addition, Wilson says, "history is not written for those who lived it and are now gone, but is constantly reshaped in terms meaningful to the living, unavoidably reflecting the concerns of the era in which it is written" (Wilson 1997:4, 11).

Because the history of the two battles of Manassas was told from a particular perspective, we have an omission from this account. This absence includes a social history and in particular, a history of the African-American community. Southern tradition contends that the impetus for the war was a states' rights issue, rather than a debate over the morality of slavery.

In addition to heritage and perspective influencing the version of history told here, in a larger and more general sense, the way in which Americans celebrate and memorialize battlefields has an effect on what is presented and how we manipulate a national history and the landscape. Edward Linenthal notes that "battle sites are civil spaces where Americans of various ideological persuasions come, not always reverently, to compete for the ownership of powerful national stories and to argue about the nature of heroism, the meaning of war, the efficacy of martial sacrifice, and the significance of preserving the patriotic landscape of the nation" (Linenthal 1993:1). Not only a heritage is at stake in Manassas, but also the power to control the story of the Civil War on a national level, for it is a national story. Landscapes often evoke powerful feelings in the individual. The return of the landscape at Manassas National Battlefield to its 1861–1862 appearance at the expense of other time periods and histories is an effort to help the visitor reflect on this event; however, not all visitors to the battlefield will take away or interpret the material culture or the landscape from the perspective in which it is presented. Not all visitors have forgotten the area's social history or African-American past. With the integration of social history from archeological evidence, the landscape at Manassas may still remain a sacred place to the African-American community.

Conclusion

In 1998 *CRM*, a publication of the U.S. Department of the Interior, dedicated an entire issue to African-American history. This periodical is intended to provide information for "Parks, Federal Agencies, Indian Tribes, States, Local Governments, and the Private Sector." This issue, entitled "Slavery and Resistance," opened with a foreword from the first African-American NPS director, Robert Stanton. In it Stanton praises the twenty-six parks that have services devoted to African-American history, a testimony to the NPS's commitment to diversity and multiculturalism. He also acknowledges that there is a rich "diversity of African-American history sites in the immediate area of our nation's capital" (Stanton 1998). Manassas National Battlefield Park is one of those sites. Archaeological investigations at the Robinson House and Nash sites, and other excavated and unexplored African-American sites in the park, have produced information that can inform us about African-American life in this community during the eras of slavery, Reconstruction, Jim Crow, and the civil rights movement.

In 1999 Manassas National Battlefield Park completely refurnished and rehabilitated its visitor center. Included in the exhibits are some information and artifacts from several domestic sites on the park, including the Robinson House. While this is the beginning of an effort to provide a more inclusive context, the subject of slavery or the struggles of the African-American community through many different time periods remains sparsely dealt with. This absence indicates that many European-Americans are still divided on the subject of slavery and the causes of the Civil War. African-American history and the Civil War are inextricably linked through the discussion of slavery, the causes of the war, and the effects its battles had on our society; however, the involvement of several Confederate organizations throughout the existence of the park has painted this history from a particular perspective. In the Southern tradition of the history of the Civil War, African-American life and slavery are separate from this story (see Horton 1998:14).

The question remains, How could we negotiate different versions of this history and expand interpretations at the battlefield? Three scholars have given suggestions that I believe may offer a solution. Josie Fernandez suggests that cultural resource managers "can facilitate commemorative celebrations that are respectful of historical fact while leaving room for visitors to frame and understand the past from their own perspectives. . . . If the past is contested terrain, perhaps the best we can do is provide a safe place to speak" (Fernandez 1998). However, I would argue that while we can provide a safe place to speak, different groups should at least have the chance to be heard, and how do we become respectful of historical "fact" if "fact" may be different for different individuals? Chris Wilson has also confronted this issue, asking "how to acknowledge the validity of diverse cultures [or versions of history] without undermining one's own beliefs." Wilson suggests a more inclusive history, contending, "Our job remains to overcome historical amnesia, challenge ethnic and tourist stereotypes, develop a sustainable economy, revitalize community, nurture myths worth believing, and foster a more humane society to pass on to coming generations" (Wilson 1997:314, 329). However, this is more an end result than a path to get there. While we can create a "safe place to speak" and encourage a "more humane society" to pass on, Steven Seidman offers an approach to a more inclusive history that acknowledges identity politics and speaks of "multiple, local, intersecting struggles whose aim is less 'the end of domination' or 'human liberation' than the creation of social spaces that encourage the proliferation of . . . voices, interests, modes of individuation and democratization" (Seidman 1993: 106). I believe that at Manassas National Battlefield we can celebrate several Manassas histories without giving up individual beliefs or ownership of a particular heritage. It will be a matter of accepting and celebrating differences.

References

Armstrong, D. V.
   1990   *The Old Village and the Great Hall: An Archaeological and Historical Examination of Drax Hall Plantation, St. Anns Bay, Jamaica.* University of Illinois Press, Urbana.
Brown, K. L., and D. C. Cooper
   1990   Structural Continuity in an African American Slave and Tenant Community. In "Historical Archaeology on Southern Plantations and Farms," edited by C. E. Orser, Jr. *Historical Archaeology* 24(4): 7–19.
Cabak, Melanie
   1990   Searching for the Meaning of Blue Beads to Afro-American Slaves. Manuscript, Department of Anthropology, University of South Carolina, Columbia.
Epperson, T. W.
   1991   Race and the Disciplines of the Plantation. In "Historical Archaeology on Southern Plantations and Farms," edited by C. E. Orser, Jr. *Historical Archaeology* 24(4): 7–19.

Fernandez, Josie
1998   Practicing History in the Public Interest. *CRM* 21(11): 3.

Foner, Eric
1998   Changing Interpretation at Gettysburg National Military Park. *CRM* 21(4): 17.

Foster, Gaines M.
1987   *Ghosts of the Confederacy: Defeat, the Lost Cause, and the Emergence of the New South, 1865–1913.* Oxford University Press, New York.

Galke, Laura
1992a   You Are Where You Live: A Comparison of Africanisms at Two Sites at Manassas National Battlefield Park, Virginia. Presentation, February. Regional Archeology Program, National Capital Region, U.S. Department of the Interior, National Park Service, Washington, D.C.
1998   "Free within Ourselves," African American Landscapes at Manassas National Battlefield Park. Paper presented at the 1998 Society for Historical and Underwater Archaeology Conference, Atlanta. January.

Galke, Laura, ed.
1992b   *Cultural Resource Survey and Inventory of a War-Torn Landscape: The Stuart's Hill Tract, Manassas National Battlefield Park, Virginia.* Occasional Report 7, Regional Archeology Program, National Capital Region, U.S. Department of the Interior, National Park Service, Washington, D.C.

Hernigle, Jacqueline
1991   You Are What You Eat: The Slaves of Portici Plantation. Paper presented at the Mid-Atlantic Archaeology Conference, Ocean City, Maryland, March.

Horton, James Oliver
1998   Confronting Slavery and Revealing the "Lost Cause." *CRM* 21(4): 14–16.

Johnson, E. H, E. R. Conner, and M. H. Ferguson
1982   *History in a Horseshoe Curve: The Story of Sudley Methodist Church and Its Community.* N.p., Hagerstown, Maryland.

Jones, Lynn
1999   Crystals and Conjuring in an Annapolis Household. *Maryland Archaeology.* 35(2):1–8.

Katz, William Loren, ed.
1969   [1940] *The Negro in Virginia.* Compiled by the Writers Program of the Work Projects Administration. Arno Press/New York Times, New York. Hampton Institute, Hastings House, New York.

Kelso, W. M.
1986   Mulberry Row: Slave Life at Thomas Jefferson's Monticello. *Archaeology* 39(5): 28–35.

Klingelhofer, E.
 1987   Aspects of Early Afro American Material Culture: Artifacts from the Slave Quarters at Garrison Plantation, Maryland. *Historical Archaeology* 21 (2): 112–19.

Lewis, Stephen Johnson
 1994   [1942] *Undaunted Faith: The Life Story of Jennie Dean, Missionary, Teacher, Crusader, Builder. Founder of the Manassas Industrial School.* Manassas Museum, Manassas, Virginia. Circuit Press, Catlett, Virginia.

Linenthal, Edward Tabor
 1993   *Sacred Ground: Americans and Their Battlefields.* University of Illinois Press, Urbana.

Logan, George C. Thomas W. Bodor, Lynn D. Jones, Marian C. Creveling, and Mark D. Leone, principal investigator
 1992   Archaeological Excavations at the Charles Carroll House in Annapolis, Maryland 18AP45. On file, Historic Annapolis Foundation, Annapolis.

Lowenthal, David
 1998   *The Heritage Crusade and the Spoils of History.* Cambridge University Press, London.

Martin, Erika K., and Mia T. Parsons
 1998   Battling beyond First and Second Manassas: Perseverance on a Free African-American Farm Site. Paper presented at the Society for Historical and Underwater Archaeology Conference, Atlanta. January.

Martin Seibert, Erika K.
 2001   Exploring the Consumerism of a Free African American Family: From the Civil War through the Jim Crow Eras, a Minimum Vessel Analysis from Manassas National Battlefield Park. In *Archeological Investigation of the Robinson House, Site 44PW288: A Free African American Domestic Site Occupied from the 1840s to the 1930s,* edited by M. Parsons. Regional Archeology Program, National Capital Region, U.S. Department of the Interior, National Park Service, Washington, D.C., and Harpers Ferry National Historical Park.

McCartney, Martha
 1992   NASH (44PW581), Historical Background. In *Cultural Resource Survey and Inventory of a War-Torn Landscape: The Stuart's Hill Tract, Manassas National Battlefield Park, Virginia,* edited by Laura Galke, 121–31. Occasional Report 7, Regional Archeology Program, National Capital Region, U.S. Department of the Interior, National Park Service, Washington, D.C.

National Park Service (NPS)
 1979 Memorandum from Manassas National Battlefield Park Superintendent to the Deputy Regional Director, National Capital Region Concerning the Research on James Peters. Ref. no. H-4215. On file, Mauassas National Park, Manassas, Virginia.

Parker, Kathleen A., and Jacqueline L. Hernigle
1990   Portici: Portrait of a Middling Plantation in Piedmont, Virginia. On file, Manassas National Battlefield Park, Manassas, Virginia.

Parsons, Mia T.
1996   A Social History of the Robinson Family and Overview of the Robinson House Site: Nearly One Hundred Years of Occupation by a Free African American Family in Prince William County, Virginia. Paper presented at the Mid-Atlantic Archaeological Conference, Ocean City, Maryland.
2001   *Archeological Investigation of the Robinson House, Site 44PW288: A Free African American Domestic Site Occupied from the 1840s to the 1930s.* Regional Archeology Program, National Capital Region, U.S. Department of the Interior, National Park Service, Washington, D.C., and Harpers Ferry National Historical Park.

Patten, Drake
1992   Mankala and Minkisi: Possible Evidence of African American Folk Beliefs and Practices. *African American Archaeology* 6:5–7.

Prince William County Deed Book
1883   Deed Book #35, 578. Prince William County Library, Manassas, Virginia. Microfilm.

Reeves, Matthew B.
1998   *Views of a Changing Landscape: An Archeological and Historical Investigation of Sudley Post Office (44PW294), Manassas National Battlefield Park, Manassas, Virginia.* Occasional Report 14, Regional Archaeology Program, National Capital Region, National Park Service, U.S. Department of the Interior, Washington, D.C.
In   Generations of Conflict: African Americans at Manassas National
press   Battlefield Park. In *Remembering Landscapes of Conflict,* edited by P. A. Shackel. *Historical Archaeology.*

Roosevelt, Franklin Delano
1938   *Public Papers and Addresses.* Random House, New York.

Ryder, Robin
1991a   Fluid Ethnicity: Archaeological Examinations of Diversity in Virginia from 1800–1900. Paper presented at the Council of Virginia Archaeology Symposium 7, Alexandria, Virginia. October.
1991b   Free African American Archaeology: Interpreting an Antebellum Farmstead. Master's thesis, College of William and Mary, Williamsburg, Virginia.

Sarles, Frank B., Jr.
1955   *A Short History of Manassas National Battlefield Park.* On file, Library Collection, Manassas National Battlefield Park, Manassas, Virginia.

Seidman, Steven
1993   Identity and Politics in a "Postmodern" Gay Culture: Some Historical and Conceptual Notes. In *Fear of a Queer Planet: Queer Politics and*

Social Theory, edited by Michael Warner, 105–42. University of Minnesota Press, Minneapolis.

Simmons, Catherine T.
1986   *Manassas, Virginia, 1873–1973: One Hundred Years of a Virginia Town.* On file, Manassas Museum, Manassas, Virginia.

Singleton, Theresa
1991   The Archaeology of Slave Life. In *Before Freedom Came: African American Life in the Antebellum South,* edited by Edward D. C. Campbell, Jr., and Kym S. Rice, 155–75. Museum of the Confederacy, Richmond.

Stanton, Robert
1998   Foreword. *CRM* 21 (4): 3.

U.S. Bureau of the Census (USBC)
1880   *Population Schedules, Prince William County, Virginia.* Prince William County Library, Manassas, Virginia. Microfilm.

Wilson, Chris
1997   *The Myth of Santa Fe: Creating a Modern Regional Tradition.* University of New Mexico Press, Albuquerque.

Zenzen, Joan
1995   *Battling for Manassas: The Fifty-Year Preservation Struggle at Manassas National Battlefield Park.* History Associates, Rockville, Maryland.

4

Remembering a Japanese-American Concentration Camp at Manzanar National Historic Site

Janice L. Dubel

Introduction

On December 7, 1941, the Japanese Navy bombed Pearl Harbor, compelling the United States to formally enter World War II. Tension ran high throughout the country as it went to battle, and rumors of infiltrators and spies spread quickly. Japanese-Americans, in the wrong place at the wrong time, were suspected of sympathizing with and spying for Japan. Judgment that they were the enemy was based solely on their race. Japanese-Americans were subsequently assembled into camps strategically placed in remote areas away from the West Coast of the United States. The emotional wounds inflicted upon these people during this time have been slow to heal.

Americans often attempt to justify the actions of the government during this time by claiming that the hysteria that gripped America immediately following Pearl Harbor was only natural for a country that had enjoyed more than twenty years of peace. For them, it was a logical assumption that some level of spying was going on within U.S. borders and some measure of security keeping had to be implemented.

Pre-War Prejudice

It is difficult to find, in America's classroom history books, mention of the forced internment of almost 120,000 Japanese-Americans during World War II. The U.S. government was responsible for setting "precedent and constitutional sanctity for a policy of mass incarceration under military auspices. . . . That . . . betrayed all Americans" (Morton Grodzins in

Daniels 1971:xiv). This historical event is seen by many as a perpetuation of racist attitudes that still endure in this country.

For decades prior to the formal entrance of the United States into World War II, anti-Asian sentiment within its borders gradually, but steadily, intensified. It began with the immigration of Chinese workers during the California Gold Rush in the 1850s. They were an unwelcome competition for employment by the late 1860s and considered by many to be less than human. Chinese immigrants were not allowed to provide testimony in courts and were legally discriminated against. By 1882, peoples of Chinese descent were barred from legally immigrating to the United States, and later the U.S. Congress passed the Immigration Act of 1924 that also barred immigration from Japan into America (Daniels 1971; Conrat and Conrat 1972).

Japanese Immigration

Immigration of Japanese peoples increased in magnitude during the late 1800s and early 1900s. Approximately 300,000 Japanese had entered the United States before the Immigration Act took effect (Daniels 1971). Discrimination against the Japanese was not entirely economically based, but it was mired in a false idea of the dominance of white people over people of color. In 1905, the *San Francisco Chronicle,* one of the most influential newspapers on the West Coast, perpetuated the campaign against the Japanese. The paper promoted the notion not only that Japanese-Americans were a menace to the safety of America, but also that all Japanese immigrants were spies (Daniels 1971).

Relations between the cultures became so strained that by the late 1930s and early 1940s, Japanese-Americans were concerned about their welfare should the United States become involved in a Pacific war. Members of Congress and clergymen made slanderous statements, including references to the offspring of Caucasian and Asian couples as "germs" and assertions that they would have such a detrimental effect upon the state of California that it would make the "black problem of the South look white" (Daniels 1971:15). Democratic congressman John Dingell summed the situation up more precisely months before the attack on Pearl Harbor. He suggested that as reprisal for any sabotage activity involving the Japanese military, the United States should "cause the forceful detention or imprisonment in a concentration camp of ten thousand alien Japanese in Hawaii" and, further, should "remind Japan that there are perhaps one hundred fifty-thousand additional alien Japanese in the United States who [can] be held in a reprisal reserve" (Daniels 1971:27–28).

A second-generation Japanese-American jeweler residing in Los Angeles spoke to Tom Treanor of the *Los Angeles Times* on August 6, 1941, four months before the bombing of Pearl Harbor. Warning of future trouble, he said, "We talk of almost nothing but this great crisis. We don't know what's going to happen. Sometimes we only look for a concentration camp" (Daniels 1971:27).

Establishing the Internment Camps

Anti-immigrant, particularly anti-Japanese, emotions were fueled not only by the attack on Pearl Harbor, but also by racist anti-Asian propaganda produced by the media and endorsed by the government. According to the *Congressional Record,* Congressman John Rankin said on February 19, 1942: "I'm for catching every Japanese in America, Alaska, and Hawaii now and putting them in concentration camps. . . . Damn them! Let's get rid of them now!" (Conrat and Conrat 1972:44; U.S. Congress 1991; Fremon 1996).

On that same day in February 1942, in what many people believe to be the worst violation of constitutional rights in U.S. history, President Franklin Delano Roosevelt signed Executive Order 9066 (Conrat and Conrat 1972; Foster 1995; Daniels 1971). The stated strategy behind the order was to provide for the continued security of the West Coast. It gave authorization to Secretary of War Henry Stimson to designate "military areas . . . from which any and all persons may be excluded, and with respect to which, the right of any person to enter, remain in, or leave shall be subject to whatever restrictions the Secretary of War or the appropriate Military Commander may impose in his discretion" (Hatamiya 1993:14; Baker 1981:12). No particular racial or ethnic group was named in the order. However, military and government officials in high standing "understood that its purpose was to authorize the evacuation and internment of Japanese-Americans" (Hatamiya 1993:14). The U.S. Census of 1940 determined the number of Japanese-Americans living in the continental United States to be less than one-tenth of 1 percent of the total population and less than 4 percent of the estimated 1,100,000 nationals of declared enemy nations residing in the country (Unrau 1996; Daniels 1971). Based on Executive Order 9066, a total of 119,803 Japanese-American citizens and Japanese resident aliens from California, Oregon, Hawaii, and Wash-

Figure 4.1. Store at Thirteenth and Franklin Streets, Oakland, California, closed in response to evacuation orders, with the I AM AN AMERICAN sign placed there by the owner on the day after the attack on Pearl Harbor. March 13, 1942. (Courtesy National Archives, photograph no. NWDNS-210–G-C519.)

ington were imprisoned (Conrat and Conrat 1972; Foster 1995; Daniels 1971).

Although voluntary evacuees had begun arriving at the hastily constructed internment camps earlier, five months after the bombing of Pearl Harbor, in May of 1942, the American government forced Japanese-Americans to assemble in the larger cities. They were then relocated to concentration camps. Many Japanese-Americans were forcibly removed from their homes, and they feared they were going to die in front of a firing squad (Okihiro 1996). Eventually these camps would officially be labeled "relocation centers" (Conrat and Conrat 1972).

Mass removal of the Japanese-Americans from mainstream society was initially handled by the military through the Wartime Civil Control Administration and customarily involved a temporary stay in one of fifteen assembly centers. Each family interviewed at any one of these stations or assembly centers had its family name replaced with an identification number. They were then herded to the permanent camps that were administered by a civilian agency created precisely for this purpose: the War Relocation Authority (WRA) (Nishimoto 1995:xxxv; Okihiro 1996:177).

Individuals destined for the camps were given only days to gather their belongings and leave their homes and businesses. Some scholars estimate that the total time allotted for some internees to evacuate was as brief as twenty-four hours (Foster 1995; Ross 1991:55). The U.S. government did not provide secure storage areas for the Japanese-American evacuees (Ross 1991:55). While they were interned, their homes, businesses, storage units, and other personal properties were ransacked (Hatamiya 1993: 132) (fig. 4.1).

The Uchida family of Idaho Falls, Idaho, picked up by the Federal Bureau of Investigation the day after the bombing of Pearl Harbor, was given "just enough time to finish breakfast" (Okihiro 1996:169). They were considered a threat to national security because they taught Japanese language classes and belonged to an organization that assisted immigrants who had trouble understanding business and legal issues (Okihiro 1996).

Permitted to take only what they could carry to the camps, Japanese-Americans were forced to sell their belongings for whatever they could get for them. Few people offered a fair price, so it was common for Japanese women to break family heirlooms in full view of prospective buyers, because they had offered such an absurd price (Conrat and Conrat 1972; Houston and Houston 1973:10; Hatamiya 1993:132; Nishimoto 1995; Okihiro 1996:177).

Some Japanese-Americans, fearing some type of retaliation for the devastation of Pearl Harbor, destroyed all items in their homes that they believed could be misinterpreted as showing allegiance to Japan. In the days following December 7, 1941, they burned or buried Japanese flags, books, records, and even written communications between themselves and family still in Japan (Houston and Houston 1973:5; Okihiro 1996:95). "Any connection, any link with Japan, any expression, any thoughts indicative of Japanese culture and ethnicity, invited others' suspicion" (Okihiro 1996:95).

Japanese immigrants (Issei), their American-born children (Nisei), and third-generation Japanese-Americans (Sansei) were all included in the evacuation (Daniels 1971:27). In fact, all peoples of Japanese descent who resided on the western coast of the United States, and many who did not, were removed, regardless of their citizen status, including American veterans of World War I. Hiro Katayama, a writer for a Nisei publication named *All Aboard,* wrote in 1944 that "the young students sing 'America,' salute the flag, and learn about democracy in the classrooms and then return to the dingy barracks 'Homes' and wonder why they can't go back to their America" (quoted in James 1987:103).

Life in the camps was made bearable by the persons who lived there. Internees built schools in order to educate their children and formed classes in the arts. They organized baseball and other recreational sports teams within their ranks. At Manzanar, the internees constructed a reflecting pool for meditation. They created war memorials and began Boy Scout troops. Gardens were coaxed out of the soil, and they landscaped the areas around the barracks. Internees also turned land within the barbed-wire fences of their new homes into cemeteries for those who died while confined. Close to six thousand children, U.S. citizens, were born in the camps (Daniels 1971) (figs. 4.2 and 4.3).

Two groups were allowed to leave the reception centers and the relocation camps during the initial evacuation, "the college students who left permanently and the farm workers who left temporarily" (Daniels 1971:110). October 1, 1942, brought "leave clearance procedures" that also granted the consequent release of many Nisei. Almost seventeen thousand internees returned to civilian life in 1942. This group consisted, primarily, of Nisei between the ages of eighteen and thirty. Military officials had determined that loyalty to America would be harder to find among the Issei and the Kibei (persons of Japanese ancestry who were born in the United States but educated or employed in Japan) than the Nisei.

Questionnaires labeled "Application for Leave Clearance" were dispensed to internees beginning February 10, 1943. The most critical problems concerning this questionnaire were created by questions 27 and 28. Question 27 was designed to test the internees' will to fight for their country by asking, "Are you willing to serve in the armed forces of the United States on combat duty, wherever ordered?" Many internees, especially the women and the elderly, were unclear about how to answer this question. Question 28 required applicants to affirm their allegiance by asking, "Will you swear unqualified allegiance to the United States of America and faithfully defend the United States from any or all attack by foreign or

Figure 4.2. Dust storm at a War Relocation Authority center. July 3,1942 (Courtesy National Archives, photograph no. NWDNS-210–G-10C-C839).

Figure 4.3. Manzanar Relocation Center, Manzanar, California, looking north between blocks of barracks. July 1, 1942. (Courtesy National Archives, photograph no. NWDNS-210–G-10C-C829.)

domestic forces, and forswear any form of allegiance or obedience to the Japanese emperor, to any other foreign government, power or organization?" (Daniels 1971:113). This was disturbing because Issei were not eligible for citizenship in the United States. Question 28 was eventually reworded to follow the regulations of the Geneva Convention, but the intent of the question remained the same and internees remained doubtful of the intentions of the government that had already betrayed them (Daniels 1971; Nishimoto 1995). The WRA ultimately used the loyalty questionnaires as the core reason for separating the "loyal" from the "disloyal" and segregating the two groups (Daniels 1971:114).

Although many volunteered for military duty, Japanese-Americans were not permitted to serve in the war effort until 1943. Secretary of War Stimson announced in January 1944 that Nisei were subject to the draft. In response, leaders of camp communities issued bulletins declaring that they were not only willing to fight in the war but also had been trying to volunteer for months (Okihiro 1996:210–11).

Periodically, protests took place within the camps; conflict between the confined and their guards was to be expected. The most serious outburst, the "Manzanar massacre" on December 6, 1942, left two prisoners dead and ten more wounded at the hands of the U.S. military police. A Caucasian soldier was also wounded; a ricocheting bullet was evidently the cause (Fremon 1996; Daniels 1971). The internees had been protesting the jailing of one of their community leaders, Henry Ueno. Ueno had discovered and reported the theft of food that was intended for internees. He accused WRA officials of the crime, maintaining that the camp employees intended to sell the food on the black market. His subsequent arrest sparked a mass protest that eventually resulted in the fatalities and injuries (Nishimoto 1995:169; Fremon 1996; Daniels 1971). This type of pilferage by Anglo-Americans was later confirmed by citizens who had lived near the camp in Owens Valley at the time (Garrett and Larson 1977).

For Japanese-Americans, wartime property losses, estimated by the Federal Reserve Bank of San Francisco in 1942, exceeded $400,000,000. Loss of professional careers, and disrupted college educations and career potential, was not calculated in the loss. In addition, Japanese culture highly values self-esteem and pride; both of these were irreparably damaged by the humiliation of being wrongly imprisoned by their own government (Hatamiya 1993:25; Conrat and Conrat 1972).

The U.S. government had ten relocation camps constructed in the harsh and desolate areas of Arizona, Idaho, Colorado, Wyoming, California,

Utah, and Arkansas (Okihiro 1996; Foster 1995). Their imprisonment in these camps left a legacy of guilt and punishment for a crime that Japanese-Americans had nothing to do with (Masumoto 1991). "No charges were ever filed against these persons, and no guilt was ever attributed to them. . . . [E]vacuation swept into guarded camps orphans, foster children in white homes, Japanese married to Caucasians, the offspring of such marriages, persons who were unaware of their Japanese ancestry, and American citizens with as little as 1/16th Japanese blood" (Morton Grodzins in Conrat and Conrat 1972:70).

After the War

V-J Day, or Victory over Japan Day, came in 1945, and the federal government closed the camps, but it did not end the racism against Japanese-Americans (Foster 1995). The Asian population was, to an extent, reluctant to return to their homes upon release from the camps. Personal experiences led them to fear attack by anti-Japanese groups and individuals. The well-publicized persecution of the Doi family upon their return home, and similar reported stories, further scared Japanese prisoners into trying to remain at the camps (Taylor 1993:260–69; Okihiro 1996:228). "Thirty-one major attacks on California relocatees were reported between January and June of 1945" (Nagata 1993:15).

As late as 1948, "an anti-Japanese proposition that would have made the alien land-ownership laws harsher" was placed on the ballot in California. The measure was defeated, but 40 percent of voters still favored harsher treatment for Asian immigrants (Daniels 1971:170). Naval intelligence went so far as to prepare a counter-intelligence report on what it called the "Japanese Situation," prompted by the "fear that communists would use discrimination against the Nisei to attract them, and other susceptible minority groups, to Marxism" (Taylor 1993:266).

Unofficial but very real restrictions prevented Japanese-Americans from continuing their careers. Trade unions would not allow Japanese-American membership, many people would not rent or sell homes to them, and shops, restaurants, and hotels refused to serve them (Fremon 1996:17). The discrimination faced by Japanese-Americans, both before the internment and continuing into the years following their forced release from the camps and the return of their personal freedom, was excessive. The U.S. Justice Department employee in charge of coordinating alien policy with California politicians reported the situation in Los Angeles as being "pretty hot" (Fox 1990:47). According to Fox, the "mounting wave of vigilantism" there "struck state and federal authorities as a menace to their own more 'efficient' antisabotage efforts" (Fox 1990:47).

Remembering Manzanar

Of the ten internment camps used during the war, Manzanar was chosen as the location for a National Historic Site because it was the best preserved (Thistlewaite 1997). The site was designated a California Register Historical Landmark in 1972, and the State Department of Park and Recreation placed a plaque on one of the two remaining sentry posts in 1973. By 1976, Manzanar was listed in the National Register of Historic Places, and by 1985, it had been designated a National Historic Landmark. Congress commemorated the site "to provide for the protection and interpretation of the historical, cultural, and natural resources associated with the relocation of Japanese-Americans during World War II" (Unrau 1996).

On March 3, 1992, President George Bush signed into law the establishment of Manzanar National Historic Site and turned control of the site over to the National Park Service (NPS), although no appropriations were part of the bill. While the site was now officially designated a historic site, the federal government did not own the land. "The Park Service formally took title of the site April 26 [1992], from its previous owner, the city of Los Angeles, which acquired the land in the 1920s for the water rights" (Fleeman 1997).

In 1996, Ross Hopkins, the sole NPS employee at the site, was assigned the job of converting 550 acres of ruin into a usable national monument (Jones 1996). As progress continues and the camp is slowly restored, this site presents an opportunity for peoples of all ages and ethnicities to understand the fear, racism, discrimination, and hatred that led to the establishment of ten American concentration camps (Thistlewaite 1997). Unfortunately, work at the site has not been as successful as originally planned. Although established in 1992, as of July 1997, one tour guide worked the site. The guide, Richard Stewart, and the tours he conducts were financed by grants from the Eastern California Museum. The NPS did not contribute to funding interpretation (Fleeman 1997). In southeastern California, summertime temperatures often top 100 degrees and desert winds can be punishing (Fleeman 1997; Daniels 1971). Stewart is stationed in an old stone sentry building at the entrance to Manzanar. The building itself "has no electricity, no running water, not even portable restrooms" (Fleeman 1997). According to National Park ranger Kari Coughlin, the situation is changing. Two privately funded guides now work the site, and the park was recently notified that they will receive NPS funds to extend the tours (Kari Coughlin, personal communication, 1999).

Remains at Manzanar

The U.S. Army Corps of Engineers used bulldozers to level the Manzanar complex in 1946. When they were finished, all that remained of the camp were two of the eight sentry posts and the wood-frame auditorium (Booth 1997). One journalist wrote that "the camp was dismantled and the remains sank back into the sagebrush. We had won the war, after all, and history is written by the winners. In this case, we decided to let Manzanar fade from memory, as if it didn't really happen" (Jones 1996).

Situated approximately three hundred miles northeast of Los Angeles in Owens Valley, California, Manzanar once imprisoned 10,046 men, women, and children (Okihiro 1996). The camp consisted of thirty-six blocks of wooden barracks (Forstenzer 1996b; Unrau 1996; Conrat and Conrat 1972). In the summer of 1945, at its peak, Manzanar was the largest city between Reno, Nevada, and Los Angeles, California. It has all but disappeared. "What you see from the road are the two gatehouses, each a small empty pillbox of a building" (Houston and Houston 1973:135).

Past the gatehouses about half a mile into the camp stands a white obelisk twelve feet high. A dozen graves are outlined in the sand, marked with small stones and surrounded with a barbed-wire fence. "The black Japanese script cut into the white face of the obelisk reads simply, 'A Memorial to the Dead'" (Houston and Houston 1973:136). A large green building that once served as a high school auditorium stands off to the right (Houston and Houston 1973).

Still visible are the concrete foundations and supports for the buildings that once served as barracks, washrooms, and mess halls, along with the stone paths that led to them. Hundreds of names and dates are carved into the concrete (Booth 1997). The garbage dump is still there with its mixture of broken china and the remains of children's toys. Also discernible is the ruin of the once magnificent reflecting pool (Okihiro 1996).

Improvements to the park continue. Manzanar has been awarded a millennium grant so that the barbed-wire fence that originally surrounded the camp can be reestablished. Additional plans are in the works for re-constructing the auditorium, restoring a guard tower, and establishing temporary visitor contact stations (Kari Coughlin, personal communication, 1999).

Controversy at Manzanar

The establishment of Manzanar as a National Historic Site continues to be a controversial issue, although more than half a century has passed since the closing of the camp (Forstenzer 1996b).

In February of 1996, the NPS released its General Management Plan for the historical interpretation of Manzanar. Although the plan includes the rebuilding of a guard tower and reinstallation of at least one of the original camp barracks, some think that the inclusion of other historical markers is deliberately intended to soften the impact of the story of the camp (Forstenzer 1996b; Jones 1996). In the years following the publicizing of the plan, the agency "has received anonymous threats that buildings erected or restored at Manzanar will be destroyed" (Forstenzer 1996b). Personal threats have also been leveled against people involved with the Eastern California Museum that has been maintaining an extensive exhibit on Manzanar (Forstenzer 1996a).

The controversy has focused primarily on a California Historical Landmark plaque that refers to Manzanar, and the other internment camps, as "concentration camps" (Forstenzer 1996a). The marker, which was placed at the entrance of the site in 1973, is appropriate, according to many Japanese-Americans, but opponents say the term is misleading. Although still in place at the site, it has been both defaced and defiled by camp opponents. One man claiming to be a World War II veteran said that he had driven more than two hundred miles for the sole purpose of urinating on it (Forstenzer 1996a).

The plaque reads:

> In the early part of World War II, 110,000 persons of Japanese ancestry were interned in relocation centers by Executive Order No. 9066, issued on February 19, 1942.
>
> Manzanar, the first of ten such concentration camps, was bounded by barbed wire and guard towers, confining 10,000 persons, the majority being American citizens.
>
> May the injustices and humiliation suffered here as a result of hysteria, racism and economic exploitation never emerge again. (Garrett and Larson 1977:73)

As of 1996, the NPS had agreed that the term "concentration camp" was inaccurate and would not be used in the future to describe Manzanar. Although Secretary H. L. Ickes of the U.S. Department of the Interior stated publicly in 1946 that he believed that is exactly what they were—concentration camps (Embrey et al. 1986)—the new official title is "war relocation center" (Booth 1997).

The 1992 edition of the *American Heritage Dictionary* defines a concentration camp as a place where people are detained or confined as prisoners of war, political prisoners, or enemy aliens. This definition accurately describes all of the American internment camps, including Manzanar. The term "concentration camp," however, has become almost synonymous with the Nazi death camps such as Auschwitz/Birkenau. Some argue that you cannot equate the American camps with those of the Nazis; there were no gas chambers, cremation ovens, or genocidal intentions at the U.S. camps. Actually, the American camps are more reminiscent of the Indian reservations fashioned a century earlier. Manzanar, during the later years, had a branch of Bank of America, a high school, a catalog outlet of Sears Roebuck, and the largest hospital in the county (Booth 1997).

Those who oppose the measure often refer to the actions of the United States as a preemptive defense measure rather than the knee-jerk reaction that it was (Baker 1981). They seem to forget that their leaders in government were slandering all Japanese, including Americans. Franklin D. Roosevelt, president of the United States, said in 1942 that the Japanese "skull pattern being less developed than that of the Caucasians, might be responsible for their aggressive behavior" (Smith 1986:79).

It was not until August 10, 1988, that the 100th Congress passed the Civil Liberties Act (Hatamiya 1993). The act's importance "lay in its direct effect on the lives of the former internees and their families . . . it reconfirmed all citizens' constitutional civil rights and civil liberties" and it addressed the notion of redress for the surviving Japanese internees (Hatamiya 1993:3). David Matsumoto, a writer whose parents were interned during the war, claims that the idea of redress, when discussed with regard to the violation of the civil rights of Japanese-Americans, also brings up discussion of Japanese civil and human rights violations.

"I'd hear someone bring up the Bataan death march," he wrote. "If 'our' government was going to address the wrongs committed against Japanese-Americans, what about 'our' boys who died at Pearl Harbor? Or the Bataan survivors? Don't they deserve compensation more than those Japanese? Fifty years later, people still can't differentiate between Americans of Japanese ancestry and the Japanese 4,000 miles across an ocean" (Masumoto 1991:13A).

The idea of redress, or monetary compensation for the imprisonment, also affected a myriad of other peoples, including veterans' groups. They opposed the payment, arguing, "Why should we pay for what happened to the Japanese-Americans if we never have been paid by Japan for what happened to the POWs?" After all, they reason, Japan started the war (Nagata 1993:205). This type of attitude convinced many Japanese-Americans that the redress movement did not have a realistic chance of succeeding. In order for Japanese-Americans to invest their time, energy, and monies into fighting for redress, they wanted to be reasonably sure that their government "would not again strip them of their fundamental rights" (Hatamiya 1993:135).

On August 10, 1988, President Ronald Reagan signed into law the Civil Rights Act, which included, among other items, a formal apology from Congress. It also covered the entitlement program that provided for distribution of the $1.25 billion settlement to the surviving internees or their heirs. The goal of the law was to complete payment by the end of the 1993 fiscal year. The amount determined proved not to be sufficient to cover all of the eligible recipients, and new legislation was passed by Congress to increase the amount to assure that all who were eligible received compensation. Each of these people received $20,000. A fund was also established for the purpose of educating the American public about the concentration camps (Okihiro 1996:240; Hatamiya 1993). In the fall of 1990, President George Bush, at the direction of Congress, sent letters of apology to tens of thousands of Americans of Japanese descent for the way the nation had imprisoned them in violation of their constitutional rights during World War II.

Manzanar critics rely, in part, on revisionist history books written by opponents such as Lillian Baker. They are convinced that the Japanese were happy to be in the relocation centers; it was the only way that the U.S. government had of protecting the Japanese from Caucasian citizens enraged about Pearl Harbor (Garrett and Larson 1977). They are unwilling to accept that Japanese-Americans were deprived of their civil rights. Critics also claim that the NPS is distorting the facts. "People in Manzanar were not confined, they were free to go any time they wanted," according to NPS opponent and World War II veteran W. W. Hastings (Forstenzer 1996a). Hastings, along with others, claims that photographs taken at the site, including those of Ansel Adams, have been doctored by the NPS in an attempt to create a tourist attraction and alter the truth of what really happened (Forstenzer 1996a). "According to the revisionist account, rather than the eight guard towers fitted with searchlights and machine guns that Park Service historians say ringed the camp, there was only one or two structures used as fire watchtowers" (Forstenzer 1996a).

Individuals and groups who are writing an alternative history of Manzanar are aided by the fact that the U.S. government concealed information about the camps during the war (Forstenzer 1996a). Gordon Chappell, an NPS senior historian, has remarked, "The War Relocation Authority made a strenuous effort to limit what could be photographed because it wanted to present the camp experience as more benign than was, in fact, the case" (Forstenzer 1996a). They are also aided by the fact that some internees were permitted to leave the camps before the end of the war on condition that they sign the loyalty oaths, renounce their homeland, and acquire a sponsor (Booth 1997). Many did leave, and some of those who did served in the famed 442nd Regimental Combat Team of the U.S. Army (Daniels 1971; Conrat and Conrat 1972; Nishimoto 1995). This segregated unit, made up solely of Japanese-Americans, was "the most decorated for its size and length of service in American military history" (Thistlewaite 1997). Approximately twenty-five thousand Japanese-American men and women fought for the United States during World War II (Okihiro 1996:215; Conrat and Conrat 1972).

Ross Hopkins, as well as being NPS's superintendent at Manzanar, is also an outspoken advocate of Manzanar as a historic site. He believes the fate of Manzanar is due more to NPS budget constraints than to local opposition. He likens Manzanar to a "very small pea in an awfully large dinner" (Fleeman 1997). The irony of Manzanar is that, as a camp, it was filled with more than 10,000 people, built into a makeshift town inside the gates, and destroyed within four years, while in the first five years that the NPS owned it, they were "unable to erect a single sign, picnic table or portable toilet. . . . Meanwhile, tourists see only the scrub land, not the story behind it" (Rogers 1997).

In 1997, Manzanar "received $225,000 to cover all studies, maintenance, office equipment, salary and benefits. By comparison, Yosemite National Park's budget is $17 million a year" (Rogers 1997). Funds for Manzanar for the 1999 fiscal year were $481,000 (Kari Coughlin, personal communication, 1999). The cost estimate to complete the restoration of Manzanar is $2.5 million, and continuing maintenance costs are about $1 million a year (Rogers 1997; Nakayama 1997).

Future Prospects

According to Congress, Manzanar was established as a National Historic Site "to provide for the protection and interpretation of the historical, cultural, and natural resources associated with the relocation of Japanese-Americans during World War II" (U.S. Congress 1991). Manzanar forces Americans to examine their country's constitutional transgressions as tangible evidence of its willingness to deny what they hold most sacrosanct, freedom. "The idea of a memorial was to remind future generations that in times of crisis, the Constitution can be dangerously fragile" (Rogers 1997).

Manzanar National Historic Site represents Japanese-Americans who were presumed guilty wholly on the basis of their race. It is important not to forget what happened at Pearl Harbor and during World War II, but it is also important to "imagine a little Japanese-American girl, a U.S. citizen, tagged with a number and herded onto a train bound for desert barracks and barbed wire." She would remain there for four years, but the emotional scars would last a lifetime (Masumoto 1991).

Accounts of what the Japanese-American internees endured are numerous yet serve no purpose if they are neither heard nor listened to. As Bill Michael, the director of the Eastern California Museum, has pointed out: "History is not just the things we like. Very seldom do the darker parts of history, and there were several at Manzanar, get commemorated. We can't learn from history if we don't acknowledge it" (Ross 1991:57). Accounts of what the Japanese-American internees endured are numerous yet serve no purpose if they are not acknowledged. "In knee-jerk furor over anything that does not support our one-nation version of cultural harmony, we are diverted from true vigilance. And we allow the seeds of further intolerance to be sown and a far more bitter future harvest to take root" (Stringer 1998:213).

References

Baker, L.
  1981   The Concentration Camp Conspiracy: A Second Pearl Harbor. AFHA Publications, Lawndale, California.
Booth, W.
  1997   A Lonely Patch of History: Japanese Americans Were Forced to Live Here. They Don't Want It to Be Forgotten. *Washington Post*, April 15, D1.

Conrat, M., and R. Conrat
1972   *Executive Order 9066: The Internment of 110,000 Japanese Americans*, sec. D, p.1. California Historical Society, San Francisco.

Daniels, R.
1971   *Concentration Camps USA: Japanese-Americans and World War II.* Holt, Rinehart, and Winston, New York.

Embrey, S. K., A. A. Hansen, and B. K. Mitson
1986   *Manzanar Martyr: An Interview with Harry Y. Ueno.* California State University Oral History Program, Fullerton.

Fleeman, M.
1997   Manzanar National Historic Site Set to Open Doors to Public. Associated Press, July 27.

Forstenzer, M.
1996a Bitter Feelings Still Run Deep at Camp. *Los Angeles Times*, April 4, A3.
1996b Manzanar: A Place That Still Divides Americans. Federal Plan to Preserve California Internment Site Is Raising Some Hostility. *Seattle Times*, May 7, A5.

Foster, D.
1995   Racism Remained after Internment Camps Closed. Associated Press, August 14, 1995 [cited December 20, 2000]. Available at http://www.detnews.com/menu/stories/13546.htm.

Fremon, D. K.
1996   *Japanese-American Internment in American History.* Enslow, Springfield, New Jersey.

Fox, S.
1990   *The Unknown Internment: An Oral History of the Relocation of Italian Americans during World War II.* Twayne, Boston.

Garrett, J. A., and R. C. Larson, eds.
1977   *Camp and Community: Manzanar and the Owens Valley.* California State University Oral History Program, Fullerton.

Hatamiya, L. T.
1993   *Righting a Wrong: Japanese-Americans and the Passage of the Civil Liberties Act of 1988.* Stanford University Press, Stanford.

Houston, J. W., and J. D. Houston
1973   *Farewell to Manzanar.* Bantam Books, New York.

James, T.
1987   *Exile Within: The Schooling of Japanese Americans, 1942–1945.* Harvard University Press, Cambridge.

Jones, R. A.
1996   Whitewashing Manzanar. *Los Angeles Times*, April 10, B2.

Masumoto, D. M.
1991   The Ghosts of Dec. 7 Still Haunt Thousands. *USA Today*, December 3, 13A.

Nagata, D. K.
  1993   *Legacy of Injustice: Exploring the Cross-Generational Impact of the Japanese American Internment.* Plenum Press, New York.
Nakayama, T.
  1997   Land Exchange Celebrated at 28th Manzanar Pilgrimage. *Rafu,* April 28, 1997 [cited November 16, 1998]. [Found at http://www.rafu.com/STORIES/manz28reun.html.]
Nishimoto, R. S.
  1995   *Inside an American Concentration Camp: Japanese American Resistance at Poston, Arizona.* Edited by L. R. Hirabayashi. University of Arizona Press, Tucson.
Okihiro, G. Y.
  1996   *Whispered Silences: Japanese Americans and World War II.* University of Washington Press, Seattle.
Rogers, P.
  1997   W.W. II Internment Camp Survivors Upset by Lack of Progress on Memorial. *San Jose Mercury News,* March 10, A1.
Ross, C.
  1991   Return to Manzanar. *Americana* 19(1): 55–58.
Smith, G. S.
  1986   Racial Nativism and Origins of Japanese American Relocation. In *Japanese Americans: From Relocation to Redress,* edited by R. Daniels, S. Taylor, and H. Kitano, 79–85. University of Utah Press, Salt Lake City.
Stanley, J.
  1994   *I Am an American: A True Story of Japanese Internment.* Crown, New York.
Stringer, L.
  1998   *Grand Central Winter: Stories from the Street.* Washington Square Press, New York.
Taylor, S. C.
  1993   *Jewel of the Desert: Japanese American Internment at Topaz.* University of California Press, Berkeley.
Thistlewaite, C.
  1997   Manzanar National Historic Site: America's Concentration Camp. Associated Press, March 9, 1997 [cited November 16, 1998]. [Found at http://www.mammothweb.com/sierraweb/lonepine/manzanar.html.]
Unrau, H. D.
  1996   *The Evacuation and Relocation of Persons of Japanese Ancestry during World War II: A Historical Study of the Manzanar War Relocation Center.* 2 vols. U.S. Department of the Interior, National Park Service, Washington, D.C.
U.S. Congress. House of Representatives.
  1991   Committee on Interior and Insular Affairs. *Establishing the Manzanar National Historic Site in the State of California, and for Other Purposes.* 102nd Congress, 1st session.

5

Wounded Knee: The Conflict of Interpretation

Gail Brown

Introduction

Commemorative battlefields, though perhaps no longer filled with the sights and sounds of battle, remain sites of confrontation today. Adversaries, old or new, continue to vie over the meaning of events that have occurred in the past. They continue to make the conflict a part of their collective memory and history. Richard Handler remarks that "a group's most prized possessions are said to be its culture and history" (Handler 1991:66). To maintain their history and therefore their identity, those groups must hold onto their version of the past or face losing their cultural identity. So as a military struggle ends, the war of words and meanings begins. Each group, the glorious victor and the vanquished foe, attempts to hold onto their version of the truth and express their story.

Edward Linenthal in his book *Sacred Ground* remarks that battlefields serve as "centers of power" where groups celebrate their sacred stories (Linenthal 1993:215). These stories and "centers of power have helped define, for numerous generations, those who are 'insiders' and 'outsiders' in American culture" (Linenthal 1993:216). Like the Little Bighorn Battlefield, Wounded Knee continues to be a battleground where Native Americans attempt to "resurrect their story from an alien patriotic landscape and an alien orthodoxy that has excluded them" for more than a century (Linenthal 1993:163).

The First Wounded Knee

It was a cold morning on December 29, 1890, when the Lakota men gathered to talk with U.S. military officials. Officers had ordered their men to surround the meeting area and the Lakota camp where the women and children were going about their daily routine (Utley 1963:204; Brown 1970:442). On a hill overlooking this expanse of prairie, four Hotchkiss guns were placed ready to rain their three-inch shells down upon any trouble that developed (Utley 1963:198–99; Mooney 1965:115; Brown 1970:441).

Events preceding this day had caused great tension between the two groups and aided in pushing them toward their fatal struggle. The Lakota reservations were in turmoil at the time. A new religious movement, the Ghost Dance, had taken hold in many Lakota camps. The Ghost Dance promised its followers a return to the good life, life as it was before the arrival of the white man (Mooney 1965:19; Kehoe 1989:7). During the Ghost Dance, followers would dance until they fell into a trance, in which they could perceive the returning buffalo and view the approaching promised land (Mooney 1965:19; Josephy 1993:16). Many Lakotas, including some from Big Foot's band, joined the movement in hopes of retaining their culture and way of life in the face of Western assimilation and oppression.

Many whites in the surrounding area feared that the Lakota were preparing to begin hostilities, as many of them were leaving the reservations to practice the Ghost Dance (Josephy 1993:17). The sizable newspaper coverage of the religious movement and the few "renegade" bands leaving the Indian agencies fueled these fears (Jensen et al., 1991:39; Beasley 1995:43). In response to the concerns of local whites and reservation officials, the federal government called upon several divisions of the U.S. Army to restore order and ease tensions.

The troops, however, had the opposite effect. Many Lakota leaders felt that the troops were there to finish them off (Green 1994:200). Tensions greatly increased after the murder, by Standing Rock reservation police, of Chief Sitting Bull, who was a Ghost Dance supporter (Mooney 1965:92; Kehoe 1989:18–20). Several chiefs began to move their bands into fortified positions throughout the reservations (Josephy 1993:18). Big Foot, fearing for the safety of his followers, acted upon a prior invitation from Chief Red Cloud and other Pine Ridge chiefs and started toward the Pine Ridge reservation.

As Big Foot and his followers began to move from the Standing Rock reservation to Pine Ridge, U.S. officers believed he was attempting to join other "hostile Indians" throughout the Pine Ridge reservation (Mooney 1965:97). General Miles believed Big Foot would reinforce the resistance of the Ghost Dancers already in the Stronghold in the northwestern corner of the Pine Ridge reservation (Utley 1963:187; Josephy 1993:21). To prevent that from occurring, he ordered troops to track down Big Foot's band, disarm the men, and move them back to the Standing Rock reservation (Josephy 1993:21; Beasley 1995:99).

Big Foot and his followers made their way from the Standing Rock reservation toward Pine Ridge starting on December 23, 1890 (Josephy 1993:21). During the trip Big Foot became seriously ill with pneumonia and eventually had to travel by wagon (Brown 1970:440; Josephy 1993:21). On December 28, 1890, Maj. Samuel Whitside from the Seventh Cavalry intercepted Big Foot's band. Wanting to avoid a fight, Big Foot notified the major of his people's peaceful intentions and agreed to follow the soldiers to their camp on Wounded Knee Creek (Utley 1963:196; Josephy 1993:22). After the Lakotas arrived at Wounded Knee, Col. James Forsyth led U.S. reinforcements into the camp and assumed command of the five hundred U.S. Cavalry troops and scouts (Utley 1963:198; Brown 1970:441).

Many of these U.S. troops were new and had never taken part in any operations. This fact, combined with the fact that many troops were part of the ill-famed Seventh Cavalry, may have added tension to the situation (Josephy 1993:24; Green 1994:201). The Seventh Cavalry, under the command of Gen. George Custer, had met disaster against the Lakota sixteen years earlier at Little Bighorn. A few of the men still in the Seventh Cavalry had been involved in that engagement (Green 1994:201).

The next morning Forsyth ordered the Lakota men to gather near the tent where Big Foot was quartered. Forsyth attempted to impress upon the Lakota their current situation (outnumbered and outgunned) by ordering his troops to deploy and surround the council area and Lakota camp (Josephy 1993:23; Green 1996:30, 34). As the meeting began, Colonel Forsyth ordered the Lakota men to surrender their weapons. When they brought forth only a few older pieces, the colonel ordered his troops to search the Lakota camp and the men. It was reported that a medicine man, Yellow Bird, was dancing around the Lakota men chanting they had nothing to fear and should be brave (Brown 1970:442; Lazarus 1991:115; Josephy 1993:24). Yellow Bird's actions undoubtedly caused a great amount of fear among the untested U.S. troops (Josephy 1993:24).

It was during the search of the Lakota men that something happened. Many accounts debate this moment as they attempt to explain what occurred. It is unclear just how the incident happened, but the outcome is clear. One report noted that a Lakota waved his rifle and shot a soldier (Lazarus 1991:115). Another report stated that a struggle to retrieve the rifle from the Lakota's hands resulted in the rifle accidentally firing (Kehoe

1989:23; Jensen et al. 1991:19; Green 1994:201). Others report that cavalry troops attempted to take the rifle of a deaf Lakota, who was unclear what was happening, when it accidentally fired (Brown 1970:442; Josephy 1993:24). Still another account reports that the Lakota planned to attack, and that Yellow Bird while dancing gave a signal for the attack to begin (Kehoe 1989:23; Jensen et al. 1991:18–19).

With the gunshot, the tension that had built between the two opposing groups led them into a desperate struggle. Soldiers began to fire their weapons indiscriminately at men, women, and children. The officers lost control of their men, and they watched as the soldiers followed the Lakotas into a ravine, killing all those in front of them. Many Lakota deaths occurred as the Hotchkiss guns fired into the Lakota camp, killing women and children. In the end 150 or more Lakota and 39 U.S. Cavalry soldiers lay dead (Beasley 1995:110; Kehoe 1989:24; Green 1994:200–01).

The number of deaths at Wounded Knee continues to be an object of debate today. In various sources, the death reports cover a range of numbers: more than 250 Lakotas and 33 U.S. soldiers (Green 1994:200); 153 Lakotas and 39 U.S. soldiers (Kehoe 1989:24); 150 Lakotas (Josephy 1993:26); 300 Lakotas and 25 U.S. soldiers dead, 39 other soldiers wounded (Brown 1970:444); 300 Lakotas killed (Gonzalez and Cook-Lynn 1999:1); and 146–250 Lakotas killed (Jensen et al. 1991:20). Though the numbers may not agree, a passage from *The Politics of Hallowed Ground* describes what the deaths have come to represent for the Lakota. "It was never about who was right or who was wrong. It was always about the deliberate genocide of a people by the European invaders of this continent who called themselves Americans. It was always a crime against humanity" (Gonzalez and Cook-Lynn 1999:296).

The Aftermath

Debate over Wounded Knee's meaning and interpretation began when the tragedy ended. Some viewed it as a victory over Native American treachery (J. V. Lauderdale, January 4, 1891, in Green 1996:51; Gonzalez and Cook-Lynn 1999:151). Others viewed it as a "wholesale massacre" (Green 1996:33).

After the engagement, General Miles, commander of the Sioux campaign and Colonel Forsyth's superior, decried the action at Wounded Knee: "Wholesale massacre occurred and I have never heard of a more brutal, cold-blooded massacre than at Wounded Knee" (Green 1996:33).

He immediately charged Colonel Forsyth with negligence for not controlling his troops and stopping the killing, and he appointed a board of inquiry to look into these charges (Green 1996:38). He also felt that Forsyth could have prevented the loss of the U.S. troops' lives by not placing them in danger of friendly fire (Green 1996:38). Some historians believe a deadly crossfire created by the U.S. troops caused many of their own deaths (Jensen et al. 1991:36; Green 1994:201; Green 1996:36).

Some historians believe that the military saw the need to persuade the public into believing Wounded Knee was a battle and not a massacre (Green 1996:39). Many in the press, however, described the engagement as a massacre, creating public outrage (Kehoe 1989:29; Josephy 1993:26). The army hoped that by changing the public's perception they could relieve some pressure.

To help change perceptions, the U.S. military nominated many men who served at Wounded Knee for the Medal of Honor and nominated several officers for brevet citations. Twenty Medals of Honor were eventually awarded. Historian Jerry Green has pointed out, however, the disproportionate number of medals awarded at Wounded Knee compared with those awarded in other U.S.–Native American engagements (Green 1994:203).

In the end, a court of inquiry found Colonel Forsyth not guilty of negligence. However, political pressure from Washington, D.C., probably aided this decision. General Miles stated: "I do not think there has ever been as marked an illustration of the suppression of the truth and false impressions published broadcast as there was in the affairs of last winter . . . not an exoneration of Forsyth, but a personal assault upon myself" (Green 1996:39).

However, most of the American populace agreed with General Miles in calling the Wounded Knee affair a massacre (Beasley 1995:137; Green 1994:204). Many people did not understand why there was so much bloodshed. Many of them believed they had civilized the American Indians, "so why kick a people when they're already down?" (Kehoe 1989:29).

Many Americans also saw this affair as the end of the Indian Wars (Utley 1963:267). America would have no more barriers and the Native-Americans could settle like other Americans and become civilized. The Lakota saw Wounded Knee as the end of their way of life. The death of Big Foot's people foreshadowed the decline of Lakota culture. Black Elk, a Lakota elder who witnessed the engagement, remarked: "I can see that something else died there in the bloody mud, and was buried in the blizzard. A people's dream died there. It was a beautiful dream" (quoted in Neihardt 1961:276).

The Second Wounded Knee

In the early 1970s Native Americans began to speak out about their subordinate position in U.S. society. Close to one hundred years after the so called "last battle of the Indian Wars," Native Americans still faced unwavering pressure to assimilate into mainstream American society (Burnette and Koster 1974:18). They had to continue abandoning their traditional ways of life and adjust to the characteristics of "American" society.

Pushed onto poor land and dealing with bureaucrats who never truly understood their traditions, they withstood the control of the dominant society. Native Americans on reservations were mostly impoverished, and many in the cities had no contact with their cultural roots (Akwesasne Notes 1974:12, 60; Dewing 1985:37; Kehoe 1989:76). After observing the black civil rights movement in the 1960s, Native Americans began to form their own groups, such as the American Indian Movement (AIM). Native Americans hoped these groups could help fight for civil rights and speak out against social and treaty abuses (Churchill 1994:254).

These activist groups attempted to speak for all tribes, and AIM's membership included individuals from multiple tribes (Akwesasne Notes 1974:60). Most of them came from the inner cities with many others from reservations. They wanted to discover their cultural roots and be proud of their Native American heritage (Kehoe 1989:51, 125). The Native American group Indians of All Tribes occupied Alcatraz Island in 1969 during their first protest against the government (Churchill 1994:253). In 1972 AIM took part in the Trail of Broken Treaties. This march gathered Native Americans from all around the country and converged on Washington, D.C., to discuss their issues with the Bureau of Indian Affairs (BIA) and the U.S. government.

When talks broke down, the marchers occupied the BIA office building and refused to surrender until the government heard their demands. The takeover ended after government officials promised to investigate their grievances. The government also agreed to pay $66,000 for the Native Americans' travel expenses back to their homes (Burnette and Koster 1974:215).

Following the BIA takeover, AIM began to support many demonstrations in the South Dakota–Nebraska area. Many viewed AIM's protests and actions supporting Native American justice as militant (Burnette and

Koster 1974:224; Dewing 1985:69; Lyman 1991:xvi). One demonstration did turn violent in Custer, South Dakota. AIM members traveled to Custer to protest the charges against a white suspect whom law enforcement officials accused of manslaughter in the killing of Wesley Bad Heart Bull (M. Crow Dog and Erdoes 1990:119; Churchill 1994:259). Protesters believed that prosecutors were going easy on the suspect by not charging him with murder, and that a Native American would have received a heavier charge (Dewing 1985:82).

The protest eventually got out of control, with AIM members and other Native Americans fighting with state police during a riot in which the police arrested many Native American protesters. The justice system later acquitted the murder suspect of second-degree manslaughter (M. Crow Dog and Erdoes 1990:121; Means 1995:248). Native Americans viewed this outcome as a slap in the face, and a demonstration of injustice toward Native Americans (Burnette and Koster 1974:223; Dewing 1985:88; M. Crow Dog and Erdoes 1990:121).

While these events unfolded throughout the country, trouble began to mount on the Pine Ridge reservation. Richard Wilson, elected in 1972 as tribal president of the Oglala Sioux tribe, started what many considered a reign of terror (Akwesasne Notes 1974:14; Lazarus 1991:301–2). Many blamed Wilson for mishandling tribal money and giving white ranchers access to the reservation's best grazing land. Others accused him of intimidation (Churchill 1994:260; Means 1995:237). They accused him of sending his GOON (Guardians of the Oglala Nation) squad, a group of hired white and Native American thugs, to silence his opposition and keep tight control on the reservation (Akwesasne Notes 1974:14; Dewing 1985:69). Wilson's opponents accused his GOON squad of firebombing houses and cars, beating people, and threatening their lives (Akwesane Notes 1974:14).

Wilson's supporters, it appears, consisted of mixed bloods and surrounding white ranchers. Those that opposed him were full bloods and traditionalists. Wilson supporters received tribal jobs and contracts. The traditionalists were usually unemployed, landless Lakota who felt they had no representation or voice in tribal government (Lazarus 1991:302).

On February 26, 1973, the Oglala Civil Rights Organization, an organization formed to fight for the rights of the Oglala Lakota, met with older district chiefs and decided to invite AIM to the Pine Ridge reservation to help in their battle against Wilson's injustice (L. Crow Dog and Erdoes 1995:187; Means 1995:252–53). After watching the outcome of events in Custer and knowing the reputation that AIM had received as militant,

Richard Wilson called on the federal government to help keep control during the eventual appearance of AIM on the reservation.

As AIM met with the Oglala Civil Rights Organization and other members of the Oglala Lakota, the U.S. marshals and tribal police prepared to defend the BIA office in the village of Pine Ridge. They feared AIM would attempt to take over the building as they had in Washington, D.C. (Akwesasne Notes 1974:23; Burnette and Koster 1974:227). In one of their meetings, AIM and the Oglala members decided to bypass the BIA building, since it was heavily defended, and move to occupy Wounded Knee (M. Crow Dog and Erdoes 1990:124).

Many of them recognized the sacred nature of Wounded Knee and the symbolic power that occupying it would achieve (L. Crow Dog and Erdoes 1995:188; M. Crow Dog and Erdoes 1990:124). As AIM, members of the Oglala Civil Rights Organization, and other supporters began to occupy and construct defenses at Wounded Knee, law enforcement officials positioned roadblocks and a fortified perimeter around the site. This began what would become a seventy-one-day siege.

AIM, masters at the media game, drew attention to the event almost immediately. The press came to see the newest Native American uprising (Means 1995:262, 274). The engagement pitted outnumbered, outgunned Native Americans fighting for their civil rights against the well-equipped, well-supported U.S. marshals and FBI.

One of the first acts of the Native American occupiers at Wounded Knee was taking over the Gildersleeves' trading post and museum. Many local Oglala felt that this white-run enterprise took advantage of their sacred past and poor situation (L. Crow Dog and Erdoes 1995:189; M. Crow Dog and Erdoes 1990:129). Many felt Gildersleeve exploited the Sioux tragedy and felt vindicated in destroying racial material in the museum and liberating sacred and traditional artifacts from the displays (Means 1995:263). The Native Americans attempted to reclaim their history and rid it of their oppressor's racial views. They now controlled the site and had the power to influence the public's memory of Wounded Knee's history.

As negotiations began, AIM gave a list of demands to the federal government. These requests included the need for the federal government to conduct investigations into the BIA and the management of the South Dakota reservations. Another demand insisted that the federal government review all treaties signed with the Lakota, including the 1868 treaty that gave the Sioux rights to the Black Hills. The demands concluded by giving the federal government two choices for resolution: (1) wipe out all the old people, women, children, and men by attacking Wounded Knee, or (2) negotiate the demands (Kehoe 1989:81–82).

As the federal government conducted negotiations with the occupiers, Richard Wilson and his GOONS stationed their own roadblocks to prevent aid from getting to Wounded Knee. Wilson also accused AIM of being supported by communist countries (Means 1995:276). Wilson and members of the John Birch Society told the country that AIM represented a communist-backed insurrection that was trying to topple the federal government (Akwesasne Notes 1974:15). Although groups were attempting to tarnish AIM's and the occupation's reputation, according to polls, most other Americans supported the occupiers' position at Wounded Knee (Kehoe 1989:85; Means 1995:276; Parman 1994:158–59).

Stanley Lyman, the BIA superintendent of the Pine Ridge reservation, felt that the press focused too much on what he called the "militant group" (Lyman 1991:53). He remarked that the Native Americans holed up in Wounded Knee did not represent the Oglala Sioux. He felt that the press should cover more stories about the elected tribal government of Wilson, and stories that would focus on the good things at Pine Ridge (Lyman 1991:53). Of course Lyman would have liked good press coverage to focus attention away from the troubles at Wounded Knee. It would not have reflected favorably on him if his superiors in Washington, D.C., saw the reservation he administrated filled with corruption and violence. Many Wounded Knee occupiers felt that Lyman was part of the government's plan to continue taking power from the traditional leaders and giving the best reservation resources to local white ranchers (Lyman 1991:11; Means 1995:251).

As the siege dragged on, support for the occupation dwindled as it appeared they would reach no agreement during negotiations. Toward the end, the federal government agreed to review the treaty of 1868 for any violations and not to arrest anyone immediately after the occupiers' surrender. The Oglala elders agreed to these points, and after seventy-one days the occupiers surrendered to the federal officers. As the marshals and FBI agents entered Wounded Knee, they approached the flagpole and tore down the AIM flag and replaced it with the U.S. flag, while firing their guns in salute (Kehoe 1989:85). The U.S. government had again reclaimed Wounded Knee.

In the end, the federal government fully addressed none of the negotiated terms. They arrested several occupiers as they exited Wounded Knee, and when investigations and discussions commenced over treaty violations, the U.S. government sent low-level representatives who had no power to deal with the issues. Many Native Americans felt that the government had broken the agreement (Means 1995:292–93).

In the years following the second Wounded Knee, however, Congress approved many acts that gave Native American tribes greater power to control and govern their reservations (Dewing 1985:358). The government also increased funding to the reservations to help improve infrastructures and create employment opportunities. In the end, the actions of AIM and other Native American groups forced the U.S. government to look at and address Native American issues. Their actions, whether "militant" or otherwise, drew attention to the problems of Native Americans (Dewing 1985:360). As Woody Kipp, a 1973 occupier, noted, "To us who were there, it is also history—a history, we hope, that created a consciousness that will reach into the lives of young Indians and perhaps white Americans" (Kipp 1994:232).

Wounded Knee Memorialization

Beginning in 1986, a group of Lakota individuals began to commemorate Chief Big Foot's journey from the Standing Rock reservation to Wounded Knee and the subsequent engagement. The Big Foot Memorial Ride, as the event became called, has participants walking or riding horseback along the trail Chief Big Foot and his followers traveled on their route to Wounded Knee. They wished to renew their stories, remember their ancestors, and remind themselves of their true history (Gonzalez and Cook-Lynn 1999:101). They also hoped the event would aid in healing the wounds left by Wounded Knee and the tragic history of U.S.–Native American relations (Beasley 1995:153). The event grew in subsequent years to include Native Americans from around the country, Euro-Americans, and others from around the world. It appeared that during these memorial rides all the participants came together, attempting to overcome past problems and work toward a better future.

This event, however, was not lacking political symbolism and conflict. An example of this occurred at the end of the ride in 1990, when the governor of South Dakota, George Mickelson, attempted to approach the cemetery at Wounded Knee. When he arrived at the gate, Russell Means, a leader of the 1973 takeover, blocked his entrance into the graves area (Beasley 1995:152; Gonzalez and Cook-Lynn 1999:102). Means's action clearly proved that old animosities remained. It displayed that some refused to have what they saw as their history appropriated by a white, U.S.

politician for the possible political gain he might garner by exhibiting concerns over Native Americans.

Means outraged other Native Americans, however, at the treatment of the governor. They felt he was there, like the rest of them, to heal the wounds of the past (Beasley 1995:153; Gonzalez and Cook-Lynn 1999:102). Mario Gonzalez noted, "They felt that Russell was using the centennial ceremonies to get media attention for himself; that he had showed no respect for their dead relatives" (Gonzalez and Cook-Lynn 1999:102).

As the centennial of the first Wounded Knee approached, interest in the Memorial Ride and other commemorative activities increased. Not only were activities carried out locally in the Pine Ridge area, but groups were busy in Washington, D.C. Beyond working with the Memorial riders, Wounded Knee survivor groups actively worked with members of Congress to pass an official apology for what occurred at Wounded Knee in 1890, and the establishment of a Wounded Knee memorial (U.S. Senate 1990:6, 1991:9). In the early 1990s Congress passed a resolution expressing the government's sorrow and regret for the event that occurred at Wounded Knee on December 29, 1890 (U.S. Senate 1991:1–2). Also in the resolution, Congress supported a memorial to Chief Big Foot's followers at Wounded Knee (U.S. Senate 1991:1–3).

The National Park Service (NPS) felt that the site was significant based on the fact that the NPS had registered the site as a National Historic Landmark in 1965. The NPS also felt it would help represent Native Americans, a group that had been underrepresented in the NPS system (U.S. Senate 1993:85, 88).

With the support of tribal Wounded Knee survivor groups, the NPS began to conduct research on the memorial park. Most of this research involved interviews and surveys of the Lakota people who wanted to have input on the memorial plan. Some members of the tribe felt the area should be left alone so the dead could rest in peace (U.S. Department of the Interior 1991:2; Van Horn et al. 1996:149). Others were concerned with issues such as commercial development, admission fees for Native Americans, and park worker qualifications (U.S. Department of the Interior 1991:2; Van Horn et al. 1996:149).

From these surveys, the NPS developed three proposals (U.S. Department of the Interior 1991:1–2; Van Horn et al. 1996:151). The major difference in these proposals lay in who managed the park. These concerns arose again during subcommittee hearings about the park. In these meetings the tribal president of the Oglala Sioux, John Yellowbird, mentioned a polarization of his people concerning turning the land over to the federal government (U.S. Senate 1993:108). On the other side, the assistant director of the NPS, Jerry Rogers, expressed his concern over who would manage and interpret the site (U.S. Senate 1993:88).

In the subcommittee meeting, we can see the continued struggle over the meaning of Wounded Knee. The NPS wanted both perspectives, Lakota oral tradition and American written tradition, to be represented to give a complete interpretation from both perspectives (U.S. Senate 1993: 88). Some tribal members wanted only the Sioux version interpreted (U.S. Department of the Interior 1991:3; Van Horn et al. 1996:150). Many people, especially the Lakota, were concerned with the possible exclusion of the word "massacre" from the interpretation (Akesasne Notes 1974: 105; U.S. Senate 1991:16). The Native Americans did not want it interpreted as a battle (Gonzalez and Cook-Lynn 1999:197). They did not want false information fed to the public, as it was in the 1890s. John Yellow Bird Steele, chairperson from the Wounded Knee District Council, expressed his views on interpreting Wounded Knee:

> We learned from that team [National Park Service study team] that there was opposition even to the word massacre. You notice I said mass murder there at one time. I did it on purpose. There is opposition. They didn't say where the opposition was to the word massacre, whether it was from the military or from within the bureaucracy somewhere, but there is still that feeling out there and opposition to saying it's a battle, the last battle. And everyone knows that it wasn't a battle. This is the reason that we would like to have local input as to how this could be developed. (U.S. Senate 1991:16)

Senator Ben Nighthorse Campbell of Colorado also expressed this sentiment as he discussed trying to revoke the Medals of Honor the government awarded after the engagement (U.S. Senate 1993:79).

Debates were occurring not only in the political channels of Washington, D.C., but also throughout the Pine Ridge reservation. The main debate centered on who had in mind the best interest of the tribe and the original Wounded Knee deceased (Sapa and Cooper 1995:5). Some Pine Ridge Lakotas felt The Wounded Knee Survivors Association no longer represented the best interest of the Lakota, the Wounded Knee area landowners, or the deceased (Sapa and Cooper 1995:3–5). They accused the survivors' association of standing to gain financially while other Lakota would lose land or voice in the historic interpretation (Sapa and Cooper 1995:4). In contrast, members of the Wounded Knee Survivors Association claimed that those opposing their movement to create a National Historic Site were themselves raising money to develop Wounded Knee commercially (Gonzalez and Cook-Lynn 1999:222).

Though a clear division was present between the groups on the reservation, both groups made the claim of better representing the descendants of Wounded Knee survivors and the Lakota people. Those opposing National Historic Site recognition with NPS involvement claimed their own cultural center would be "intended to help Lakota rediscover their traditional culture, and the strengths, and benefits it provides. The traditionalists hope to preserve the present memorial and grave-site in memory of their ancestors. The traditionalists do not wish the dead to be disturbed" (Sapa and Cooper 1995:5). Supporters of the Wounded Knee Historic Site and the Wounded Knee Survivors Association claim: "The proposed monument at Wounded Knee not only honors the Lakota dead. It honors the Lakota ideal of its own storytellers. A nation whose story has been under foreign domination cannot express its nationhood, and such a condition will not be tolerated by the men and women of the First Nations of America" (Gonzalez and Cook-Lynn 1999:231). Both sides claim to help the Lakota people and claim to be against the commercialization of Wounded Knee (Sapa and Cooper 1995:4; Gonzalez and Cook-Lynn 1999:55, 222). What is clear between the two is their hope of doing what is best for the Lakota people and Wounded Knee. Both sides want to tell the "true story," but what they cannot agree upon is who can tell it. Each side believes it has the sole responsibility and right to protect and interpret the past at Wounded Knee.

In trying to create a memorial for those killed at Wounded Knee, we can see the struggle of several groups attempting to dictate what the interpretation should be, and who should have the right to control the memory. Years of government oppression of Native American culture created strong feelings of mistrust that do not help in solving this problem. The continued bickering and dissension among various groups within the tribe also pose a major hurdle. Perhaps these reasons along with the continued debate over whether to call Wounded Knee a battle or a massacre are what has caused Congress not to approve the establishment of the Wounded Knee Historic Site.

References

Akwesasne Notes
  1974   *Voices from Wounded Knee 1973.* Akwesasne Notes, Rooseveltown, New York.
Beasley, Conger, Jr.
  1995   *We Are a People in This World: The Lakota and the Massacre at Wounded Knee.* University of Arkansas Press, Fayetteville.
Brown, Dee
  1970   *Bury My Heart at Wounded Knee: An Indian History of the American West.* Holt, New York.
Burnette, Robert, and John Koster
  1974   *The Road to Wounded Knee.* Bantam Books, New York.
Churchill, Ward
  1994   The Bloody Wake of Alcatraz: Political Repression of the American Indian Movement during the 1970s. *American Indian Culture and Research Journal* 18(4): 253–300.
Crow Dog, Leonard, and Richard Erdoes
  1995   *Crow Dog: Four Generations of Sioux Medicine Men.* HarperCollins, New York.
Crow Dog, Mary, and Richard Erdoes
  1990   *Lakota Women.* HarperCollins, New York.
Dewing, Rolland
  1985   *Wounded Knee: The Meaning and Significance of the Second Incident.* Irvington Publishers, New York.
Gonzalez, Mario, and Elizabeth Cook-Lynn
  1999   *The Politics of Hallowed Ground: Wounded Knee and the Struggle for Indian Sovereignty.* University of Illinois Press, Chicago.
Green, Jerry
  1994   Medals of Wounded Knee. *Nebraska History* 75(2): 200–8.
  1996   *After Wounded Knee.* Michigan State University Press, East Lansing.
Handler, Richard
  1991   Who Owns the Past. In *The Politics of Culture,* edited by Bret Williams, 66–74. Smithsonian Institution Press, Washington, D.C.
Jensen, Richard, R. Eli Paul, and John Carter
  1991   *Eyewitness at Wounded Knee.* University of Nebraska Press, Lincoln.
Josephy, Alvin, Jr.
  1993   Wounded Knee: A History. In *Wounded Knee: Lest We Forget,* edited by Alvin Josephy, Jr., Trudy Thomas, and Jeanne Eder. Buffalo Bill Historical Center, Cody, Wyoming.
Josephy, Alvin, Jr., Trudy Thomas, and Jeanne Eder
  1993   *Wounded Knee: Lest We Forget.* Buffalo Bill Historical Center, Cody, Wyoming.

Kehoe, Alice Beck
 1989 *The Ghost Dance: Ethnohistory and Revitalization.* Holt, Rinehart, and Winston, Chicago.
Kipp, Woody
 1994 "The Eagles I Fed Who Did Not Love Me." *American Indian Culture and Research Journal* 18(4): 213–32.
Lazarus, Edward
 1991 *Black Hills, White Justice: The Sioux Nation Versus the United States, 1775 to the Present.* HarperCollins, New York.
Linenthal, Edward
 1993 *Sacred Ground: Americans and Their Battlefields.* University of Illinois Press, Urbana.
Lyman, Stanley David
 1991 *Wounded Knee 1973.* Edited by June Lyman, Floyd O'Neil, and Susan Mckay. University of Nebraska Press, Lincoln.
Mattes, M. J.
 1952 *Report on the Historical Investigations of the Wounded Knee Battlefield Site, South Dakota.* Department of the Interior, Region Two, National Park Service, Omaha, Nebraska.
Means, Russell
 1995 *Where White Men Fear to Tread.* St. Martin's Press, New York.
Mooney, James
 1965 *The Ghost Dance Religion and the Sioux Outbreak of 1890.* University of Chicago Press, Chicago.
Neihardt, John G.
 1961 *Black Elk Speaks: Being the Life Story of a Holy Man of the Oglala Sioux.* University of Nebraska Press, Lincoln.
Parman, Donald L.
 1994 *Indians and the American West in the Twentieth Century.* Indiana University Press, Indianapolis.
Sapa, Wanbli, and William Cooper
 1995 *Wounded Knee: Are We About to Do It Again?* [Found at http://www. dickshovel.com/wkc.html.]
U.S. Department of the Interior, National Park Service.
 1991 *The Wounded Knee Update, Cankpe Opi Wonahuna.* Issue 1, September. U.S. Government Printing Office, Washington, D.C.
 1992 *The Wounded Knee Update, Cankpe Opi Wonahuna.* Issue 2, March. U.S. Government Printing Office, Washington, D.C.
U.S. Senate
 1990 Select Committee on Indian Affairs. Wounded Knee Memorial and Historic Site Little Big Horn National Monument Battlefield hearing. 101st Congress, 2nd session. September 25. Doc. nos. 101–1184.
 1991 Select Committee on Indian Affairs. Wounded Knee Park and Memorial hearing. 102nd Congress, 1st session. April 30. Doc. nos. 102–93.

1993   Subcommittee on Public Lands, National Parks and Forests. Committee on Energy and Natural Resources. Truman Farm Home; Wounded Knee National Memorial; Bodie Bowl, Preservation of Taliesin Site; and Alaska Peninsula Subsurface Consolidation Act hearing. 103rd Congress, 1st session. July 29.

Utley, Robert M.
 1961   *The Last Days of the Sioux Nation.* Yale University Press, New Haven
Van Horn, Lawrence F., Allen R. Hagood, and Gregory J. Sorensen
 1996   Wounded Knee, 1890 and Today: A Special Resource Study for Planning Alternatives. *Landscape and Urban Planning* 36: 135–58.

Part II

Commemoration and
the Making of a Patriotic Past

Commemoration and the Making of a Patriotic Past

One way to control the past is to create a public memory that commemorates a patriotic past. Patriotic histories promote and preserve the ideals of cultural leaders and authorities. They develop social unity and try to maintain the status quo. Officials present the past in a way that helps to reduce competing interests (Bodner 1992:13). Government agencies often advance the notion of "community of the nation while suppressing authentic local group memories and collective identities" (Glassberg 1996:12).

When histories develop to support a patriotic past, the process comes at the expense of other histories. In order to participate in a dominant collective memory, people from subordinate groups must reinterpret or abandon their own memories (Thelen 1989:1123–24). They must negotiate these meanings and incorporate them into their ongoing daily lives.

Two of the chapters in this section show that the creation of commemorative activities and memorial landscapes occurs within a dialogue that can be highly contested. As Martha Temkin relates in chapter 6, in the case of Antietam National Battlefield Park, there is a plan, approved by the State of Maryland and the National Park Service, to commemorate the battle by "freezing" the landscape. Time-freezing the Antietam landscape to the day before the battle is highly political and controversial. Choosing an era or a day to commemorate excludes the histories of many other groups who occupied the lands before and after that time.

The Robert Gould Shaw Memorial is also about creating a patriotic past, although the degree that specific groups embrace the monument has changed significantly, as Paul A. Shackel explains in chapter 7. It was originally created to honor the white officer who led the first Northern-organized African-American troops into Civil War battle. By the late twentieth century the monument had become an important symbol to the African-American community.

Another chapter in this section shows that some American sacred grounds can be left ambiguous because of the diverse competing memories of different factions. Monuments and landscapes can serve as an example of "collected memory" rather than of collective memories. A collected memory occurs when divergent memories converge on a common space. It is a place where various voices are heard and a dialogue can be fostered (Glassberg 1996, 1998). In chapter 8, Laurie Burgess describes the situation at Arlington National Cemetery and the Robert E. Lee Memorial, where the National Park Service is left with the dilemma of which past to commemorate. Lee's grounds, used as a cemetery for the Union dead, were later known as Arlington National Cemetery. The mansion where Lee lived has become his memorial. The message at this national shrine appears to be more inclusive and diachronic, although ethnic tensions and gender biases have challenged this notion.

The examples presented in this section show that events, monuments, and landscapes create a patriotic past that is politically charged. At Antietam, at the Shaw Memorial, and at Arlington National Cemetery, groups are continually competing for the control of memory. When officials create a patriotic past by commemorating a particular history, the history that is seen and interpreted on the American landscape comes at the expense of excluding other memories.

References

Bodner, John

1992   *Remaking America: Public Memory, Commemoration, and Patriotism in the Twentieth Century.* Princeton University Press, Princeton, New Jersey.

Glassberg, David

1996   Public History and the Study of Memory. *Public Historian* 18(2): 7–23.

1998   Presenting History to the Public: The Study of Memory and the Uses of the Past. Understanding the Past. *CRM* 21(11): 4–8.

Thelen, David

1989   Memory and American History. *Journal of American History* 75 (4): 1117–29.

6

Freeze-Frame, September 17, 1862: A Preservation Battle at Antietam National Battlefield Park

Martha Temkin

Introduction

Antietam National Battlefield Park is located in Washington County, Maryland, about seventy-five miles northwest of Washington, D.C. The park is a beautiful piece of the American agricultural landscape, yet also the place where the Civil War's bloodiest day occurred. It is a place full of contradictions and mixed feelings, a good place to look at issues of change in the managing and interpreting of a historic landscape over time, specifically the issue of "landscape freezing." This term refers to the maintenance of a landscape at a particular point in time and is an especially relevant issue to historic battlefield sites. Landscape freezing not only affects the decision making of the professionals involved in the management of the site, but also influences how they interpret the history of the site to the public.

Early Commemoration and the War Department Years

After the Battle of Antietam, the single bloodiest day of the Civil War, more than twenty-three thousand soldiers were dead, wounded, or missing. The battle began at dawn on September 17, 1862, and by the next day Confederate general Robert E. Lee withdrew his army back over the Potomac. Many historians see the Battle of Antietam as a major turning point in the war. While neither side could claim a clear victory, Lee's inability to move the war into Northern territory removed the threat of foreign recognition of the Confederacy. This encouraged President Lincoln to issue the Emancipation Proclamation, which came only five days after the battle. From that point on, the purpose of the war was not only to preserve the Union, but to end slavery.

Commemoration began on the site three years after the battle when the State of Maryland established Antietam National Cemetery, a burial place for the federal dead. It was officially dedicated on September 17, 1867, the fifth anniversary of the battle. In 1877, Maryland granted stewardship of the property to the U.S. War Department (Snell and Brown 1986: chapter 1).

By the 1880s veterans from both the Union and Confederate armies were considering how best to commemorate and preserve the battlefields of the Civil War. As part of this commemorative movement, an act of Congress established Antietam National Battlefield Site in 1890. The act included an appropriation of funds to locate, survey, and mark the "lines of battle" (U.S. House of Representatives 1890) of the U.S. Army, and to purchase land related to the battle. This action was the beginning of the preservation of the battlefield landscape as opposed to the honoring of the heroic dead with proper burial and memorials. An 1891 report noted that the battlefield at Antietam was virtually intact and should be maintained as such to clearly understand "the field and illustrate for historical purposes, the unparalleled deadly fighting which distinguishes it from all others" (Snell and Brown 1986:72). This unaltered quality of the landscape becomes a theme that resurfaces through the years, right up to the present.

The War Department had almost completely surveyed and mapped the battle lines by the end of 1894. In an essay to Congress, Secretary of War Daniel S. Lamont set into motion a preservation policy that was to have a great impact, not only at Antietam, but also on battlefield preservation overall. Lamont recommended that to best preserve the landscape of Antietam, the land should remain in the hands of the farmers in residence, ensuring the rural character of the land. In addition it would cost less for the government to purchase "several lanes or avenues along which the most severe fighting occurred" than to purchase whole farmsteads (Snell and Brown 1986:89). This policy would create a site that was easier to maintain over the long term. In addition, the government built roads on these strips of land so that historical markers erected upon them were accessible to visitors (Snell and Brown 1986:89–93). Governmental reliance on local farmers and landowners to maintain the battlefields in their original state actually worked and continues to serve as a successful management strategy today.

By the close of the nineteenth century, the War Department completed the road system and erected almost four hundred informational markers. The department also built a stone tower overlooking the battlefield at

Bloody Lane. Veterans' associations or states raised more than a dozen monuments. During the early years of the twentieth century, the War Department did not add to the commemorative landscape (Davis 1898). Veterans' groups continued to construct monuments, such as one honoring President McKinley after his assassination. By 1931, Antietam's commemorative landscape included ninety-one monuments (List of Monuments 1931; Snell and Brown 1986:119).

National Park Service Management: 1933–1942

Management of Antietam National Battlefield Park and Cemetery was transferred from the War Department to the National Park Service (NPS) in 1933. This transition was not without tension. The War Department was very reluctant to give up its historic military sites, in part because the department thought the NPS would not treat them with the respect due to places where sacrifices of blood had been made. Some members of the department expressed concern about the transformation of the sites into "playgrounds," places of recreation, not reverence (U.S. House of Representatives 1929). In essence, the NPS pledged not only to preserve the battlefield but also to interpret it to the greater public. Under the War Department this was a landscape where veterans honored their dead and relived their personal past. It was a place where young soldiers in training learned the lessons the Battle of Antietam had to teach. The general public came to this place to honor and remember their war dead, not to learn about the history of the Civil War. The NPS claimed it not only would continue to preserve these sites, but also would add an educational aspect in order to make them mean more to the people of this country (Snell and Brown 1986:144).

Interpretive services for the public were an improvement over what the War Department had offered but were still minimal by today's standards. The NPS became concerned with the potential lack of "historical correctness" (Annual Report 1934) that unsupervised self-appointed guides to the battlefield might display in telling their stories about the battle. In response to this concern, the NPS hired ranger-historians, but only for a few summers between 1933 and 1942. In addition, the NPS management devised a self-guiding leaflet and proposed trailside maps (Snell and Brown 1986:146, 183–96). Also, during this period, the museum and library at Antietam developed. However, the NPS regional director in 1941 felt that a museum was not needed because the "purpose at Antietam is to interpret the field action . . . [and] an elaborate museum display is not necessary in doing this" (Allen 1941).

During the 1930s the NPS created the first master plan for Antietam. Produced in Washington, D.C., it did not rely on any historical research. The master plan was minimal in scope; it consisted of a land acquisition program, map, and interpretive program (Snell and Brown 1986:199). The seventy-fifth anniversary of the battle occurred in 1937 and was commemorated with a reenactment in the Bloody Lane area and a visit by President Franklin Roosevelt. More than fifty thousand people attended this event (Beckenbaugh 1938).

Postwar Management: 1942–1950

In the postwar period between 1942 and 1950 the park continued to be understaffed in the areas of interpretation and research (Snell and Brown 1986:246). NPS management expressed concern that as a park it was "little more than a ribbon of road," that the War Department had made a mistake in its planning and it was up to the NPS to fix it (Appleman 1947). The donation of farmland near Burnside Bridge added more than one hundred acres to the park. In an effort to maintain the "historic scene," the NPS razed several farm buildings that, while more than seventy years old, were built shortly after the battle (Tolson 1944).

While interpretation improved, maintenance continued to be the main focus of management. Not everyone saw this failure to develop the park and its interpretation as negative. In an evaluation report, a historian wrote that while interpretive programs had been neglected, "the lack of interest in this park and consequent failure of government agencies to develop and promote it have been a blessing . . . for the absence of modern improvements Antietam battlefield has retained an atmosphere of authenticity" (Lattimore 1941).

Park Management: Mission 66

With the development of Mission 66, the interpretive and research focus on the military history of the battle shifted. Mission 66 was a ten-year plan initiated in 1956 to "properly rehabilitate, develop, interpret, and maintain every park in the system" (Snell and Brown 1986:247). This program enabled the master plan at Antietam to be fully developed. The park acquired the Dunkard Church property, and research began in order to reconstruct the building. Both the superintendent and the summer ranger-historian gave lectures and orientations, and a self-guided tour was printed on the back of the free map leaflet. The NPS erected ten new trailside exhibits along the driving route and improved the museum exhibits (Snell and Brown 1986:260–74).

As a direct result of Mission 66 and in part due to the impending 1962 centennial of the battle, park management hired a full-time historian. This hiring became necessary because monies from Mission 66 could not be used for restoration unless the buildings were "restored accurately" (Snell and Brown 1986:284). This policy precipitated a change in attitude toward historical and architectural research. The NPS no longer saw this research as peripheral to interpretive and visitor contact work. The historian laid out a very clear and detailed research program and suggested a new research topic: the effects of the battle on the nearby town of Sharpsburg. The research would include investigation into "damage and destruction of property, what the inhabitants did during the battle, what changes occurred as a result of the engagement, and whether citizens favored the North or the South" (Snell and Brown 1986:288–89).

The new historian also uncovered the story of Clara Barton and her contributions to the history at Antietam, bringing women into Antietam's interpretation for the first time. A prospectus for exhibits to be included in the newly funded visitor center contained a suggestion that the Battle of Antietam's influence on President Lincoln's decision to issue the Emancipation Proclamation should be interpreted to the public. This was the first time the park interpretive staff considered the Emancipation Proclamation in the interpretation of the battle. Other proposed exhibits included themes such as "Care of the Wounded" and "The Significance of the Battle." It is in this period that the interpretive focus began to widen to include more than just the twenty-four hours of the battle (Snell and Brown 1986:292–307).

In the 1960s, development at Antietam gathered momentum. In 1962 the park completed the reconstruction of the Dunkard Church. The building's rededication was part of the centennial commemorative activities. The 1962 ceremonies also included a reenactment of the battle, involving more than two thousand "troops," and the dedication of a monument to Clara Barton. Three states erected monuments in the 1960s—Texas, Georgia, and Delaware—and the new visitor center and museum opened. While some were concerned that the building intruded on the historic scene, the park staff and public generally met its erection with enthusiasm (Snell and Brown 1986:321–35). NPS historians conducted a great deal of historical research in the 1960s. In spite of the shift in research focus suggested in the 1950s, it continued to be concerned more with "romantic studies of troop movements and actions, than with the prosaic consideration of farm houses, buildings, fences and chains of title" (Snell and Brown 1986:382).

In this period, the scope of the park's mission broadened to include recreation, an addition to the NPS traditional missions of preservation, conservation, and interpretation. Some within the NPS did not agree with the use of historic sites as places for recreation. They worried that important (and in a sense sacred) sites would become playgrounds, just as the War Department had feared back in the 1930s (Snell and Brown 1986:309).

Park Management: 1970s and 1980s

In the 1970s and 1980s new interpretive themes arose. A museum revision plan suggested that soldier life and human aspects of the battle be explored, and that the battle be illustrated in terms of the entire Maryland campaign, the issuance of the Emancipation Proclamation, and the war as a whole. Implementation of these themes included a living-farm exhibit illustrating historic agricultural techniques. An interpretive emphasis on women began, as did the use of costumed interpreters. Other themes included the events leading up to and including the battle itself, the effect it had on the local people, and what life was like in the area at the time of the battle. Special events at the park occurred year-round and included, in addition to activities directly related to the battle, foot races, seminars, and exhibits (Snell and Brown 1986:394, 440–41, 501–5).

Also in this period, the NPS became concerned with protecting areas surrounding the park from development that would threaten the integrity of the historic landscape. As a result, Congress passed a bill in 1978 that substantially increased the extent of the park boundaries (Snell and Brown 1986:459–65).

The 1982 General Management Plan

In 1982 the park began to develop its General Management Plan (GMP) for the 1990s (U.S. Department of the Interior 1991:1), and it sparked controversy. In the mid-1980s, a section of battlefield outside the park boundaries was rezoned for commercial use. This rezoning created a very real development threat to the park (Nelson 1990). Also, in 1990, the National Trust for Historic Preservation listed Antietam as one of the nation's top eleven most endangered historic places. The trust identified growth and development pressures due, in part, to the site's proximity to

Washington, D.C., as a major threat to this historic landscape (Downey 1990). Nearby Manassas National Battlefield Park in Virginia had been fighting different kinds of development threats over this same period, and this fostered a sense of urgency and high concern over these issues (Downey 1990).

The final GMP reflected these concerns over out-of-control development. In 1989 the park released a scoping document to publicly announce the beginning of the GMP planning process. This document stated that a primary focus of the new GMP would be to "determine the extent of restoration necessary to fulfill the 1960 legislative mandate" (U.S. Department of the Interior 1991:62). This mandate called for maintaining and/or restoring the battlefield to its 1862 appearance (U.S. Department of the Interior 1991:66).

Following public hearings on the issue, the NPS made available for public review a list of alternatives (U.S. Department of the Interior 1990). Alternative A called for maintaining the status quo (U.S. Department of the Interior 1991:8). Alternative B called for restoring the historic scene "to the maximum extent possible on the eve of the battle" (U.S. Department of the Interior 1991:11). This alternative called for many changes: the removal of the 1890s military road system, the eventual demolishing of the visitor center, a moratorium on the raising of monuments, and the replanting of more than three hundred acres of woods. Alternative B also severely restricted recreational use (U.S. Department of the Interior 1991:11–17). Alternative C was similar to B except that it recognized the period of commemoration as also significant. It left the 1890s road system in place and included the commemorative period in the interpretation of the park's history to the public. Also, the creation of new monuments remained a possibility under C (U.S. Department of the Interior 1991:20).

In 1992, the NPS chose as its GMP a slightly altered Alternative B. Not surprisingly, many preservation groups supported this alternative. These included the Maryland Historic Trust, the Advisory Council of Historic Preservation, and the National Parks and Conservation Association. Many Civil War Round Tables and similar organizations also favored Alternative B (U.S. Department of the Interior 1992:67–109).

Many local landowners, however, did not support the choice of Alternative B. They felt threatened by the possibility of the park usurping control of the management of their private property. These local people thought that private landowners in and around the park had been doing a good job of preservation over the years and the park should leave well enough alone. Some area residents saw Alternative B as "a large-scale tourist construction project that would have negative impacts on the battlefield and the local inhabitants" (U.S. Department of the Interior 1992:153). Farmers and residents of Sharpsburg were also concerned about what effect road changes and closures would have on their daily activities (U.S. Department of the Interior 1992:86, 89, 149; Downey 1990; Nelson 1990 25 March). Also, many people expressed complaints about the recreation restrictions (U.S. Department of the Interior 1992: 77, 80, 86, 110–12, 114).

The Park Today

Antietam battlefield is a beautiful, rural locale (fig. 6.1). As Linenthal remarks about Gettysburg battlefield, it is a great irony how peaceful these places of terrible carnage, tragedy, and suffering have become (Linenthal 1993:89). The story being told at Antietam is still primarily the one of that single bloody day in 1862. Lincoln's Emancipation Proclamation features prominently in the movie shown to orient visitors to the battlefield and what happened there. Yet there is little mention of the farmers and their families and no mention of their slaves. Women are represented only by the Clara Barton memorial on the field and some books in the gift shop. The commemorative landscape remains. No roads have been removed. The West Woods have been replanted, and a ranger told me to bring my grandchildren back in thirty years to see what they looked like at the time of the battle.

Alternative B is a GMP honored more in the breach than in the observance. Parts of it are being implemented, for example, the replanting of the West Woods. The park has obtained many if not most of the scenic easements thought to be required to maintain the historic scene. The chief historian of the NPS, Dwight Pitcaithley, who backed Alternative C due to the significance of the commemorative landscape, told me that he thought that the superintendent then was very concerned about development encroaching on the battlefield. That superintendent saw freezing as a way to stop such encroachment (Pitcaithley, personal communication, 1998). Here is another instance of the interpretive stance being influenced by current social conditions and concerns. The idea of preservation through freezing can result in a terrible erasure and silencing of events and people affected by both past events and present interpretations. Returning Antietam battlefield to the eve of the battle also takes us back to the time when the enslavement of human beings was accepted in the United States. Is that the past we choose to enshrine?

Figure 6.1. Antietam Battlefield. (Photo: Martha Temkin.)

There is a new superintendent at Antietam now, and he may be less worried about the encroachment of suburban development. The staff I spoke to at the battlefield had great respect for the commemorative landscape: monuments and roads. One ranger told me that if veterans of the Civil War saw fit to put the monuments up, who are we to take them down. He also suggested that GMPs are not written in stone, and that even the ban on future monuments could be lifted in the right circumstances.

Interpretation and Freezing

The interpretation of history at Antietam National Battlefield Park has always focused on the events of September 17, 1862. The battle forever changed this ordinary rural landscape into one laden with meaning. Civil War veterans were the first to recognize its power and mark it in commemoration. Initially their concern was to care for fallen comrades respectfully. The creation of Antietam National Cemetery by the State of Maryland achieved this. Once the dead were honored with proper burial and monuments, the veterans turned to the battlefield. They wanted the battle site marked upon the land so that the great sacrifices made there would not be forgotten. In order to assist in the research and mapping of the battle lines, memories were called upon before they could be lost to time and old age. The observation tower was built so that future military leaders could be brought to this place and learn from their predecessors (U.S. Department of the Interior 1992:4). Veterans placed monuments on this now sacred ground not only to ensure remembering, but to give the survivors and the families of the dead a *place* to gather and remember together.

Under post–World War II NPS management, the intellectual climate and public events of the time influenced public interpretation programs at Antietam. The focus on the Emancipation Proclamation arose in the 1950s and 1960s, during the civil rights movement. During the 1970s and 1980s the emphasis on individual histories of ordinary soldiers coincided with the development of the new social history movement. And while the accent on Clara Barton predates the feminist movement of the 1970s, the inclusion of ordinary women in the interpretations at Antietam appears at this time.

Antietam battlefield has always been regarded as an excellent example of a site with high historic integrity. As defined by the NPS, integrity is "the authenticity of a property's historic identity, evidenced by the survival of physical characteristics that existed during the property's historic or prehistoric period. The seven qualities of integrity as specified by the National Register Program are location, setting, feeling, association, design, workmanship, and materials" (Birnbaum 1996:5). Antietam fits the bill. This feeling of integrity has led finally to a GMP that embraces the concept of time freezing as a historic preservation method. If this plan were to be followed to the letter, only one history would be told at Antietam. The story would be limited to events of the eve of September 17, 1862.

The freezing of historical sites is commonplace. At Harpers Ferry National Park in the 1950s, the NPS decided to restore the town to its Civil War period and to this end removed any buildings that did not fit into this time scheme (Shackel 1996:5). This same approach was undertaken at Colonial Williamsburg, where Rockefeller restored the town to its 1770s appearance (Handler and Gable 1997:223). In fact, this approach is used in many living-history presentations, where visitors are invited to step back in time and experience the lives of past peoples. Examples include such common tourist destinations as Mystic Seaport in Connecticut and Plimouth Plantation in Massachusetts.

Cultural landscapes are not static things, but dynamic accumulations of human activity interacting with the natural environment and shaped by the myriad of meanings given to a place through time. The preservation policy of freezing is not fully endorsed by the NPS today. This is partly a result of the emphasis on cultural landscape preservation and analysis that the NPS has developed over the past fifteen years (Ahern 1992). One NPS publication suggests that battlefields should be considered as a "continuum through history" (Birnbaum 1996:22). Another claims, "Battlefields cannot be frozen in time" (Andrus 1992:11).

Other authors have also dealt with the issue of freezing. Handler and Gable suggest that it is impossible to present the past, except in terms of the present. There is no real and true history; there are only the tales we, in the present, tell. These tales reflect our present voices, our concerns, and our knowledge (Handler and Gable 1997:223). David Lowenthal speaks of the dangers of trying to restore or preserve our past too completely and suggests that it can be a way of blinding ourselves to the reality of our alteration of the past. In fact, he states that it is this very alteration that keeps the past "real, alive and comprehensible" (Lowenthal 1985:411).

Freezing the landscape at Antietam could result in a form of purposeful amnesia, a way of returning to a past in which we remember only the golden times and put away any reminder of the darkness that may have also existed. Michael Kammen describes this as "heritage syndrome." This approach to the presentation of the history of a cultural landscape can only result in what he terms an "oversimplification and tendentiously selective memories—which means both warping and whitewashing a fenced-off past" (Kammen 1997:220, 221).

Edward Linenthal presents another point of view. In his book on battlefields, *Sacred Ground: Americans and Their Battlefields,* he remarks that in order to preserve the sanctity of a place deemed sacred, it must be separated from secular space. At battlefields, this freezing of the landscape is necessary to give visitors an authentic landscape where they can then properly understand the important events that took place. Freezing becomes a form of veneration (Linenthal 1993:5). It creates a situation wherein only one story of the battle is "true"; only one story is important and all others are silenced. At this point, not only is any attempt to change the physical aspects of the place seen as defilement, but even redefinition of the story can be taken as heresy (Linenthal 1993:5). At Antietam any redefinition (including the issuance of the Emancipation Proclamation, for example) has not led to much controversy. At other battlefields, such as the Little Bighorn site, history and whose story should be told have been much more fiercely contested (Linenthal 1993).

This issue of sanctification is further explored by Kenneth Foote in his 1997 book *Shadowed Ground: America's Landscapes of Violence and Tragedy.* He describes sanctification of violent landscapes as the creation of a "sacred" place by consecration in terms of the erection of a durable monument or memorial. He goes on to suggest that violent landscapes treated in this manner are designed to serve as a reminder or warning to future generations. They tend to be places that are set clearly apart from the surrounding environment, are carefully maintained for a long period of time, have been transferred from private to public ownership, remain places of ongoing commemoration and rituals, and "attract additional and sometimes even unrelated monuments and memorials" (Foote 1997:9). Most of these characteristics exist at Antietam, and the last two would be changed by freezing the landscape. Sanctified sites are meant to speak to successive generations in part because the concepts and ideals they represent are thought to be timeless. Freezing a landscape could result in making it irrelevant to future generations. Continued ritualized activity, including the addition of what people in the present see fit to memorialize, may be necessary in order to maintain the sanctification of the site.

Interestingly, there was little public comment on how the application of Alternative B would affect this landscape. The Maryland Historical Trust expressed concern over the removal of "the 1890s commemorative roads" (U.S. Department of the Interior 1992:69). In a letter to the park superintendent, a representative of the Sons of Confederate Veterans pointed out that the participants in the conflict are not equally represented. There are far more monuments to the soldiers of the Union Army than to those of the Confederate Army. To deny future monuments would "illustrate an amazing insensitivity toward the descendants of soldiers who were killed, wounded, or risked their lives during the Sharpsburg conflict" (U.S. Department of the Interior 1992:106). The current assistant superintendent of the park, Susan Trail, also suggested that removing the roads and leaving the monuments would take the monuments out of context. They were built in conjunction with the roads and were not meant to stand alone. She also said that circumstance denied certain groups the right to put up monuments in the initial years after the battle. The South was devastated by the war and had little money to spend on memorials (Trail, personal communication, 1998). In a similar vein, the chief historian at NPS, Dwight Pitcaithley, suggests that this "no new monuments policy" also denies the commemoration of events at Antietam by modern people. For example, an African-American group might want to commemorate Antietam's role in the issuance of the Emancipation Proclamation (Pitcaithley, personal communication 1998).

In a 1990 newspaper article titled "The Second Battle of Antietam: Farmers against Preservationists," reporter Kristin Downey suggests that local farmers felt that the preservationists were just "pursuing an intellectual exercise in restoration" (Downey 1990). In doing this research I began to feel the same way. It became clear to me that even though the GMP was supposed to be the guiding document for the management of Antietam National Battlefield Park, the idea of landscape freezing was recognized by the park staff as very problematic and probably would not be acted upon in its entirety.

Dwight Pitcaithley (personal communication, 1998) remarks that the reality in historic preservation is that a line needs to be drawn somewhere and sites managed to some point in time. While each site must be examined within its own context and some decisions need to be made, we must remain aware that fixing a place in one particular time "destroys other dimensions." Where possible, he advises, it is wise to take an evolutionary point of view. He felt that drawing the line on the eve of the 1862 battle was unrealistic and that, in a sense, the whole argument was esoteric at Antietam because the landscape had really changed so little. Another problem he saw with Alternative B was that it limited the engagement of visitors with the battlefield in a physical and emotional sense. Taking out

Figure 6.2. Bloody Lane, circa 1880, and a house built after the battle. (Courtesy Antietam National Battlefield Park.)

Figure 6.3. Bloody Lane, circa 1956, and a white house razed by the National Park Service a few years later. (Courtesy Antietam National Battlefield Park.)

the 1890s roads would change the ability of visitors to wind their way through the landscape of the battlefield. The planned tour, under Alternative B, would tend to keep people on the edges, and this physical limitation would, in turn, limit emotional engagement.

The problem with freezing as a preservation policy for Antietam National Battlefield Park is twofold. First, returning the landscape to the eve of the battle is 1862 is impossible. Things change over time and cultural landscapes are an especially dynamic form of material (see figs. 6.2 and 6.3). The 1992 GMP recognizes this in that there is no suggestion that the postbattle monuments themselves will be removed. It recognizes that only certain elements of the Antietam battle landscape can be frozen. As pristine as the site appears, many changes have taken place there and cannot be reversed. Second, in presenting only one "true" history, all other histories are silenced. If only the story of the battle is told at Antietam, so much more is left unsaid. The battlefield was not an empty place, filled up by soldiers on that September day and emptied the following day. It was peopled—before, during, and after the battle—by farmers, their slaves, wives, and children, generals and infantry, and later, wounded soldiers and those that nursed them. In the decades to follow, the landscape continued to be farmed and called home by the local people. It became a place of reverence and memory for those who came to mourn and remember. To the War Department, it became a place of military training and education. To others it has become a place of rural beauty and to many a place of recreation. And it remains home to the people who continue to live on and work the land. As Kevin Lynch claims, "Preservation is not simply the saving of old things, but the maintaining a response to those things" (Lynch 1972:53). In order to speak meaningfully, Antietam and other historic places need to speak in many voices.

References

Ahern, Katherine
   1992   *Cultural Landscape Bibliography: An Annotated Bibliography on Resources in the National Park System.* U.S. Government Printing Office, Washington, D.C.
Allen, Thomas J.
   1941   Regional Director for Region 1, memorandum in letter to the Director, November 4, 1941 (copy to Superintendent Coleman). Record Group 79, Box 2606, File 840, Inspection of Interpretation Program, Antietam National Battlefield Site, Antietam, Maryland. April 11. National Archives, Washington, D.C.
Andrus, Patrick W.
   1992   *Guidelines for Identifying, Evaluating and Registering America's Historic Battlefields,* U.S. Department of the Interior, National Park Service. Cultural Resources. Interagency Resource Division. Washington, D.C.
Annual Report for Fiscal Year Ending 30 June
   1934   Record Group 79, Box 2602, File 207.01.4, Antietam National Battlefield Site, Antietam Maryland. National Archives, Washington, D.C.
Antietam–South Mountain Centennial Association
   1962   *Battle of Antietam Centennial and Hagerstown Bicentennial: Official Program and Historical Guide, Aug. 31 through Sept. 17, 1962.* Hagerstown, Maryland.
Appleman, Robert.
   1947   Memorandum to Regional Director, Region 1, November 12. Record Group 79, Box 2603, File 207.03, National Archives, Washington, D.C.
Beckenbaugh, John K.
   1938   Superintendent's Annual Report for the Fiscal Year Ending June 30, 1938 [Antietam National Battlefield] Record Group 79, Box 2602, File 207.01.4 National Archives, Washington, D.C.

Birnbaum, Charles A., ed.
  1996   *The Secretary of the Interior's Standards for the Treatment of Historic Properties with Guidelines for the Treatment of Cultural Landscapes.* U.S. Department of the Interior, National Park Service, Washington, D.C.

Davis, George W.
  1898   Letter to Secretary of War, March 18. Record Group 92, Entry 707, Box 230, File 697, National Archives, Washington, D.C.

Doust, Harry W., and Robert L. Lagemann.
  1958   *Antietam National Battlefield Site, Maryland.* U.S. Department of the Interior, National Park Service, Washington, D.C.

Downey, Kirstin
  1990   The Second Battle of Antietam: Farmers Against Preservationists. *Washington Post.* June 9.

Foote, Kenneth E.
  1997   *Shadowed Ground: America's Landscapes of Violence and Tragedy.* University of Texas Press, Austin.

Frassanito, William A.
  1978   *Antietam: The Photographic Legacy of America's Bloodiest Day.* Scribner, New York.

Handler, Richard, and Eric Gable
  1997   *The New History in an Old Museum: Creating the Past at Colonial Williamsburg.* Duke University Press, Durham, North Carolina.

Hartwig, D. Scott
  1990   *The Battle of Antietam and the Maryland Campaign of 1862: A Bibliography.* Heckler, Westport, Connecticut.

Heysinger, Isaac W.
  1912   *Antietam and the Maryland and Virginia Campaigns of 1862: From the Government Records—Union and Confederate—Mostly Unknown and Which Have Now First Disclosed the Truth.* Heale, New York.

Kammen, Michael
  1997   *In the Past Lane: Historical Perspectives on American Culture.* Oxford University Press, New York.

Lattimore, Ralston B.
  1941   Inspection of Interpretive Program, Antietam National Battlefield, Record Group 79, Box 2606, File 840. National Archives, Washington, D.C.

Linenthal, Edward
  1993   *Sacred Ground: Americans and Their Battlefields.* University of Illinois Press, Urbana.

List of Monuments, Markers, and Tablets on the Antietam National Battlefield
  1931   Record Group 79, War Department, Box 2606, File 688. National Archives, Washington, D.C.

Lowenthal, David
1985   *The Past Is a Foreign Country.* Cambridge University Press, New York.
Luvass, Jay, and Harold Nelson, eds.
1996   *Guide to the Battle of Antietam: The Maryland Campaign.* University
        Press of Kansas, Lawrence.
Lynch, Kevin
1972   *What Time Is This Place?* MIT Press, Cambridge.
Maryland Department of Education
1962   The Centennial Commemoration of the Civil War: 1962, *Antietam Com-
        memoration Year.* Prepared by a state committee in cooperation with the
        Maryland Department of Education.
Murfin, James V.
1982   *The Gleam of Bayonets: The Battle of Antietam and Robert E. Lee's
        Maryland Campaign, September, 1862.* Louisiana State University Press,
        Baton Rouge.
Nelson, W. Dale
1990   Antietam Battlefield Under Fire as Development Peppers the Area; Pres-
        ervation: Those Who Want to Protect the Past Are Divided on How to
        Accomplish Their Goal. Associated Press/*Los Angeles Times.* March 25.
Sears, Stephen W.
1983   *Landscape Turned Red, The Battle of Antietam.* Popular Library, New
        York.
Shackel, Paul
1996   *Cultural Change and the New Technology: An Archaeology of the Early
        American Industrial Era.* Plenum Press, New York.
Snell, Charles W., and Sharon A. Brown
1986   *Antietam National Battlefield and National Cemetery: An Administra-
        tive History.* U.S. Department of the Interior, National Park Service,
        Washington, D.C.
Tilberg, Frederick
1960   *Antietam National Battlefield Site, Maryland.* U.S. Department of the
        Interior, National Park Service Series 31, Washington, D.C.
Tolson, Hillory A.
1944   Acting Director, memorandum to Regional Director, Region 1, April 24.
        Record Group 79, Box 2607, File 900—Part 1, National Archives,
        Washington, D.C.
URS Greiner, Inc.
1998   *Management Summary: Archaeological Investigations at Antietam Na-
        tional Battlefield, Sharpsburg, Maryland, Prepared for: National Capital
        Area National Park Service.* URS Grenier, Florence, New Jersey.
U.S. Department of the Interior. National Park Service.
1941   *Antietam, National Battlefield Site, Maryland.* U.S. Government Print-
        ing Office, Washington, D.C.

1977 *Proposed Antietam National Battlefield Site, Maryland/ Submitted as an/and Accompanying Part of the Communication to the Secretary of the Interior.* U.S. Government Printing Office, Washington, D.C.

1988 *Antietam National Battlefield: Analysis of the Visible Landscape.* U.S. Government Printing Office, Denver.

1990 *Alternatives: Antietam National Battlefield.* U.S. Government Printing Office, Washington, D.C.

1991 *Draft Environmental Impact Statement and General Management Plan: Antietam National Battlefield Park.* U.S. Government Printing Office, Denver.

1992 *Summary General Management Plan and Final Environmental Impact Statement Antietam National Battlefield.* U.S. Government Printing Office, Denver.

U.S. Congress. House of Representatives.

1890 *Appropriations Bill.* 10830, 51st Congress, 1st Session, June 7.

1929 Committee on Military Affairs. *Transfer of National Military Parks: Hearings before the Committee of Military Affairs.* 70th Congress, 2d Session, January 31, S4173.

7

The Robert Gould Shaw Memorial: Redefining the Role of the Fifty-Fourth Massachusetts Volunteer Infantry

Paul A. Shackel

Introduction

A highly respected art historian describes Augustus Saint-Gaudens, a well-known American sculptor during the Victorian era, as "an American Michelangelo, a superb craftsman, a poet and philosopher" (Dryfhout 1982:25). He is best recognized for his memorial to Col. Robert Gould Shaw that sits on the Boston Common (fig. 7.1). Shaw led the first African-American Northern volunteer regiment into battle during the American Civil War. He was immediately immortalized by Americans after he and nearly half of his troops died in an attempt to capture Fort Wagner, outside Charleston, South Carolina. Saint-Gaudens unveiled the Shaw monument in 1897. It displays the colonel in the foreground, on horseback; his African-American troops, the Fifty-Fourth Massachusetts Volunteer Infantry, march in step next to him. The foot soldiers serve as a background to Shaw, who occupies the central portion of the monument.

The memorial stood for more than a century with its public meaning controlled by the white community. It demonstrates and reinforces the memory of their community's historic abolitionist commitment, a heritage that has been cherished by many liberal Northerners for more than a century. Some critics claim that "Saint-Gaudens' memorial to Shaw demonstrates how one vastly gifted, socially responsible white artist, operating on intractable material with an objective eye, and absolute control over hand and eye" (Benson and Kirstein 1973). Others critics (see for instance Boime 1990) disagree with this assessment. They claim that Saint Gaudens

Figure 7.1. The Robert Gould Shaw Memorial on the Boston Common. (Photo: Paul A. Shackel.)

was not socially responsible and dedicated to a social cause—the abolition of slavery. In fact, they see the memorial as reinforcing social and racial inequalities.

The Robert Gould Shaw Memorial is a multivalent object that is politically and socially charged. The memorial has different meanings to various people and different social groups, and its message has changed as groups vie for control over the memory of the event. While some have hailed Saint-Gaudens's sculpture as a magnificent piece of art that commemorates the deeds of Shaw, its public memory changed in the late twentieth century. With the strengthening of the civil rights movement, the African-American community has strongly embraced the memorial, since it is one of only a few Civil War memorials with African-American representation. Robert Gould Shaw's symbolic role has gradually diminished in the official memory in favor of recognizing and commemorating the African-American soldier of the Civil War.

Robert Gould Shaw and the Making of the Fifty-Fourth Massachusetts Infantry

With Lincoln's Emancipation Proclamation during the Civil War, many Northerners initially saw black soldiers playing a limited support role for the white troops. Governor John A. Andrew of Massachusetts had a strong desire to form the first "model regiment" of African-Americans (Duncan 1992:26). In February 1863, he asked Robert Gould Shaw to lead the Fifty-Fourth Massachusetts, an infantry unit composed solely of African-Americans. Shaw eventually consented, and his family, with a strong abolitionist commitment, was overjoyed by his decision. His mother wrote him, "Now I feel ready to die, for I see you willing to give your support to the cause of truth that is lying crushed and bleeding" (quoted in Duncan 1992:23). Shaw wrote his fiancée, Annie, on February 8, 1863, "I feel that what I have to do is to prove that a negro can be made a good soldier." Later in the letter he explained, "I shan't be frightened out of it by its unpopularity; and I hope you won't care if it is made fun of" (Duncan 1992:285–86).

The raising of African-American troops along with the publication of the Emancipation Proclamation jeopardized the balance of power in the war. Upon learning about the Emancipation Proclamation, and threatened by the raising of African-American troops, General Pierre G. T. Beauregard called for the "execution of abolition prisoners [captured Union soldiers and officers] after 1st of January. . . . Let the executions be with the garrote" (quoted in McPherson 1988:565–66). Jefferson Davis, in a message to the Confederate Congress, stated that captured Union officers leading black troops should be punished for "inciting servile insurrection, and shall, if captured, be put to death or be otherwise punished at the discretion of the Court" (Emilio 1969 [1894]:7; also see McPherson 1988:566). In May of 1863, the Confederate Congress sanctioned this policy (McPherson 1988:566), although these threats did not discourage Shaw's efforts to establish his regiment.

On May 18, 1863, ceremonies were held before the Fifty-Fourth Massachusetts Volunteer Infantry left Boston. Frederick Douglass, William Lloyd Garrison, and Wendell Phillips spoke to a crowd of about three thousand spectators. The governor presented the battle flag to Shaw, who responded, "May we have an opportunity to show you that you have not made a mistake in intrusting the honor of the State to a colored regiment— the first State that has ever sent one to war" (Duncan 1992:333). On May 28, Shaw and the Fifty-Fourth Massachusetts Volunteer Infantry marched to Battery Wharf, where they set sail for the Sea Islands off Charleston, South Carolina.

The world followed the Fifty-Fourth Massachusetts, including abolitionist supporters and Democratic detractors. The Fifty-Fourth Massachusetts met its first contest on James Island on July 16. The island, a strategic land mass that was key to holding Fort Wagner, guarded the main shipping channel to Charleston, South Carolina. Though outnumbered, the Fifty-Fourth Massachusetts rescued the Tenth Connecticut Regiment from defeat by routing the rebels (Duncan 1992:49–50). Word spread of the heroics of the Fifty-Fourth in battle. Newspapers in the North reported that African-Americans could fight, and fight well.

After the Fifty-Fourth made a two-night march through rain and shifting sands, with insufficient rations, an exhausted Shaw accepted the order to lead an attack on Fort Wagner. An attempt to capture Fort Wagner had failed the week before. At dusk, on July 18, the Fifty-Fourth Massachusetts led the assault. "More was riding on the Fifty-Fourth's first big action than the capture of a fort, important as that might be" (McPherson 1988:686). Colonel Shaw led only six hundred troops across a narrow spit of sand against a strong earthwork. A large camp guard remained behind. Shaw was one of the first to fall, but his troops pressed on. More than half reached the inside of the fort, and they held Wagner's parapet for an hour before being driven off by the Confederates (McPherson 1988:686) (fig. 7.2). Some white regiments attacked the fort that night, but they also failed. The assault on Fort Wagner that day left 1,515 Union casualties compared with 181 on the Confederate side (Burchard 1965:149).

A Confederate lieutenant, Iredell Jones, reported, "The dead and wounded were piled up in a ditch together sometimes fifteen in a heap, and they were strewn all over the plain for a distance of three-fourths of a mile" (quoted in Benson and Kristein 1973). In the Fifty-Fourth Massachusetts, two-thirds of the officers and nearly half the enlisted men who took part in the attack were killed, wounded, or missing. This tragedy was only compounded by the wounded receiving poor medical attention. Confederate commanders refused the assistance of the Union army to care for the wounded and the burial of the dead. They shipped the captured soldiers upriver to Charleston, where they forced them to parade through the streets amid jeers and catcalls (Burchard 1965:142).

John T. Luck, an assistant surgeon, who wrote the only surviving Northern account of the battle's aftermath, reported, "All the officers killed in the assault were decently buried, excepting Colonel Shaw" (Burchard 1965:142). Captain H. W. Hendericks, a Confederate officer, remarked that Shaw's "body was carried through our lines; and I noticed that he was stripped of all his clothing save under-vest and drawers. . . . His watch and chain were robbed from his body by a private in my company" (quoted in Emilio 1969 [1894]:98). Hoping to disgrace him, the Confederates buried Shaw in a mass grave with his troops. "Colonel Shaw

Figure 7.2. *The Attack on Fort Wagner, South Carolina,* an 1890 lithograph. (Courtesy U.S. Department of the Interior, National Park Service, Saint-Gaudens National Historic Site, Cornish, New Hampshire.)

was the only officer buried with the colored troops" (quoted in Emilio 1969 [1894]:98).

When the federals asked for Shaw's body for proper burial, a Confederate general reportedly said, "We have buried him with his niggers" (quoted in McPherson 1969). Brigadier General Hagood, commander of the Confederate forces at Wagner, supposedly said, "I knew Colonel Shaw before the war, and then esteemed him. Had he been in command of white troops, I should have given him an honorable burial; as it is, I shall bury him in the common trench with the negroes that fell with him" (from Emilio 1969 [1894]:101; Burchard 1965:143). Hagood later denied he said those words.

News of the assault on Fort Wagner by the Fifty-Fourth Massachusetts spread widely in the North, and Shaw and his fallen men were transformed into martyrs. Henry James wrote Shaw's parents, "I feel for you all, in truth, exactly what I should feel for myself—profound pity: and yet such a pride in the noble and beautiful boy, such a grateful sense of his finished manhood, as disdains that pity" (from Benson and Kirstein 1973). The *New York Tribune* reported that the battle "made Fort

Wagner such a name to the colored race as Bunker Hill had been for ninety years to the white Yankees" (from McPherson 1988:686). The author of an article in the *Atlantic Monthly* wrote, "Through the cannon smoke of that black night the manhood of the colored race shines before many eyes that would not see" (from McPherson 1969). The courage that the Fifty-Fourth Massachusetts displayed during the assault on Wagner proved that African-Americans could fight honorably. Enlistment of African-American troops increased dramatically after the attack on Fort Wagner, and by the end of the year sixty black regiments had been organized (Duncan 1992:53).

Postbattle Memorialization

Immediately after the Fifty-Fourth Massachusetts's failed attack on Fort Wagner, Northerners began to memorialize Robert Gould Shaw. Shaw represented the gallantry of the regiment, not only because he was the commander, but also because he came from the Boston Brahman elite. His death was a family loss and, for Boston, a moral contribution to preserve the Union and fight for emancipation (Lauerhass 1997:5).

As part of the creation of Shaw's martyrdom, influential writers remarked on Shaw's great sacrifice. Charles Lowell wrote that Robert Gould Shaw's death was "a perfect ending. I see now that the best Colonel of the best black regiment had to die, it was a sacrifice we owed—and how could it have been paid more gloriously?" (quoted in Emerson 1907:285). Lowell later wrote that Shaw's death was for "a cause greater than any National one" (quoted in Emerson 1907:288). Lydia Maria Child wrote to Shaw's mother and echoed the sentiment of many abolitionists. She said that Shaw "died nobly in the defense of great principles, and he has gone to join the glorious army of martyrs" (quoted in Meltzer and Holland 1982:433).

Shaw became one of the Civil War's most celebrated legends. Newspapers published a selection of his letters that explained his abolitionist intentions (Duncan 1992:375). More than forty poems were written about Shaw to help solidify his martyrdom. The most famous is by James Russell Lowell (from Emilio 1969 [1894]):

Right in the van,
On the red rampart's slippery swell
With heart that beat a charge, he fell
    Forward, as fits a man;

But the high soul burns on to light men's feet
Where death for noble ends makes dying sweet.

Plans for a Shaw Memorial began almost immediately after his death. Shaw's own regiment, although still unpaid at the time, raised $2,832 for a monument. T. W. Higginson's regiment, an African-American regiment also stationed in South Carolina, added $1000. The African-American population of Beaufort, South Carolina, contributed $300. Shaw's father wrote: "It seems to me that the monument, though originated for my son, ought to bear, with his, the names of the brave officers and men, who fell and were buried with him. This would be simple justice" (quoted in Benson and Kirstein 1973). Because of the general hostility to the idea of a monument to the Fifty-Fourth Massachusetts by the local white South Carolina population, it was never erected near Fort Wagner. Instead, the funds were used to create the first free African-American school in Charleston, named after Shaw (from Benson and Kirstein 1973).

After the Civil War a monument-building craze erupted in the United States, commemorating the bravery of fallen soldiers and their leaders— although one African-American veteran, George R. Williams, perceptively noted that this monument building did not extend to the black participants:

> Nowhere in all this free land is there a monument to brave Negro soldiers, 36,847 of whom gave up their lives in the struggle for national existence. Even the appearance of the Negro soldier in the hundreds of histories of the war has always been incidental. These brave men have had no champion, no one to chronicle their record. (Williams 1969[1888]:328)

Williams proposed that a monument be placed in front of Howard University in Washington, D.C. He predicted that one day a painter would commemorate the assault on Fort Wagner, but Americans would remember only one name, Col. Robert Gould Shaw (Williams 1969[1888]:202). His proposed monument contrasted sharply with those that existed. While contemporary sculptures of African-Americans often portrayed them as "dreamy-eyed and fatigued" (Boime 1990:212), Williams proposed one that represented them as standing erect, proud, and tall. The monument would stand in a park named after Col. Robert Gould Shaw and contain four figures including "a Negro artilleryman, . . . a cavalryman in full-dress uniform, . . . an infantry man in full-dress uniform . . . and musket at in-place rest [and], a Negro sailor in uniform standing by an anchor or mortar" (Williams 1969[1888]:328–29). His dream of a monument to African-American soldiers remained a dream until almost a century later, when such a monument was finally erected in Shaw's neighborhood in Washington, D.C., in 1998 (Shackel 1997).

Saint-Gaudens and the Making of the Shaw Memorial

Plans for a Shaw monument in Boston began with a formal meeting held in Boston in the autumn of 1865. Joshua Smith, a carter, formerly a fugitive slave and once a servant of the Shaw family, was one of the original movers. He pledged $500 of his own money and raised additional funds in the African-American community (Savage 1997b:196–97). Progress slowed after Governor Andrew and Senator Charles Sumner of Massachusetts died, the chief political supporters of the memorial. The Shaw family did not press the project. By the 1870s Smith's role had diminished significantly, and leadership of a commemorative project that developed in the African-American community was usurped by Boston's Brahman elite (Savage 1997b:197). A new, predominantly white committee raised more than $16,000 by the early 1880s, and on February 23, 1884, more than twenty years after the assault on Fort Wagner, the commission appointed a young, well-known artist, Augustus Saint-Gaudens, for the Shaw Memorial project (Benson and Kirstein 1973).

Saint-Gaudens initially planned a conventional equestrian monument to commemorate Shaw. However, Shaw's family objected, stating that the monument would be pretentious since their son's inexperience hardly merited such high praise. They also felt that a single equestrian monument ignored the role of the African-American troops that died beside him (Saint-Gaudens 1913:332). The family believed that the monument should not show a status difference between the colonel and the troops. They remarked that Shaw did not lead the charge mounted but on foot, with his men beside him (Boime 1990:212; Benson and Kirstein 1973).

Saint-Gaudens labored sporadically on the monument for thirteen years, and he finally unveiled it on Decoration Day, May 31, 1897. At the ceremony sixty-five veterans of the Fifty-Fourth Massachusetts marched up Beacon Hill to the memorial (fig. 7.3). Saint-Gaudens remarked: "They seemed as if returning from the war, the troops of bronze marching in the opposite direction, the direction in which they left for the front, and the young men there represented now showing these veterans the vigor and hope of youth. It was consecration" (Saint-Gaudens 1913, vol. 2:83). Also

Figure 7.3. Veterans of the Massachusetts Fifty-Fourth Regiment marching past the Shaw Memorial at its dedication, May 31, 1897. (Courtesy U.S. Department of the Interior, National Park Service, Saint-Gaudens National Historic Site, Cornish, New Hampshire.)

present were African-American veterans of the Fifty-Fifth Massachusetts and the Fifth Cavalry (Lauerhass 1997:26–27).

The memorial was the first soldier's monument to honor a group rather than a single individual (Dryfhout 1982:226). Colonel Shaw is in the center among his troops and on horseback with his fatigue cap on. The African-American soldiers serve as a backdrop. They are ready for battle with rifles over their shoulders, and the procession is led by a drummer boy. Above them is an allegorical figure with laurel branches in one hand and poppies in the other (Dryfhout 1982:222).

For more than a century the monument has stood as a multivalent object. For instance, Lorado Taft (1969 [1924]:302), in his pioneering history of American sculpture, wrote that "there is nothing like it or even suggestive of it, in the annals of art." He then explained that he saw the monument as an "adequate expression of America's newborn patriotism" (Taft 1969 [1924]:304). In 1897, a columnist in *Century Magazine* remarked, "No poet's dream of heroism, glory, or devotion . . . could be realized in material form as this is . . . this beautiful work of art" (Lauerhass 1997:53).

In 1916 Freeman Murry lauded the sculpture as a "memorial to man, race, and a cause." He later noted that it seemed "strangely providential that the greatest of American military memorials should have been inspired primarily by the valor and devotion of Negro-American soldiery" (Murry 1916:172). Murry remarked that Saint-Gaudens's work will "tower above the color line" (Murry 1916:166).

Murry's interpretation—that the Shaw monument would help dismantle the racial boundaries so prevalent in the early twentieth century—puzzles some scholars. For instance, Albert Boime (1990:205–6) points out Saint-Gaudens's racist tendencies. He created the Shaw monument in the context of strong racial and ethnic tensions in the late-nineteenth-century United States. He developed the sculpture in an era when many Americans felt threatened by the massive waves of immigrants entering the United States. Although freed and American born, African-Americans did not receive any better treatment than immigrants. The development of Jim Crow legislation in the late nineteenth century made it increasingly difficult for African-Americans to achieve equality—in the North and the South.

While creating the monument, Saint-Gaudens filled his studio in New York with African-American subjects from the surrounding neighborhood. He remarked that while many African-Americans in his studio were born after the Civil War, and they did not even know how to hold a gun, they "described to me in detail the battle of Fort Wagner and their part in it" (Saint-Gaudens 1913:335). Reinforcing a contemporary stereotype, Saint-Gaudens remarked that "they are very likable, with their soft voices and imaginative, though simple, minds" (Saint-Gaudens 1913:334–35; see Boime 1990:208).

Saint-Gaudens's son, Homer, described an incident of his father's substandard treatment of an African-American. In *The Reminiscences of Augustus Saint-Gaudens* (1913:133), Homer noted, "I believe he could detect a change of two degrees from his favorite amount of heat, when woe betides the darkey who tended stove."

While contemporary critics claimed that the sculpture was an act of "newborn American patriotism" (Taft 1969 [1924]:304) and that it would "tower above the color line" (Murry 1916:166), other contemporary voices contested their claims. They believed that the Shaw Memorial is just that, a memorial to Robert Gould Shaw, and the African-American troops serve as a background to the subject. It is a monument that remembers one of Boston's Brahman elite and the role that the elite played in the abolitionist movement.

Charles Caffin wrote in 1913 that Saint-Gaudens

portrays the humble soldiers with varying characteristics of pathetic devotion. [The sculpture is] distinguished by virile contrasts and repetition of line and by vigorous handsomeness of light and shade. Mingled with our enjoyment of these qualities is the emotion aroused by intent and steadfast onward movement of the troops, whose doglike trustfulness is contrasted with the serene elevation of their white leader (Caffin 1913:11) (fig. 7.4).

There is no doubt that the white officer is the central figure in the monument. Shaw is on horseback and "sharing the upper zone with the allegorical Angel of Death who bears Victory and Sleep" (Boime 1990:209). Shaw, the troops, and the allegorical angel all move laterally, in differing levels of relief. Shaw is portrayed as noble and sits erect in his saddle. He is a three-dimensional figure, while the troops are farther from view and take on less of a three-dimensional quality (fig. 7.1). The soldiers are cropped out on both sides of the memorial as the memorial's framing columns hide part of the soldiers' bodies and equipment (Dryfhout 1982:x). The horse's head is rearing and complements Shaw's torso. His rumpled-looking troops, according to Albert Boime (1990:209), are somewhat listless. Their postures are less certain and less energetic than Shaw's. The troops' stride is in sync with the horse's hind leg. The horse

Figure 7.4. Detail of the Shaw Memorial. (Photo: Paul A. Shackel.)

and Shaw's torso block the image of many in the regiment. Some of them are visible only by their boots. The net result, according to Boime (1990:209), "is to visually promote the identification of troops and animal, who moved in obedience to Shaw's command, further reinforced by his diagonally thrusting riding crop."

Saint-Gaudens's inscription on the relief honors only Shaw. It reads "OMNIA RELINQUIT SERVARE REPUBLICAM" (He foresook all to preserve the public weal). Saint-Gaudens added the following inscription to the section underneath the relief:

ROBERT GOULD SHAW
COLONEL OF THE FIFTY FOURTH REGIMENT OF MASSA-
CHUSETTS INFANTRY BORN IN BOSTON 10 OCTOBER
MDCCCXXXVII KILLED WHILE LEADING THE ASSAULT
ON FORT WAGNER
SOUTH CAROLINA 18 JULY MDCCCLXIII

Boime (1990:211) concludes that Saint-Gaudens was successful "in establishing a visual 'color-line' that guarded white supremacy."

Until 1981, only Shaw is recognized in the official public memory, and the rest of the members of the Fifty-Fourth Massachusetts Volunteer Infantry are anonymous characters that fill the background of the composition. A rededication of the monument placed a stone on the back of the monument with the names of the 281 soldiers who died in the assault on Fort Wagner (Lauerhass 1997; Dryfhout 1982:226). The list does not include those who died afterward of wounds and diseases, or those who were listed as missing after the battle.

Transforming the Shaw Memorial into the Fifty-Fourth Massachusetts Regiment Memorial

After the Civil War, monuments were commissioned by governments or other powerful groups to reinforce a set of values in order to justify their own existence and consolidate their power. These monuments became very important in a late-nineteenth-century American society dominated by xenophobia. The heroes usually "stood out against a backdrop of nationalism, inventions, industrialization, and great wealth" (Dryfhout 1982:28).

Ever since the unveiling of the Shaw monument, its memory has been challenged and it has had different meanings for different groups of people. For Murry (1916) and Williams (1969[1888]), both writing at the turn of the twentieth century, the creation of a monument with African-American representation was important for the African-American community, which increasingly lost rights during the Jim Crow era. A monument with some African-American representation would give them visibility and representation in the public memory. While Saint-Gaudens used African-Americans to help commemorate the deeds of Robert Gould Shaw, many feel that his monument serves to reinforce the differences between whites and blacks (Caffin 1913; Boime 1990:217). For Caffin (1913) and Boime (1990) the hegemony of the powerful is explicit and noticeable.

In the late twentieth century the tone and meaning associated with the monument changed significantly. In May 1997, Boston held a symposium and public ceremony that celebrated the 100th anniversary of the unveiling of the Shaw Memorial. The event was inclusively titled "Hope and Glory: Centennial Celebration of the Augustus Saint-Gaudens Monument to Robert Gould Shaw and the Fifty-Fourth Massachusetts Regiment." In the symposium, historians Barbara Fields (1997) and William McFeely

(1997) remarked that the memorial is very significant since it was the first monument that showed that black men participated in the war. They noted that this representation is significant for that era, and for today.

Art historian Kirk Savage (1997b) also sees the memorial as an excellent blend between soldier and colonel. Shaw is not in the lead of the procession, and the soldiers look well drilled. Each soldier looks very different. They are individuals who wear their uniform in various fashions. The horse glides and towers, and the soldiers are weighed down by their equipment as they lean forward. Savage argued that they are not "listless," as Boime described them (1990), but determined. The troops do not lose their humanity. "Saint-Gaudens was able to elevate the white hero without demoting the black troops" (Savage 1997a:203). African-Americans never had this representation of individuality before; if the soldiers represented had been white, they may not have been interpreted as listless by art critics. Savage (1997b) also remarked that Charles Caffin's 1913 description of "dog-like trustfulness" is a misreading of the monument. Savage (1997a:201, 1997b) proposes that what Saint-Gaudens was thinking about had no bearing on his sculpture. He notes that Saint-Gaudens "treated racial differences openly and with dignity, asserting a 'brotherhood' of man. And yet it registered, compellingly and beautifully, the transcendence of the white hero in that brotherhood" (Savage 1997a:204).

Several prominent African-Americans spoke at this 100th-anniversary rededication public ceremony. President Benjamin Payton of Tuskegee University, Professor Henry Louis Gates, Jr., of the Du Bois Institute, Harvard University, and Gen. Colin Powell all spoke about the splendid beauty of the monument and saw the portrayal of the troops in a positive and uplifting light. Powell, commenting on the monument, remarked:

> Look at them. Look at them one more time. Soldiers looking to the front, marching solidly and straight ahead on a perpetual campaign for righteousness, led by their brave colonel. So let us too follow these heroes. Let us carry on the work to make this God-given beloved country of ours an even more perfect Union. A land of liberty and justice for all. (1997:1–2)

The events of the civil rights movement of the late twentieth century gave African-Americans greater representation in our public memory. The events of the Shaw Memorial centennial celebration also helped to solidify and sanctify a new meaning and official memory for the memorial. For instance, *USA Today* reported on the ceremonies, and it did not even mention Robert Gould Shaw when describing the event and the memorial.

It stated that the members of the Fifty-Fourth Massachusetts "were honored during the weekend in a celebration of the 100th anniversary of the dedication of a memorial to them here" (Larrabee 1997).

No longer do public-funded institutions like the City of Boston and National Park Service speak about the Robert Gould Shaw Memorial; they now include the name of the Fifty-Fourth Massachusetts Infantry when referring to the monument. It is part of the new and changing official memory of the Civil War. This new attitude about the Fifty-Fourth Massachusetts has become part of popular culture, especially after the creation of a successful late 1980s movie, *Glory*, portraying the feats of the regiment.

Remembering Soldiers

Augustus Saint-Gaudens, creator of the memorial, held the derogatory views toward African-Americans that were commonly held by whites in the late nineteenth century. At best, these people saw African-Americans as passive children who needed to be guided. At worst, they saw African-Americans as shiftless subhumans who needed to be controlled and subjugated. Saint-Gaudens's attitudes appear to fall between these two negative views, and some critics have argued that the Robert Gould Shaw Memorial is an expression of these feelings. For instance, one group sees the soldiers as following in "dog-like trustfulness" (Caffin 1913) and as "listless" (Boime 1990). Contrary to this opinion, others see the soldiers as "determined" (Savage 1997b) and the monument as a "memorial to man, race, and a cause" (Murry 1916).

The memorial is embraced by many groups today, including African-Americans. The question is then, why and how can African-Americans and other groups embrace a monument that can be interpreted as racist? First, the Shaw Memorial is one of only a few memorials that portray African-American soldiers. It fills a void in the memorialization of African-American soldiers. Second, beyond the monuments of solitary soldiers poised with a musket that stand at town centers throughout this country, the Shaw Memorial is one of only a few memorials that celebrate a group of foot soldiers. It stands with the Iwo Jima and Vietnam Veterans memorials as highly acclaimed memorials that portray a group of foot soldiers. Both of these memorials have inspired such strong emotions as to transform them into symbols of the wars they represent, something rarely inspired by the hundreds of statues of war leaders, or the solitary statues of foot soldiers that dot the American landscape. Therefore, the popularity of the Shaw Memorial may also rest in the fact that it is part of a small subset of memorials that represent a group of forgotten foot soldiers.

The monument is an object that is politically and socially charged. Is the statue about Saint Gaudens's racist tendencies, is it about honoring one of Boston's antislavery Brahmin members—Robert Gould Shaw—or is it about the Massachusetts Fifty-Fourth Infantry? The Shaw monument's meaning, I think, will always be in flux, since different groups will view it in contrasting ways. Its meaning will always be challenged and changed, depending on who is reading the object and the social and political context within which they are reading it.

References

Benson, Richard, and Lincoln Kirstein
  1973   *Lay This Laurel: An Album on the Saint-Gaudens Memorial on Boston Common Honoring Black and White Men Together Who Served the Union Cause with Robert Gould Shaw and Died with Him July 18, 1863*. Eakins Press, New York.
Boime, Albert
  1990   *The Art of Exclusion: Representing Blacks in the Nineteenth Century.* Smithsonian Institution Press, Washington, D.C.
Burchard, Peter
  1965   *One Gallant Rush: Robert Gould Shaw and His Brave Black Regiment.* St. Martin's Press, New York.
Caffin, Charles H.
  1913   *American Masters of Sculpture: Being Brief Appreciations of Some American Sculptors and of Some Phases of Sculpture in America.* Doubleday, Page, New York.
Dryfhout, John H.
  1982   *The Works of Augustus Saint-Gaudens.* University Press of New England, Hanover, New Hampshire.
Duncan, Russell, ed.
  1992   *Blue-Eyed Child of Fortune: The Civil War Letters of Colonel Robert Gould Shaw.* University of Georgia Press, Athens.
Emerson, Edward W.
  1907   *Life and Letters of Charles Russell Lowell, Captain Sixth United States Cavalry, Colonel 2nd Massachusetts Cavalry, Brigadier General United States Volunteers.* Houghton Mifflin, Boston.
Emilio, Luis F.
  1969   [1894] *A Brave Black Regiment: History of the Fifty-Fourth Regiment of Massachusetts Volunteer Infantry, 1863–1865.* Arno Press and New York Times, New York.

Fields, Barbara
  1997   The Impact of African American Soldiers on the Civil War. Paper pre-
          sented at the symposium "Hope and Glory: Centennial Celebration of
          the Augustus Saint-Gaudens Monument to Robert Gould Shaw and the
          Fifty-Fourth Massachusetts Regiment." Boston, May 29.
Higginson, Thomas Wentworth
  1971   [1870] *Army Life in a Black Regiment*. Corner House, Williamstown,
          Massachusetts.
Larrabee, John
  1997   Blacks Claim Share of Civil War Glory: The Growing Number of Blacks
          in Reenactment Groups Recalls the Sacrifices of Thousands Who Fought
          and Died. *USA Today*, June 2, 3A.
Lauerhass, Ludwig
  1997   *The Shaw Memorial: A Celebration of an American Masterpiece*. East-
          ern National, Conshohocken, Pennsylvania.
McFeely, William
  1997   The Impact of African American Soldiers on the Civil War. Paper pre-
          sented at the symposium "Hope and Glory: Centennial Celebration of
          the Augustus Saint-Gaudens Monument to Robert Gould Shaw and the
          Fifty-Fourth Massachusetts Regiment." Boston, May 29.
McPherson, James M.
  1969   Foreword to *A Brave Black Regiment: History of the Fifty-Fourth Regi-
          ment of Massachusetts Volunteer Infantry, 1863–1865*, by Luis F.
          Emilio. Arno Press and New York Times, New York.
  1988   *Battle Cry of Freedom: The Civil War Era*. Oxford University Press, New
          York.
Meltzer, Milton, and Patricia Holland, eds.
  1982   *Lydia Maria Child: Selected Letters, 1817–1880*. University of Massa-
          chusetts Press, Amherst.
Murry, Freeman H. M.
  1916   *Emancipation and the Freed in American Sculpture: A Study in Interpre-
          tation*. Freeman Murry, Washington, D.C.
Powell, Colin
  1997   General Colin Powell on the 100th Anniversary of the Shaw Monument.
          Museum of Afro American History, September, 1–2.
Ruffins, Fath Davis
  1992   Mythos, Memory, and History: African-American Preservation Efforts,
          1820–1990. In *Museums and Communities: The Politics of Public Cul-
          ture*, edited by Ivan Karp, Christine Mullen Kreamer, and Steven D.
          Lavine, 506–611. Smithsonian Institution Press, Washington, D.C.
Saint-Gaudens, Homer
  1913   *The Reminiscences of Augustus Saint-Gaudens*. 2 vols. Century, New
          York.

Savage, Kirk
  1997a The Monument to Robert Gould Shaw and the Fifty-Fourth Massachu-
        setts Regiment. Paper presented at the symposium "Hope and Glory:
        Centennial Celebration of the Augustus Saint-Gaudens Monument to
        Robert Gould Shaw and the Fifty-Fourth Massachusetts Regiment."
        Boston, May 29.
  1997b *Standing Soldier, Kneeling Slaves: Race, War, and Monument in Nine-
        teenth-Century America*. Princeton University Press, Princeton, New Jer-
        sey.
Shackel, Paul A.
  1997 A Long-Overdue Salute: African American Troops Who Fought in the
        Civil War Are Being Honored in a National Monument. *Atlanta Journal-
        Constitution*, November 2, C2.
Sturman, Shelley
  1997 August Saint-Gaudens' Memorial to Robert Gould Shaw and the Massa-
        chusetts Fifty-Fourth Regiment, 21 September through 14 December
        1997. Brochure. National Gallery of Art, Washington, D.C.
Taft, Lorado
  1969 [1924] *The History of American Sculpture*. Arno Press, New York.
Thompson, Benjamin F.
  1903 *An Authentic History of the Douglass Monument*. Rochester Herald
        Press, Rochester, New York.
Williams, George W.
  1969 *A History of the Negro Troops in the War of the Rebellion, 1861–1865*.
        [Originally published in 1888.] Negro University Press, New York.

Acknowledgments

Matthew Reeves remarked on an earlier version of this study. Paul Mullins
and James Delle also provided insightful review comments. I value their
kindness and willingness to help make this a better essay. I also appreciate
Steven Pendrey's willingness to share information on the 1997 Centennial
celebration.

8

Buried in the Rose Garden: Levels of Meaning at Arlington National Cemetery and the Robert E. Lee Memorial

Laurie Burgess

Introduction

Cemeteries need to be viewed as cultural landscapes; they are open cultural texts to be read (Meyer 1993:2). Serving multiple purposes, they represent an intentional structuring of space that appears to carry the past forward to the present, but in fact carries forward only a past that meets current needs. Remembering is an active process that reconstructs the past in terms of the present (Schwartz 1982:374), and the structuring of the past at sites of national significance takes places on many levels.

Overlooking Washington, D.C., Arlington National Cemetery, surrounding the Robert E. Lee Memorial, which is also known as Arlington House, serves as a repository for the U.S. military dead and draws millions of visitors each year (Jackson and Vergura 1989:26). Does the significance and the enduring pull of this landscape go beyond its role as repository for the war dead? While visitors flock to Arlington's peaceful and manicured plots, an underlying tension still exists in the perception, use, and designation of this physical space. The meanings of the landscape are still contested today on several levels and by many groups despite the overt trappings of heroic veneration and the transformation into a national sacred grove to honor the dead of the Civil War and other wars.

Maintained by the National Park Service (NPS), Arlington House sits at the top of a hill overlooking Washington, D.C., and its monuments; it forms a "meaningful terminus to the landscape of patriotism lying before it," both in Lee's day and in ours (Jackson and Vergura 1989:27). Even before the Civil War, the house was a significant cultural marker during the nineteenth century as the home of one of the area's most prominent and historic families, the Custis family, but the conversion of the property into a cemetery spurred transformations of meaning across the cultural landscape that continue to grow and change today.

I believe that the landscape at Arlington served as a symbolic battlefield for the Civil War; the use of the land itself became a weapon in the end whose impact resonated long after the actual fighting stopped. Many of the Civil War battlefields themselves became cemeteries when the dead were buried where they fell, but here the landscape became a battlefield through the act of burial. Symbolic and physical possession of the house and the surrounding lands, the seizing of and use of those lands as a cemetery for Union soldiers, were used as acts of domination during wartime, but their effects extended far beyond those of most military maneuvers. And different groups today continue to play out various conflicts through the cultural landscape of Arlington. Issues of power can be negotiated through burials and their rituals (McGuire 1988:436), and here the scripted presentation of death and the past serves the needs of many groups in the present.

The official interpretations of the site's creation, the structuring of the landscape, the tacit designation of Arlington as sacred and male space, the hesitant inclusion of women—these issues represent conflicting and multiple levels of meaning that underlie the peaceful, reflective experience that visitors are meant to draw from their time spent here.

Arlington's Beginnings

Although it is a military cemetery created during wartime, Arlington Cemetery has its roots in the rural cemetery movement of the nineteenth century. The creation of space reminiscent of a park or of a Romantic-period English landscape garden began with the creation of Mt. Auburn cemetery, Massachusetts, in 1830 (Ames 1981:642; Bender 1974:196). While Arlington represents a far more structured and regulated space, especially as it began to spread farther and farther from its original center, the influence of the rural cemetery movement can still be seen in its rolling hills, with graves shaded by mature trees. Rural cemeteries gave way to lawn cemeteries following the Civil War (French 1974:52), when the fencing of individual plots was prohibited, resulting in a more homogeneous and uninterrupted landscape, an aspect very visible at Arlington, where not only are fences prohibited, but headstones are standardized as well. It is ironic, and deliberate, that aspects of Arlington reflect more pastoral and bucolic cemetery movements, since its beginnings were anything but peaceful. While Arlington did begin as a Southern plantation, a landscape that dominated the view south from Washington, D.C., its transformation into a cemetery both sanctified and defiled the landscape in an act of war that created a symbolic battlefield.

The physical landscape that became Arlington Cemetery and the house began as a plantation built by George Washington Parke Custis. Raised by George and Martha Washington, Custis was the grandson of Martha Washington from her first marriage; his daughter, Mary Anna Randolph Custis, was thus the great-granddaughter of Martha Washington (Andrews 1985:21). Custis, in 1802, hired architect George Hadfield, initial architect of the Capitol, to build what became known as Arlington House, where Robert E. Lee married Mary Anna Randolph Custis on June 30, 1831 (Nelligan 1955:70, 205). The house not only served as home to Custis and to the Lee family, but it also became a main repository of the possessions Custis inherited from Washington (Andrews 1966:16). Upon Custis's death his will transferred the property to Mary for her lifetime, to pass to her eldest son upon her death (Nelligan 1941:6). Although Lee traveled back and forth to his various army posts, they lived there with their children until April 1861 when Lee resigned his federal army commission to lead the Confederate forces (Andrews 1966:17). On April 22, 1861, Lee left for Richmond; he would not return to his house again (Nelligan 1955:455). In a letter to his wife dated May 11, 1861, he wrote, "It is sad to think of the translation, if not ruin, [the war] may bring upon a spot so endeared to us" (Nelligan 1955:460). Mrs. Lee left the following month, but packed in haste, leaving many of the Washington possessions (Andrews 1966:18). Federal troops occupied the house and land throughout the war, and in January 1864 the government levied a tax upon the property and ruled that the owner must pay in person. Mrs. Lee was in poor health and would have had to go behind enemy lines to comply, so the government seized the property for $92.07 in delinquent taxes and then, as the sole bidder, acquired it through auction for the sum of $26,800 (Andrews 1966:20, 1985:7).

With very little space available to bury the ever-increasing number of Civil War dead, President Lincoln ordered Secretary of War Edwin Stanton to acquire cemetery grounds near Washington, D.C.; he in turn assigned the duty to his quartermaster general, Montgomery Meigs (Andrews 1966:19). Meigs recommended Arlington as the site and on June 15, 1864, Stanton signed an order designating two hundred acres around Lee's house to be used for burying soldiers (Andrews 1966:21).

Figure 8.1. Roses, gravestones, and the east side of Arlington House. (Photo: Laurie Burgess.)

But Meigs had already begun the burials: On May 13, 1864, Private William Christman of the Sixty-Seventh Pennsylvania Infantry was the first Civil War casualty to be buried at Arlington (Andrews 1966:21).

Meigs discovered that the troops had buried the bodies a half-mile from the house and immediately had "a long row of graves made on the east side of Mrs. Lee's flower garden" (Nelligan 1955:492). These and the previous burials began the creation of Arlington National Cemetery (fig. 8.1).

In 1870, after the deaths of Robert E. Lee and later Mary Lee, their eldest son, Custis Lee, sued the government, alleging illegal seizure of Arlington. The U.S. Supreme Court ruled in his favor and returned the title to Lee. But since the lands surrounding the house were filled with graves of Union soldiers, Lee agreed to accept $150,000 from the government instead of taking physical possession of the property (Andrews 1966:22).

Transformation of the Landscape

The burial of the Union dead changed the lawns, fields, and gardens of Arlington and altered the larger landscape of Washington, D.C. A highly visible Southern landmark had become the bounty of the North. The funerary landscape of Arlington evokes issues of veneration and defilement, but although these ideas have been applied to many battlefields and repositories of the dead, at Arlington both occurred simultaneously and within the same act. The land was transformed from secular to sacred space by the burials of the soldiers, while at the same time the burials of these men were used to defile a symbol of the South, the home of the South's leading general, Robert E. Lee. Although by then the Union had physically seized the house and lands, it was the actual interment of the men that was the more significant act for both sides. Similar to sowing fields with salt to render them useless, here the fields and even Mrs. Lee's rose garden were sowed with the dead of the opposing side, transforming one of Washington's most visible properties, one that dominates the view south from the city, into a physical and symbolic possession of the North. Burial was an act of war; an army of the dead took the battlefield.

There have been multiple interpretations of the events leading to the creation of Arlington National Cemetery, from the time of its establishment to today. On June 18, 1864, the *National Intelligencier,* a newspaper whose editors were friends of the Lees, "barely mentioned the new cemetery," but the more liberal *Morning Chronicle* praised "the righteous use of the estate of General Lee" on June 17, 1864, and also stated that "the people of the entire nation will one day not very far distant, heartily thank the creator of this monument" (Nelligan 1955:492). Ironically, the people of this nation do come by the millions to Arlington, but not to gloat over the spoils of war and the seizure of Lee's home. They come to justify these deaths through venerating the sacrifices of war; they come to connect with the past; they come to commemorate the dead; they come to draw their own versions of the past from the cultural landscape of Arlington. The landscape then takes on a kind of functional symbolism.

Landscape might be seen in this light as a sort of communicational resource, a "system of signs and symbols, capable of extending the temporal and spatial range of communication. In effect the physical durability of landscape permits it to carry meaning into the future" (Foote 1997:33)— and into the past as well, in terms of new interpretations through which visitors are to view a specific past. Arlington's 612 acres expand the spatial range of communication, and its highly visible placement on the edge of the nation's capital and on the lawns of the military leader of the South intensifies its physical symbolism. It extends the temporal range of communication into the past as well as into the future, but here the text is written in bodies and headstones and neatly ordered graves.

Meaning and the Past

"The need for burial space was great, and what better place than in the lawns of the hero of the South?" reads one interpretation that acknowledges symbolic intent on the part of the federal army in appropriating Arlington (Andrews 1966:21). Another speaks of the government's decision to maintain national cemeteries following the war as being driven by logistical needs—there were so many unidentified bodies that the army could not have returned all of them to their families (Sloane 1991:232). And historian Murray Nelligan offered a softer interpretation: Using Arlington as a cemetery for the war dead would mitigate criticism for having seized the land (Nelligan 1955:489).

The NPS has offered its own interpretations of the site, which it has owned since federal legislation was passed in 1925 designating it the Lee Mansion National Memorial. The legislation stipulated that the mansion be restored to the period just preceding the Civil War (Nelligan 1955:503). The 1941 official NPS handbook for the site presents a sequence of events that I have found nowhere else. It claims that Meigs, while riding through Arlington, which was used as a field hospital, saw large numbers of bodies awaiting transport to the cemetery at the Old Soldiers Home in Washington, D.C., and that upon seeing them ordered them buried on the spot (Nelligan 1955:26). No corroborating sources are offered, nor are specific dates cited, despite the fact that historical records show that Meigs began burying dead at Arlington on May 13, 1864, a month before Stanton signed the orders on June 15, 1864 (Andrews 1966:21). This questionable interpretation casts Meigs in an almost noble light, making it seem as if he took pity on the unburied dead and immediately gave them their military due, a burial. It sidesteps the issue of the seizure of the land and the potential meaning behind the actions of Stanton and Meigs.

In 1962, during the centennial of the Civil War, the NPS changed the handbook's interpretation to a more biased approach that claims Arlington was "a most appropriate national monument to one of America's greatest men, Robert E. Lee . . . it is maintained by the nation in his honor and in the years to come will serve as a constant reminder of his nobility and greatness" (Nelligan 1962:1). It may well be, as Davies suggested for Confederate veterans of an earlier time, that in the face of the hundred-year anniversary, idealization helped offset defeat for the South, that in the 1960s, as he suggested for the post–Civil war era, "commemoration would attempt to make meaningful their loss" (Davies 1982:2). The NPS handbook continues its praise, alleging that its thousands of visitors each year come because of "the universal admiration for its former master," Robert E. Lee, and that "only the long rows of white headboards gleaming in among the trees and the desolate house now used only for the cemetery office bespoke the bitter strife that had wrought such a profound change at Arlington" (Nelligan 1962:26, 1). It allows for no interpretation other than that of venerating Lee, not even venerating the war dead.

While continuing to venerate Lee, the 1985 official handbook extends this softened interpretation, referring to the creation of the cemetery in reference to the Supreme Court's return of the title to Custis Lee: "By then, however, several thousand war dead had been buried in Arlington's hills," and again as a caption: "Meigs selected 200 acres surrounding the house as a national cemetery for the Union dead" (Andrews 1985:7, 31). At least this version acknowledges the creation of the cemetery, although by muting it the NPS creates a contradiction in downplaying the hundreds of thousands of graves that define the landscape and ends up emphasizing missing elements. This muted interpretation encourages the perception that the house and land just happened to be selected as a cemetery, as if the two spaces, the house and the cemetery, were unconnected and separate now, not linked as an act of war in the sowing of the dead in the lawns of the Lee family. It is as if we are supposed to accept the concept that in the interpretive time period chosen by the NPS, 1861, the landscape was joined and whole, but now we are to view the graves and the house as discrete domains.

This interpretation encourages a reading of the landscape, where "the cemetery has become codified space in thrall to both knowledge and power," that

> produces the authoritative instrumental practices that engender "the silences of the 'uses' of this space." The abstract and self-referential codes of such space are among the techniques of power of the disciplinary state. Augustus Saint-Gaudens captured this when he said of Arlington National Cemetery, "Nothing could be more impressive than the rank after rank of white stones, inconspicuous in themselves, covering the gentle wooded slopes and producing the desired effect of a vast army in its last resting place." (Ferguson and Turnbull 1996:7)

One of the silent uses of Arlington includes minimizing the reality of death. The fact that the viewer perceives the headstones as inconspicuous is all the more chilling; it leads to the negation of individual death, replacing it instead with the quiet veneration of the mass sacrifice of the army in celebration of the living state. And the fact that Saint-Gaudens perceives the space and the dead this way is not coincidental. As mentioned before, the NPS 1962 handbook refers to grave markers by using the nineteenth-century term "headboards," which evokes images of beds and sleep, in lieu of "headstones" or "tombstones," which clearly evoke graves and death (Nelligan 1962:26,1). This interpretation deliberately conjures images of soldiers sleeping peacefully in pastoral beds, rather than of skulls and long bones and scraps of fabric lying in graves in Lee's lawns and gardens.

Interestingly, the tacit interpretation of graves as a dead army at rest is similar to that of the nineteenth-century rural cemetery movement. In a sense, those in control at Arlington are promoting a nineteenth-century view of death. In that time period, death was presented as sleep, and its ugly realities were veiled, helped in part by the bucolic setting of the rural cemetery (Ames 1981:654). The presentation of death as sleep during the last century had ecclesiastical overtones as well, implying "that the sleep of death preceded the last great awakening" (Farrell 1980:57). These strategies at Arlington allow the visitor to reconcile the contradictions apparent in the devastating numbers of graves by justifying this expenditure of lives as being necessary and worthy. Sanctification of the remains of war helps to mask the realities and contradictions for both winner and loser of the conflict, especially for the Civil War that killed more soldiers than any that preceded it. It does away with the question of cost.

Sacred Space

Chidester and Linenthal (1995:29) wrote that "American historical experience has produced a national orientation, supported by specific national sites, that has been saturated with a distinctive kind of sacrality." In a way, we create the myths or stories of our past from sites like these and, especially in sites where death is involved, begin to perceive them as sacred. Battlefields can operate as "sacred centers," and visitors to them "often use religious language to express their awe, having stood on ground sanctified by the 'blood of our fathers'" (Linenthal 1993:215, 3). At Arlington the ground was not sanctified by the blood of soldiers shed in battle, but by the fact that it received, and receives still, their bodies.

Historic sites, notably battlefields, have taken on shrinelike qualities and have become areas that groups try to possess symbolically (Utley 1993:x). These sacred places have become "centers of power . . . where power has and will continue to be, contested; they are places where the struggle for ownership, for the right to alter the story, is a vibrant part of the site's cultural history" (Linenthal 1993:215). And, even more, these struggles are an integral part of the site's contemporary interpretation as well. It is the contemporary visitor that brings meaning to the site, meaning created in a contemporary context and used to view the past.

It is as if, to return to the concept of a textual landscape, messages have been written on these sites that are central to how groups, large and small, and individuals want to interpret the past (Foote 1997:5). The past is read in terms of the present, and especially in terms of the needs of the present. An interpretation of the veneration of heroic death, framed in sacred space, is what visitors are expected to read into the funerary landscape. This interpretation operates within the framework of a negative dialectic, where ideological strategies override the harsh deaths of young men. As Ferguson and Turnbull (1996:7) have written: "When space is taken as a transparent medium, cemeteries are places where the bones and other remains of the dead are invisible and underfoot, present but absent, and it is personal feelings and decorum that are visible and socially regulated." At Arlington the hideousness of death in war is masked and celebrated in the form of heroic veneration and in the perception that the dead merely sleep. This version of the past, written upon Arlington's landscape, is used for a purpose.

Ferguson and Turnbull invoke Hegel in their article on the National Memorial Cemetery of the Pacific, writing that he provides

> conceptual tools for successfully shaping memory and grief and reverence into contours acceptable to the state. Hegel, the battle monuments commission, and the modern nation state all speak the same language, a language that projects a grand national destiny onto the future and then reads that destiny back into the past to provide a narrative of legitimacy and reassurance. (Ferguson and Turnbull 1996:7)

The NPS's interpretations imply legitimacy and reassurance for a number of reasons. First, the NPS is part of the government, the same entity that seized Arlington for delinquent taxes, and now is steward of the Robert E. Lee Memorial. The interpretation of avoidance reconciles the contradictions inherent in the government's seizing Lee's home, creating a cemetery there for the enemy dead, and then promoting a memorial that venerates Lee today. In selecting 1861 as the interpretive date, which is appropriate for a site whose role is to celebrate Lee, the NPS can sidestep the more controversial aspects of the history of the site and direct the visitor's focus to what the NPS presents as a happier time. But freezing history to a single point in time can be dangerous, since "time freezing provides one history at the expense of other histories" (Shackel 1996:11). What we see of the house today recreates the days of Lee and Custis, with a few of George Washington's possessions placed in the dining room, leading us back to a past far from that of Union soldiers lounging on the portico, with the raw earth of graves turned in the rose garden.

This interpretation allows the house, and the NPS, to claim ownership of the Washington past, to incorporate it into their stories, to further legitimize the present's use of the past. Even in 1861 the house's association with Washington through Custis was powerful enough to instill perceptions of the house and grounds as sacred space. The *New York Times* reported on May 29, 1861, after federal troops had crossed to Virginia, "These grounds are hallowed as once being the estate of the Custis family from whence sprang the wife of Washington" (Nelligan 1955:465).

And all these interpretations minimize the presence of death in the cemetery. By muting death, the interpretations at Arlington discourage the possibility of questioning, of outrage, of the grief that usually accompanies death. Not only is the past reconciled with the present, and the living

Figure 8.2. Headstones among trees, Arlington National Cemetery. (Photo: Laurie Burgess.)

with the sometimes untimely deaths of those in the military, but overt mourning is discouraged in this landscape as well.

Matturi characterizes other cemeteries similarly, invoking a landscape of reconciliation, saying, "the rural and lawn plan cemeteries that embody this ideal seek to engender this reconciliation not through maintaining a strongly particularized memory of the dead, but rather through subduing that memory and its associated grief—by eliciting contemplation of the integration of the dead into what was seen as a beneficent natural order" (Matturi 1993:15). The rows of uniform headstones winding over hills and among trees, the images of soldiers sleeping in their beds of earth, present a reconciliation of the mass death of war as part of the natural order. The neat and orderly graves, the regulated headstones, the constantly tended grounds, all encourage quiet contemplation of the landscape, especially of the landscape as a whole, and not of individuals who are buried there. It mitigates the possibility of unrestrained, and therefore possibly dangerous, expressions of grief in lieu of compliant veneration. Grief of this nature could also be dangerous in that it could represent an intrusion of femaleness upon the structured, male, and restrained space of Arlington (fig. 8.2).

Gendered Space

Sacred places define insiders and outsiders and function as places where the marginalized can write their own text onto the past in a way that will alter their status in the present (Linenthal 1993:216). These sites frequently involve issues of gender and status and role (Carmichael et al. 1994:2). Sacred sites have defined groups as outsiders both symbolically and physically, especially women. As gendered space, Arlington is and has been male.

Oddly enough, although officially named the Robert E. Lee Memorial, the house and land at Arlington were never owned by Lee at all. Instead, the property had been willed to his wife, Mary, when George Washington Parke Custis died, and only for the remainder of her life. Upon her death, it was to transfer to her eldest son (Nelligan 1941:6). But women have been more obviously excluded from this sacred space. Ferguson and Turnbull (1996:1) call the National Memorial Cemetery of the Pacific and its associated memorial "tacitly gendered spaces," claiming that the cemetery is "an implicitly masculine space, one that is planned, controlled, disciplined, orderly. . . . Feminine figures are incorporated into supporting roles in the narration of manly conquest." The orderly masculine space of

Arlington seems also to reaffirm the transformation of grief, construed as emotional and therefore feminine, into contemplation, with the perceived restraint and discipline of the inherently male soldier.

Mitchell describes what he calls a "credo of masculinity, maturation and military service" through which boys are transformed into men and civilians into soldiers, in a ritual of proving manhood (Mitchell 1992:44). But this cult of manhood at Arlington has recently been offset by the creation of the Women in Military Service for America Memorial. Constructed at what the brochure refers to as the ceremonial entrance of Arlington, the memorial reaches back to early American history to also claim symbolic possession of this part of the past, honoring the military history of women, which, the brochure states, began "more than 220 years ago with the women who served during the American Revolution and continues with those who serve today" (Women in Military Service Foundation 1997). Text on the wall of the monument interior refers to the honoring of "the lost history" of women's military contributions and is accompanied by World War II mementos.

Examining gender in terms of women's military history in this constructed, male space can answer a question raised in an archaeological context: "Do objects reflect and reinforce gender-based differences in power or status?" (Spector 1993:8). Here they do, directly reflecting and reinforcing the very constructs that the women's memorial was designed to offset.

The monument was built into what is called the Hemicycle, the original entrance of Arlington Cemetery that had lain uncompleted since the 1930s. Space is short at Arlington and the unused Hemicycle provided a setting of prominent and monumental architecture for the women's memorial (fig. 8.3). This use of the Hemicycle inscribes the landscape of Arlington in a new way, acknowledged in the official literature, which describes the Hemicycle as having been "a retaining wall, a barrier that literally held back the earth and established a change of level between the land of the living, extending towards Washington and the land of the past behind the hemicycle" (Women in Military Service Foundation 1997). So here, at a point of transition between what the literature construes as areas of the living and areas of the dead, a monument for women has been placed. I believe this division of space is also between the secular and sacred rather than just between the living and dead, an interesting spot for a women's memorial. It is a location that highlights the possible relationships between the tangible and intangible aspects of gender (Spector 1993:8). Apart from honoring their achievements and sacrifices in the standard patriotic vernacular of war, are women perceived here as media-

Figure 8.3. The center of the hemicycle and its reflecting pool at the Women in Military Service Memorial. (Photo: Laurie Burgess.)

tors between the kinds of spaces? Between the living and the dead, or the sacred and the secular? Between the military and the not-so-military? Also intriguing is the placement of the monument at the entrance, in a space more clearly associated with the secular landscape of Washington, D.C., outside the sacred space, tying into Linenthal's interpretation of sacred space being used to define outsiders. It may well have been a question of logistics, of available space for the placement of this memorial, but despite assertions of acceptance it appears that the women are still outside of, or at least on the edge of, the sacred masculine space contained behind and above the Hemicycle.

Other marginalized groups have also struggled for the right to be buried at Arlington, including Native American, Hispanic, and African-American veterans. At times these veterans were only buried—or commemorated—after political intervention (Andrews 1966:59; Green 1991:32; Sanchez 1989; Wheeler 1996). With these groups, as with women, the sacred space of Arlington was used to reinforce insider/outsider status (Linenthal 1993:216). Often, groups use the dead, and burial practices can reflect their idealized relationships (Parker Pearson 1982: 110). Status in death may be able to provide one more step toward equal status in life, or toward a more inclusive rewriting of the past.

Conclusion

The latest competition over the sacred space of Arlington centers on an area known as Section 29, which is the last pre–Civil War landscape within the cemetery. Different groups are competing for the use of the land. Since Arlington is running out of room for grave sites, the army has requested that the NPS return the parcel to them for additional interment space (Thomas 1996). The Sierra Club, the Arlington Historical Society, and others are pitted against the army, protesting the use of the twenty-four acres for more burials. The Sierra Club has argued that it will destroy trees and habitat, and the Arlington Historical Society has objected on the grounds that it would impact the historical value of the property (Nakashima 1996). Virginia Senator John Warner favored turning the land over to the army and former Senator Charles Robb favored the transfer with the stipulation that future transfers be approved by Congress. The positions have been argued in the press, with *Los Angeles Times* writer George Thomas asking questions such as "What does the present owe to the future?" when the land in question will provide grave sites for only five additional years, but "when the forest is gone, there will be no undoing their decision" (Thomas 1996).

Linenthal writes that physical preservation maintains the "sanctity of the site," but here we have competing versions of sacred space (Linenthal 1993:5). The burial of the Union soldiers transformed Arlington into sacred space, and presumably the burial of the military dead of today would do the same for Section 29. But, depending on the viewpoint, burials could be seen again as a type of defilement in that they would destroy the last antebellum landscape of Arlington Cemetery. The pre–Civil War landscape of the area has different meanings, though I would argue sacred ones as well, especially since it is the last tract of land left in the cemetery that dates to this time. Ironically, this landscape physically represents the 1861 interpretation date the NPS uses for the Lee mansion and grounds, yet the destruction of all or part of it remains a possibility. A final report on the matter has not yet been released; a decision is still pending.

The transformations of meaning and the conflicts they have created began with the use of Robert E. Lee's lawns as burial space and continue today. The sacred aspects of the land, the muted presence of death, and the use of a space to exclude and include different groups, all contribute to the tensions that underlie the kempt lawns with their rows of white headstones. In fact, the Section 29 dispute summons echoes of the original act that created Arlington cemetery: The last remaining landscape that dates to Lee's time may be filled in with graves. Whatever the outcome of this most recent fight involving the cemetery, the contested role of Section 29 will not be the last disputed use of the past here, whether physical or symbolic. Different groups will continue to use the sacred space as a way to lay claim to the stories of the past. The burials at Arlington and the complex landscape they occupy require a deeper reading than those presented in the official handbooks. No longer—if it ever was—is Arlington simply the nation's sacred grove for the military dead. As time passes, new meanings will be inscribed on its landscape, and the physical text of the land will need to be read in new ways.

References

Ames, Kenneth
  1981   Ideologies in Stone: Meanings in Victorian Gravestones. *Journal of Popular Culture* 14(4): 641–56.
Andrews, Peter
  1966   *In Honored Glory: The Story of Arlington.* Putnam, New York.
  1985   *Arlington House: The Robert E. Lee Memorial, Official National Park Handbook.* U.S. Department of the Interior, National Park Service, Washington, D.C.
Bender, Thomas
  1974   The "Rural" Cemetery Movement: Urban Travail and the Appeal of Nature. *New England Quarterly* 47:196–211.
Carmichael, David L., and Jane Hubert, Brian Reeves, and Audhild Schanche
  1994   *Sacred Sites, Sacred Places.* Routledge, New York.
Chidester, David, and Edward T. Linenthal, eds.
  1995   *American Sacred Space.* Indiana University Press, Bloomington.
Davies, Stephen
  1982   Empty Eyes, Marble Hand: The Confederate Monument and the South. *Journal of Popular Culture* 16(3): 2–21.

Farrell, James J.
  1980   *Inventing the American Way of Death*. Temple University Press, Philadelphia.
Ferguson, Kathy E. and Phyllis Turnbull
  1996   Narratives of History, Nature and Death at the National Memorial Cemetery of the Pacific. *Frontiers: A Journal of Women's Studies* 16 (2/3):1–19.
Foote, Kenneth E.
  1997   *Shadowed Ground: American Landscapes of Violence and Tragedy*. University of Texas Press, Austin.
French, Stanley
  1974   The Cemetery as Cultural Institution: The Establishment of Mount Auburn and the Rural Cemetery Movement. *American Quarterly* 26(1): 37–59.
Green, George N.
  1991   The Felix Longoria Affair. *Journal of Ethnic Studies* 19(3): 23–49.
Jackson, Kenneth T., and Camilio Jose Vergura
  1989   *Silent Cities: The Evolution of the American Cemetery*. Princeton Architectural Press, New York.
Linenthal, Edward T.
  1993   *Sacred Ground: Americans and Their Battlefields*. University of Illinois Press, Urbana.
Matturi, John
  1993   Windows in the Garden: Italian-American Memorialization and the American Cemetery. In *Ethnicity and the American Cemetery*, edited by Richard E. Meyer, 14–34. Bowling Green State University Popular Press, Bowling Green, Ohio.
McGuire, Randall
  1988   Dialogues with the Dead: Ideology and the Cemetery. In *The Recovery of Meaning*, edited by Mark P. Leone and Parker Potter, 435–80. Smithsonian Institution Press, Washington, D.C.
Meyer, Richard
  1993   Strangers in a Strange Land: Ethnic Cemeteries in America. In *Ethnicity and the American Cemetery*, edited by Richard E. Meyer, 1–13. Bowling Green State University Popular Press, Bowling Green, Ohio.
Mitchell, Reid
  1992   A Northern Volunteer. In *Divided Houses: Gender and the Civil War*, edited by Catherine Clinton and Nina Silber, 43–54. Oxford University Press, Oxford.
Nakashima, Ellen
  1996   Plan to Expand Cemetery Angers Preservationists. *Washington Post*, June 22, B5.

Nelligan, Murray
    1941   *Park Service Handbook: Lee Mansion National Memorial.* U.S. Department of the Interior, National Park Service, Washington, D.C.
    1955   *Old Arlington: The Story of the Lee Mansion National Memorial.* U.S. Department of the Interior, National Park Service, Washington, D.C.
    1962   *Custis-Lee Mansion: The Robert E. Lee Memorial, Handbook Series No. Six.* U.S. Department of the Interior, National Park Service, Washington, D.C.

Pearson, Michael Parker
    1982   Mortuary Practices, Society, and Ideology: An Ethnoarchaeological Study. In *Symbolic Structural Archaeology,* edited by Ian Hodder, 99–114. Cambridge University Press, New York.

Sanchez, Carlos
    1989   Another Unknown Soldier. *Washington Post,* May 28, B1.

Schwartz, Barry
    1982   The Social Context of Commemoration: A Study in Collective Memory. *Social Forces* 61:374–402.

Shackel, Paul
    1996   *Culture Change and the New Technology.* Plenum Press, New York.

Sloane, David Charles
    1991   *The Last Great Necessity: Cemeteries in American History.* Johns Hopkins University Press, Baltimore.

Spector, Janet
    1993   *What This Awl Means.* Minnesota Historical Press, St. Paul.

Thomas, George E.
    1996   Resolving the Past. *Los Angeles Times,* July 14, M1.

Utley, Robert
    1993   Foreword to *Sacred Ground: Americans and Their Battlefields,* by Edward T. Linenthal, ix–xi. University of Illinois Press, Urbana.

Wheeler, Linda
    1996   Remembering Forgotten Heroes. *Washington Post,* September 11, C1.

Women in Military Service for America Memorial Foundation
    1997   *The Memorial: Women in Military Service for America Memorial Brochure.* Brochure. Arlington National Cemetery, Washington, D.C.

Part III

Nostalgia and the Legitimation of American Heritage

Nostalgia and the Legitimation of American Heritage

With only a few exceptions, until the late nineteenth century Americans did little to foster their heritage. People were not generally concerned with issues related to historic preservation or to creating a national collective memory. In the 1890s, Congress finally authorized the establishment of five Civil War battlefields and several Revolutionary War sites. Shortly afterward, Congress passed the Antiquities Act in 1906, which allowed for the protection of prehistoric ruins. These milestones are often seen as part of America's growing need and desire to create nostalgia and a useable heritage. By the middle of the twentieth century, Americans increasingly depended on building a useable heritage, a strategy that allowed them to make the past useable in the present (Lowenthal 1997:xv). Michael Kammen (1997:214–19) calls this conscious historic preservation movement since the 1950s the "heritage phenomenon."

The chapters in this section are related to the development of heritage and nostalgia. Like many of the chapters in the other sections, they can comfortably fit into another section in this book. The development of heritage activities is noticeable in the case of the creation and fabrication of the Lincoln cabin, as Dwight Pitcaithley explains in chapter 12, and the George Washington birthplace, as Joy Beasley makes clear in chapter 10. Their development comes at a time when commemoration and memorialization became popular in this country. While the Lincoln's cabin is not authentic, Americans in the late nineteenth century saw a need to create a symbol to represent the humble beginnings of a national hero. At the George Washington birthplace home the local community and experts could not agree on the structure's original location, and the Memorial House was constructed on outbuilding foundations, rather than on the foundations of the Washington house.

In the case of Camden Yards, discussed by Erin Donovan in chapter 11, the City of Baltimore developed a sports complex and waterfront area that reminisces about a pastoral past often associated with baseball, while forgetting about the horrors of the labor strife associated with the property. One of the most violent Baltimore & Ohio Railroad strikes occurred at Camden Yards, but the city has chosen to forget this event and commemorate baseball and its ideals of a pastoral past. In another case, as Matthew M. Palus discusses in chapter 9, nostalgia is used as a tool for segregating classes. Carriage roads developed by John D. Rockefeller, Jr., in Acadia during the rise of the democratization of the automobile were to be used exclusively by the elite who owned carriages. Those who could not afford the leisure and expense of these outdated modes of transportation could not participate—in other words, the new middle-class vacationers.

In all of these cases, nostalgia and heritage are important vehicles for establishing a national consciousness. In the case of the Lincoln cabin and the Washington birthplace home, patriotism is evoked. The development of Camden Yards in Baltimore is about remembering a pastoral past. And the development of carriage roads in the 1930s by Rockefeller is a case of using nostalgia to reinforce economic exclusion.

References

Kammen, Michael
    1997 *In the Past Lane: Historical Perspectives on American Culture.* Oxford University Press, New York.
Lowenthal, David
    1997 History and Memory. *Public Historian* 19(2): 31–39.

9

Authenticity, Legitimation, and Twentieth-Century Tourism: The John D. Rockefeller, Jr., Carriage Roads, Acadia National Park, Maine

Matthew M. Palus

> "Parks are for the people" is the public relations slogan, which decoded means that the parks are for people-in-automobiles. Behind this slogan is the assumption that the majority of Americans, exactly like the managers of the tourist industry, expect and demand to see their national parks from the comfort, security, and convenience of their automobiles.
>
> —Edward Abbey

Introduction

Between 1913 and 1940, an elaborate system of carriage roads was constructed on Mount Desert Island, on the rocky seacoast of southern Maine, largely within what is now Acadia National Park. This network of narrow, broken-stone or macadam paved roads meanders through some of the most spectacular scenery on the island and was planned and executed by John D. Rockefeller, Jr., who purchased a summer home on the island in 1910. Rockefeller was the principal private benefactor of Acadia National Park for more than forty years (Ernst 1991:4; Foresta 1984:22), and the carriage roads, which were financed and maintained by Rockefeller until the time of his death in 1960, are now administered by the National Park Service (NPS).

The Rockefeller carriage roads are suggestive of a basic aspect of tourism in the twentieth century. As with much archaeological interpretation, the public is invited to visit history at the national parks as tourists. Dean MacCannell (1976) writes that *authenticity* is fundamental to the experience of tourism. Authenticity is defined by need, in that representations of history that more or less satisfy our needs today are viewed as authentic. If accuracy is ever a concern, then accuracy is established as an aspect of staging, to support the authenticity of a representation. Viewed in this way, the Rockefeller carriage roads were authentic representations, in exactly the same way that the restored carriage roads are "authentic" and represent certain needs in the park today. The second, equally important issue in modern tourism is control: An authentic production must be seamless. The tourist is never taken backstage so long as the production remains a production, an authoritative relation between the guide and the tourist (MacCannell 1976). Authentic presentations of history are thus authoritarian and lend themselves to mass consumption. This is the paradigm for representation that has generally dominated the NPS, and it is another important issue in the case of the carriage roads.

The Rockefeller carriage roads, which consist of fifty-seven miles of roadway (fifty-one miles of which occur within the park reserve), seventeen stone and concrete bridges, two gate lodges, innumerable culverts and roadside features, and a carefully planned landscape of scenic vistas and forested areas (U.S. Department of the Interior 1989a:5), were intended for public use and enjoyment (fig. 9.1). They are used today for recreation by park visitors, and by park maintenance and fire suppression crews, as an important means of access to the interior of the park. However, through heavy use and general neglect, substantial negative impacts were sustained by this historic property during the years between Rockefeller's death and recent efforts to save the roads (U.S. Department of the Interior 1989b). Within the last five years, the park has made great progress in correcting this neglect; nearly 100 percent of the road surface occurring within the park has been reconstructed to its original design specifications, and the park has initiated studies toward reestablishing scenic vistas and landscapes, and the repointing and repair of park bridges (AcadiaNet 2000).

The initiation of restoration activities at this historic property in the last decade of the twentieth century has been accompanied by a new interest in interpreting the historic carriage roads to the public. Dramatically, Acadia National Park has reestablished control over the property and its meaning, both as a significant historical site and as an attraction for recreation and tourism.

In order to understand this new policy of interpretation, and the concomitant seizure of the site as a symbol, it helps to have a context for the creation and management of the Rockefeller carriage roads at Acadia National Park that pays particular attention to the actors involved in this

Figure 9.1. The Carriage Road Bridge at the head of Hadlock Pond Inlet, July 1935. (Courtesy National Park Service, Historic Photograph Collection, ACAD 171.)

production. The creation and management of these roads by John D. Rockefeller, Jr., was not only philanthropy but also stagecraft. And their more recent elevation and enshrinement by the NPS, in a sense their becoming historic and significant, involves a similar stagecraft that is intended to maintain an ideology among tourist-visitors to Acadia National Park.

Mount Desert Island, the Rockefeller Carriage Roads, and Acadia National Park

Mount Desert Island was sparsely inhabited by subsistence farmers, fishermen, and loggers until the latter half of the nineteenth century, when the picturesque scenery and isolated setting began to attract artists and writers, as well as clergy and educators who sought a simpler country lifestyle. Some of the Hudson River School painters discovered the island and advertised its rugged beauty (Shepard 1991:94). These summer residents, the first "rusticators," were joined by the very wealthy, and the island quickly became characterized as a resort (Rhodes 1983:22–23). By 1905 there were well-defined populations of seasonal summer residents, dwelling in mansions (called "cottages") on estates set into wilderness and coastal areas, and permanent residents of the island who lived primarily by providing support services to the resort communities. The "summer people," who were part of a relatively new, extremely wealthy class in America, fulfilled a nostalgic attachment to a leisured, genteel country lifestyle at Mount Desert Island and were protective of the island's natural resources and beauty (Bunce 1994:44–86). The Hancock County Trustees of Public Reservations, a coalition of influential island residents, assembled and donated five thousand acres of land to the federal government in 1914. This reservation of land became Sieur de Monts National Monument in 1916, renamed Lafayette National Park in 1919 and later Acadia National Park in 1929 (U.S. Department of the Interior 1992:1).

In 1910, John D. Rockefeller, Jr., son of the Standard Oil titan, and his wife, Abbey Aldrich Rockefeller, purchased a summer house overlooking Seal Harbor on the southern coast of eastern Mount Desert Island (Ernst 1991:5). Rockefeller had recently recovered from a nervous breakdown, returning from travels in southern Europe, and sought the healthful atmosphere of the ruggedly beautiful island (U.S. Department of the Interior 1989a:24); perhaps more importantly, his image was recovering from the labor violence that occurred at Ludlow, Colorado, in 1914, and he "gravitated towards philanthropic projects that would directly improve the family name and provide support and involvement in seemingly non-controversial conservation, health and social problems" (Goldstein 1992:20). Rockefeller was approached by the Hancock County Trustees for financial support.

John D. Rockefeller, Jr., had a passion for park driving, which was an extremely popular sport in the first part of the twentieth century, when automobiles were still relatively new and shared roadways with a variety of horse-drawn vehicles, such as buckboards, cut-unders, coach teams, and carriages. At that time, automobiles were unpopular on Mount Desert Island, and until 1915 they were barred from several towns, as was allowed by state law (U.S. Department of the Interior 1989a:22–23). It was in 1915 that Rockefeller first petitioned to expand carriage roads located on his property onto adjacent park property, embarking on a partnership of park road building with Charles Eliot, the noted landscape architect who had initially organized the Hancock County Trustees to preserve and donate land on Mount Desert Island to the federal government, and George B. Dorr, who would become the park's first superintendent (Ernst 1991:5).

Both John D. Rockefeller, Jr., and his father had a fascination with road building. This interest was characterized by one biographer: "Acadia needed roads, and Mr. Rockefeller, who shared his father's passion for road-building, was only too anxious to help meet this requirement. Before Acadia National Park was created, he had built miles of carriage roads on his own property just as he had done at the Pocantico estate, and he took great satisfaction in the excellence of their design and construction" (Fosdick 1956:305).

John D. Rockefeller, Jr., studied road building in Yellowstone on visits to the park and enjoined the park superintendent, Horace M. Albright, to drive him into the most rugged and unprepared road construction sites so that he could examine the techniques and machinery. Rockefeller and his family toured many western natural parks as well, and frequently these park visits resulted in letters of advice from Rockefeller and charitable gifts to help in implementing them (Ernst 1991:3–20). John D. Rockefeller, Jr., was also intimately involved in the construction of the carriage roads in Acadia:

> JDR Jr. approached road-building as an art and a science. Before beginning he had careful surveys made; then having studied every mile and worked out each unit on paper, he followed each step with unremitting vigilance, finding it a great satisfaction, even in later years, to jolt over the roughest kind of terrain and then stand in the midst of blinding dust and deafening noise to watch the process of road building at first hand. (Fosdick 1956:305)

"Unremitting vigilance" is an apt characterization of the attention Rockefeller paid to his roads in Acadia National Park, which included even the review of all billed expenses and not infrequent disputes or requests for more detailed explanation of charges (U.S. Department of the Interior 1989a).

Between 1916 and 1922, John D. Rockefeller, Jr., received an enormous sum of money, totaling approximately one-half billion dollars, from his father, who had redistributed his fortune partly in response to recently passed income tax laws. Rockefeller became increasingly ambitious and enthusiastic about the philanthropic work of park-road building (U.S. Department of the Interior 1989a:70). Eliot and Dorr were the political arm in Acadia National Park, complementing John D. Rockefeller's financial power; it was they who carried proposed developments through Congress and the White House for approval (Goldstein 1992). Rockefeller was also supported by Horace M. Albright, who became director of the NPS in 1929 (Ernst 1991).

The majority of the carriage roads on Mount Desert Island were constructed between 1930 and 1935. All parts of the road system, and nearly ten thousand acres of undeveloped land that now comprise one-third of the total area of the park, were donated to the NPS by Rockefeller (U.S. Department of the Interior 1989a:70). After 1940, construction ceased, though Rockefeller continued to see that the roads, including planted landscapes and vistas designed with the help of noted horticulturalist and garden designer Beatrix Farrand, were carefully maintained (Deitz 1997). He was instrumental in replanting efforts after a fire ravaged the interior of the park in 1947 (Ernst 1991:17; U.S. Department of the Interior 1989a:247), though it is uncertain whether Farrand's original plans for planting and landscaping were followed (U.S. Department of the Interior 1991:245–46). Acadia National Park accepted responsibility for maintaining the carriage roads in 1960 upon Rockefeller's death. They fell into neglect, being maintained on an as-needed or emergency basis until the early 1990s, when a project of complete restoration and maintenance was initiated, funded by an endowment from the federal government and a matching grant for future maintenance from the Friends of Acadia Foundation.[1]

With this historical overview in mind, a review of the history of management of the Rockefeller carriage road system by different agencies can be examined as a history of creating a built landscape that is socially constructive and meaningful (Eco 1986; Ernstein 1998; Leone 1984, 1992; Potter 1994; Shackel and Little 1992), and also as the careful framing of the past in contemporary programs of interpretation of this historic property (Bunce 1994; Casteñeda 1996; MacCannell 1976). The processes at work in both of these instances are actually very much the same.

A Private Park within a Public Park

John D. Rockefeller initially came to Mount Desert Island seeking the same experience sought by the rusticators of the previous century: the sublimity of nature as antidote to technology and the squalor of the urban setting (Fosdick 1956; U.S. Department of the Interior 1989a:5). He was not among the first summer people to come to the island, which was well established as a resort by 1910, having been "discovered" by the painters of the Hudson River School, who helped to create and promote the pastoral ideal that Rockefeller would eventually fulfill (Shepard 1991:94).

Rockefeller participated in the phenomenon of touring, and in the idealization of the rustic wilderness landscape, in particular the segment of this activity that satisfied a sense of nostalgia. Motor vehicles were still barred from the towns on Mount Desert Island and were very unpopular in 1910 when John D. and Abbey Aldrich Rockefeller purchased "The Eyrie" above Seal Cove (U.S. Department of the Interior 1989a).

Rockefeller was involved in the conservation of natural and historic sites from the very beginnings of the national park system. Such natural settings as are found in the national parks have always been carefully selected arrangements of sights and scenery (MacCannell 1976:82). "Nineteenth-century tourists entered a setting designed to dramatize nature in terms of the sublime" (Nye 1997:26). Rockefeller also entered this scene at a time when the meaning of touring and tourism was on the verge of a great change, which, according to David Nye, was largely due to improvements in transportation infrastructure. Thus, "a particular gaze emerged from the dominant tourist ideology of each time: conspicuous leisure in the age of capital accumulation and the grand tour, mass consumption in the age of capital disaccumulation and the short holiday" (Nye 1997:23–24).

Improvements in rail and automobile transportation in the early twentieth century were creating a new base of consumers for tourist experiences, and consequently a new product, as Michael Bunce has suggested (1994:86–87):

> Although the twenties were the heyday of summer residences for the affluent they also marked the beginning of what was to become a mass-movement. The key factors in this were the growth of paid leisure time . . . and the automobile. In many ways it was the automobile which provided the main impetus for the acquisition of more modest country retreats by somewhat less affluent urbanites. It had an immediate impact on countryside recreation and made it possible for families to travel freely between vacation or weekend homes and their urban residences.

Rockefeller of course had to negotiate with this technological change. "One of the things that attracted Mrs. Rockefeller and me most to Mount Desert Island some twenty years ago," he told one reporter in 1928, "was that there were no motors on the island. I greatly deplored the pressure to open the island roads to motors and was one of those who opposed their admission to the last" (Fosdick 1956:305).

Rockefeller inarguably broke the back of elite recreation on Mount

Figure 9.2. A new motor road at Acadia National Park. September 1926. (Courtesy National Park Service, Historic Photograph Collection, 73–778[.4].)

Desert Island in helping to create the national park. He also helped bring automobiles to the park by financing the construction of thirty-five miles of very scenic automobile road around the park (fig. 9.2), but this was considered by many to be a concession intended to keep automobiles off his carriage roads (Foulds 1996:13). As he was creating a public park, he manufactured a landscape that contained a statement of resistance to the new popular countryside recreation, and to the changes occurring in American society in the early twentieth century.

The carriage road system, including all bridges, vistas, and gate lodges, includes nearly all of the formal elements of a private garden or park. Though explicitly these roads and landscapes were public property, Rockefeller exerted much control over how the roads were enjoyed, requiring that they be traveled by horse-drawn vehicles only (Fosdick 1956; U.S. Department of the Interior 1989a). This could be viewed as implicitly reserving use of the roads for those with certain resources: Tourists experienced the park from one of two crowded loop roads (as they primarily do today), while a separate, potentially exclusive network of carriage roads allowed more refined enjoyment of the island.

The carriage roads feature many elements that are adapted from classic park landscape design, and this property has been studied as an example of the "Natural Style" school of landscape architecture that was extremely popular in the early decades of the twentieth century. The style is typified by the nineteenth-century work of Frederick Law Olmstead (Steinitz et al.

1988), who also played a key role in the development of the national park system and authored the organization's paradoxical mission statement. The roadways meander leisurely through the landscape, allowing "cultivated and refined access to natural areas," blending or becoming transparent against the landscape (U.S. Department of the Interior 1989a:39). Such designed landscapes had clear associations with leisure and personal status in the nineteenth and early twentieth centuries (Marx 1964:76–89; Shepard 1991:94).

Particularly significant in this regard are the two gate lodges that were constructed in 1932 and deeded to Acadia National Park in 1939, Jordon Pond Gate Lodge and Brown Mountain Gate Lodge. These lodges were initially constructed to allow visitors to the park to stable and secure horses at reasonable prices; however, they are also evocative symbols of prestige borrowed from private park architecture. In an upper-class residence, the gate lodge would be located at the entrance to the grounds and would be occupied by servants and groundskeepers, functioning as working-class housing and placed at some distance from the main house. The journey to the house itself took the visitor through the carefully groomed landscape of the owner's estate. As such, the gate lodge greeted visitors, demarcated and controlled access to the property, was more impressive than a simple gate, and housed a number of servants at the entrance to the property, bordering on a public space. The Jordon Pond and Brown Mountain Gate Lodges are massive stone structures that clearly incorporate these ideas (U.S. Department of the Interior 1989a:55–58). And so, "just as park design reflected the English landscape or Natural Style of landscape gardening popular for country estates, the gate lodge was adapted to serve as park entrances" (U.S. Department of the Interior 1989a:58) (fig. 9.3).

It is evident that, more than a nostalgic refuge, the carriage roads at Acadia National Park are an expression of Rockefeller's mastery and control over important symbols of pastoralism as understood by the elite. Writing on landscape, Leo Marx (1964:4) describes "the uses of the pastoral ideal in the interpretation of the American experience" as a metaphor of contradiction, a way of ordering meaning and values that is shared by most Americans. Michael Bunce (1994) calls it "the countryside ideal," this need to idealize a simple, rural environment in opposition to the industrial, urban environment, which is also described by Paul Shepard (1991), David Nye (1997), and David Lowenthal (1968, 1975). This ideal is the root of the fresh-air movement of the late nineteenth and early twentieth centuries, and the outdoor organizations such as Ernst Thomas

Figure 9.3. Stone Gate Lodge at Acadia National Park soon after construction, with electrical lines in the background. 1935. (Courtesy National Park Service, Historic Photograph Collection, 73–923 [174].)

Seton's League of Woodcraft Indians and the Boy Scouts of America (Foulds 1996:4). In planning and constructing these roads, Rockefeller created an explicitly public space (though perhaps an implicitly private one) that contained all of the most important symbols of personal wealth *from his past*. In those images of countryside lay their authenticity. This designed pastoral landscape functioned, through nostalgic connotations, to authenticate the carriage roads for Rockefeller himself, and to maintain a separation between Rockefeller and the middle-class tourists who flocked to Mount Desert Island in the early twentieth century.

By the time the last carriage road was completed in 1940, they were a technological anachronism inappropriate to modern conveyances. "I was criticized at one time for being rather selfish," Rockefeller once commented, "but the roads that I built can be hard-surfaced very easily because they have excellent foundations, and while they are narrow, there are enough of them so that you can make them one-way roads" (quoted in Fosdick 1956:305). The meaning of the carriage roads, for Rockefeller, was contained within the anachronism that they represented.

The carriage roads at Acadia National Park were not simply a work of philanthropy, as they are frequently characterized. Nancy Newhall (1957:ix) in recording the conservation activities of John D. Rockefeller, Jr., writes: "He rejected the delusion that wealth was personal and turned his thoughts and energies toward discovering ways through which the fruit of wealth . . . could be enjoyed by the greatest number of people. It is a wonderful and heartening fact that this attitude toward the responsibilities of private fortune has, to a large degree, become prevalent and may indeed be said to have become characteristic of 'the American way.'" In addition to being a work of philanthropy, the carriage roads contain associations with a nostalgic and pastoral lifestyle that for Rockefeller legitimated the undertaking of making a public facility for recreation while maintaining his own position as inheritor of the landscape. As such, the carriage roads, and to an extent the whole of Acadia National Park, were and continue to be a very complex symbol.

Restoration and Contemporary Meanings

The first General Management Plan (GMP) for the park, which enumerated and discussed the treatment of cultural and natural resources, was produced in 1992 (U.S. Department of the Interior 1992). Two studies of historic cultural resources were conducted within Acadia National Park in anticipation of preparing this document. These included an inventory of historic structures (Arbogast 1984) and a study of the historic carriage road system (U.S. Department of the Interior 1989a), which was amended to treat potential restoration of the carriage roads to their historic condition, and to evaluate the potential for successful maintenance in light of a variety of contemporary uses (U.S. Department of the Interior 1989b). Though the historic carriage roads have been listed on the National Register of Historic Places since 1979 (U.S. Department of the Interior 1992:18), the historic context study appears to be the first thorough treatment of the carriage roads as a historic resource, and it remains the definitive work on the history of this property. William Rieley and Roxanne Brouse (U.S. Department of the Interior 1989a) synthesize and present in great detail historical data on the roads, information drawn from numerous sources, including (but not limited to) the Rockefeller Archives at Pocantico Hills, the National Archives, the Maine State Library and Archives, and several Bar Harbor–area and NPS repositories. Their work has been the basic source for all subsequent interpretation of the carriage roads.

In interpreting the carriage roads today at Acadia National Park, these narratives are brought to life through reenactments performed by park staff and volunteers during carriage rides and other events. Three themes dominate interpretations of the carriage roads:

(1) Rockefeller is represented as a wealthy visionary, a philanthropist and humanitarian who worked with George Dorr to create the carriage roads for the public to have access to the most scenic locales in Acadia National Park.

(2) The construction of the roads, though not reenacted, is represented as interpreters discuss the roads from the points of view of the local landscapers, architects, and laborers. Thus multiple voices contribute to the story of this property, and engineering values in the roads are also communicated.

(3) The battle of the automobiles is described as a third theme, presented as a struggle to keep a rural, clean, and natural atmosphere on the island: a very green message.

Thus, the restoration and partial remanufacture of the property has been accompanied by an established significance, and this interpretation is intended to reflect well on current park management; the positive spin placed on the Rockefeller carriage roads extends to portray what is essentially a driving park in a positive light.

Dean MacCannell (1976:7) interprets the packaging of history and the idyllic landscape as a substitute heritage: Tourism is seen as an attempt to reconstruct a cultural heritage and social identity by alienated urbanites, a ritual of sightseeing and a shared experience. Through MacCannell's view of modern tourism, one can see how cultural heritage sites in particular would be important as instruments of cultural production. This idea of national parks as socially constructive landscapes with a nationalist bent has been echoed in archaeological literature (for example, see Fowler 1987), as well as by those involved in public history (Linenthal 1993; Linenthal and Engelhardt 1996). However, MacCannell does not separate historical landmarks from other landscapes—all are simply viewed as attractions, or spectacles. All attractions, be they historical landmarks or natural wonders, are equally institutionalized for sightseers in America as segments of our national identity.

In the current interpretation, Rockefeller is presented as a humanitarian who sought to preserve a wondrous natural landscape for the enjoyment of all Americans. The crisis of the introduction of automobiles to the island is interpreted as the relentless push of progress, which corrupts with noise, chemicals, and crowds. However, the campaign of road building that Rockefeller conducted was considered by some a serious intrusion, and he was fought by conservationists on several fronts (Eliot 1928). This dichotomy is explicit in the purpose of the NPS, which is charged both with preserving natural and historic sites for posterity, and with making these sites available for the enjoyment of the American people (U.S. Department of the Interior 1992). Reflected in this dichotomy is a basic conflict that grew in the American conservation movement as the national park system was being conceived and created. One school, inspired by the romantic primitivism and Transcendentalism of Emerson and Thoreau, saw in the nation's remaining wilderness the possibility of true worship of God, and ultimately national health and reform, and believed that the wilderness had to remain unadulterated. This position was promulgated most notably by John Muir, and also by Robert Underwood Johnson, Charles Sargent, and Aldo Leopold, and was at the core of a number of early preservation societies including the Sierra Club, the National Parks Association, and the Wilderness Society. At the same time, progressive conservationists such as Theodore Roosevelt, Gifford Pinchot, Charles Eliot, and Frederick Law Olmstead saw the importance of the national forests and parks for recreation, but also for the resources that they contained: All natural resources were to be put to their best use (Foresta 1984:2–47; Nash 1973:44–123; Sellars 1997:15–32; Wilson 1992:24–44).

This conflict has generally favored those on the side of development and utilitarian meanings for national park lands (Abbey 1968; Sax 1980; Wilson 1992). While initially the national parks were most threatened by extractive industries, in the postwar period, tourist development has come to be equally threatening, both to the resources of the parks and to the quality of visitor experiences in the outdoors. The restoration and augmentation of the carriage road system proposed by the 1992 GMP reflects the adoption of a plan for improving the quality of visitor experiences at Acadia National Park by dispersing visitors through the less-developed western portion of the park (U.S. Department of the Interior 1991:35–54). Under this management strategy, the historic carriage roads are instrumental in decreasing crowding at Acadia by spreading visitors into the less developed and less accessible western portion of the park, and thus the significant improvements to the carriage roads became necessary as they had been assigned a new function. This decision was adopted despite concerns over the carrying capacity of the park, terrible traffic on the two loop roads, crowding in campsites and on trails, and the quality of visitor experience voiced as the draft GMP was being reviewed.

Additionally, some comments expressed concern with the vast balance of attention being paid to John D. Rockefeller, Jr.'s carriage roads, at the expense of other cultural resources within the park (U.S. Department of the Interior 1991:195–229). However, from a historical standpoint, the carriage roads are clearly integral to the identity of Acadia National Park, more than any other property that it contains. Inscribed within the carriage roads is the development of the park by Rockefeller, under the "best use" philosophy popular with Rockefeller's supporters such as Dorr and Eliot. By convincing park visitors to accept the construction of the carriage roads by Rockefeller, visitors also learn to accept the current state of the park as dominated by automobile transportation (fig. 9.4).

The Rockefeller carriage roads clearly have an *ideological* function under their current use and interpretation, in addition to the practical one already described. The positive interpretation of Rockefeller's construction and development on the island, depicted as an extended project of humanitarianism, promotes an ideology that favors additional development of the park and combats criticism of development and increased accessibility. Furthermore, by drawing attention toward the struggle between conservationists and the various extractive industries that would prey on the parklands, tourists are led away from the fact that they themselves comprise a significant threat and a negative impact to the natural and historical resources in our national parks. In this way Acadia uses the Rockefeller carriage roads as a symbol and a metaphor to negotiate the contradiction within its mission, while visitors are led to accept the cur-

Figure 9.4. Bubble Pond Bridge at Acadia National Park. 1928. (Courtesy National Park Service, Historic Photograph Collection, 73–763 [43].)

rent state of the park as dominated by automobile transportation and the promotion of the park as a tourist attraction with no defined visitor or vehicle capacity.

The Rockefeller carriage roads, and possibly all historic sites associated with modern tourism, are unique in that they have never really been saved, salvaged, or enshrined. Rather, they have always been commodities: They were conceived already historic and already authentic. Yet, in all representations of history, there are interests at work. Rockefeller faced an impossible conflict—to develop a site for tourism but to retain the qualities that he and his peers considered to be authentic, significant, and meaningful. In order to accomplish this he translated elite pastoral symbols into a public park, with tremendous skill. Similarly, the modern park uses the carriage roads in order to negotiate conflict among various interests, while maintaining the authenticity, and therefore the authority, of their spectacular production: Acadia National Park itself.

Note

1. Information presented in this chapter regarding current practices and interpretations at Acadia National Park was derived from material presented on-line in various forms at http://www.acadia.net/anp (written in November 1995 and cited on December 20, 2000) and at http://www.nps.gov/acad/history/htm (updated September 28, 2000) as well as from discussion with park staff.

References

Abbey, Edward
  1968   *Desert Solitaire: A Season in the Wilderness.* Ballantine Books, New York.
AcadiaNet
  2000   The Carriage Roads, 1996. [Found at http://www.acadia.net/anp.]
Arbogast, D.
  1984   *Inventory of Structures, Acadia National Park.* Prepared for the U.S. Department of the Interior, National Park Service, Division of Cultural Resources, North Atlantic Regional Office, Boston.
Bunce, Michael
  1994   *The Countryside Ideal: Anglo-American Images of Landscape.* Routledge, New York.
Casteñeda, Quetzil E.
  1996   *In the Museum of Maya Culture: Touring Chichén Itzá.* University of Minnesota Press, Minneapolis.
Deitz, Paula
  1997   "Open to All Real Plant Lovers": Beatrix Farrand's Invitation to Reef

Point Gardens. In *The Bulletins of Reef Point Gardens,* by Beatrix Farrand, the Island Foundation, Bar Harbor, Maine. Sagapress, Saga-ponack, New York.

Eco, Umberto
1986   Function and Sign: Semiotics of Architecture. In *The City and the Sign: An Introduction to Urban Semiotics,* edited by Mark Gottdiener and Alexandros Lagopolous, 55–86. Columbia University Press, New York.

Eliot, Charles W.
1928   *The Future of Mount Desert Island: A Report to the Plan Committee, Bar Harbor Village Improvement Association.* Bar Harbor Village Improvement Association, Bar Harbor, Maine.

Ernst, Joseph W.
1991   *Worthwhile Places: Correspondence of John D. Rockefeller, Jr., and Horace M. Albright.* Published for the Rockefeller Archive Center by Fordham University Press, New York.

Ernstein, Julie H.
1998   *Nostalgia and the Perpetuation of an Historic Ideal: Two Views from a Twentieth-Century Maryland Suburb.* Paper Delivered at the Council for Northeast Historical Archaeology Meeting, Montreal. October 17, 1998.

Foresta, Ronald A.
1984   *America's National Parks and Their Keepers.* Resources for the Future, Washington, D.C.

Fosdick, Raymond B.
1956   *John D. Rockefeller, Jr.: A Portrait.* Harper, New York.

Foulds, H. Eliot
1996   *Cultural Landscape Report for Blackwoods and Seawall Campgrounds, Acadia National Park.* Cultural Landscape Publication No. 11. Olm-stead Center for Landscape Preservation. U.S. Department of the Inte-rior, National Park Service, Boston.

Fowler, Don D.
1987   Uses of the Past: Archaeology in Service of the State. *American Antiquity* 52(2): 229–48.

Goldstein, Judith S.
1992   *Tragedies and Triumphs: Charles W. Eliot, George B. Dorr, John D. Rockefeller, Jr.: The Founding of Acadia National Park.* Port-in-a-Storm Bookstore, Somesville, Maine.

Leone, Mark P.
1984   Interpreting Ideology in Historical Archaeology: Using the Rules of Per-spective in the William Paca Gardens in Annapolis, Maryland. In *Ideol-ogy, Power, and Prehistory,* edited by Daniel Miller and Christopher Tilley, 25–36. Cambridge University Press, New York.

1992   Epilogue: The Productive Nature of Material Culture and Archaeology. In *Meanings and Uses of Material Culture*, edited by Barbara J. Little and Paul A. Shackel. *Historical Archaeology* 26(3): 130–33.

Linenthal, Edward T.
1993   *Sacred Ground: Americans and Their Battlefields*. University of Illinois Press, Urbana.

Linenthal, Edward T., and Tom Engelhardt, eds.
1996   *History Wars: The* Enola Gay *and Other Battles for the American Past*. Holt, New York.

Lowenthal, David
1968   The American Scene. *Geographical Review* 58(1): 61–88.
1975   Past Time, Present Place: Landscape and Memory. *Geographical Review* 65(1): 1–36.

MacCannell, Dean
1976   *The Tourist: A New Theory of the Leisure Class*. Schocken Books, New York.

Marx, Leo
1964   *The Machine in the Garden*. Oxford University Press, New York.

Nash, Roderick
1973   *Wilderness and the American Mind*. Yale University Press, New Haven.

Newhall, Nancy
1957   *A Contribution to the Heritage of Every American: The Conservation Activities of John D. Rockefeller, Jr.* Knopf, New York.

Nye, David E.
1997   *Narratives and Spaces: Technology and the Construction of American Culture*. Columbia University Press, New York.

Potter, Parker B., Jr.
1994   *Public Archaeology in Annapolis: A Critical Approach to History in Maryland's Ancient City*. Smithsonian Institution Press, Washington, D.C.

Rhodes, Diane Lee
1983   *Archaeological Investigations at Fabbri Memorial, Acadia National Park, Bar Harbor, Maine*. U.S. Department of the Interior, National Park Service, Denver Service Center, Northeast Team, Denver.

Sax, Joseph L.
1980   *Mountains Without Handrails: Reflections on the National Parks*. University of Michigan Press, Ann Arbor.

Sellars, Richard West
1997   *Preserving Nature in the National Parks: A History*. Yale University Press, New Haven.

Shackel, Paul A., and Barbara J. Little
1992   Post-Processual Approaches to Meanings and Uses of Material Culture

in Historical Archaeology. In "Meanings and Uses of Material Culture," edited by Barbara J. Little and Paul A. Shackel. *Historical Archaeology* 26(3):5–11.

Shepard, Paul

1991 *Man in the Landscape: A Historic View of the Esthetics of Nature.* Texas A&M University Press, College Station.

Steinitz, C. F., A. Wiley, and V. Wiley

1988 *Toward the Design of Sustainable Landscape with High Visual Preference and High Visual Integrity: A Case Study in Acadia National Park.* On file, Acadia National Park, Bar Harbor, Maine.

U.S. Department of the Interior. National Park Service.

1989a *Historic Resource Study for the Carriage Road System, Acadia National Park, Mount Desert Island, Maine.* North Atlantic Regional Office. Rieley and Associates, Charlottesville, Virginia.

1989b *Recommended Guidelines for the Restoration, Maintenance, and Use of the Carriage Roads at Acadia National Park.* North Atlantic Region. Rieley and Associates, Charlottesville, Virginia.

1991 *Draft General Management Plan, Acadia National Park, Maine.* Denver Service Center. Denver.

1992 *General Management Plan, Acadia National Park, Maine.* North Atlantic Region. Boston.

Wilson, Alexander

1992 *The Culture of Nature: North American Landscape from Disneyland to the Exxon Valdez.* Blackwell, Cambridge, Massachusetts.

10

The Birthplace of a Chief: Archaeology and Meaning at George Washington Birthplace National Monument

Joy Beasley

Introduction

> This national shrine, which will bring to the thousands of visitors who come here a fresh appreciation of the life of George Washington, is one of the most sacred and valuable possessions of the government. . . . Wakefield makes us all feel closer to the Father of Our Country.
> —Virginia Secretary of State Ray Lyman Wilbur

The history of memorialization at George Washington Birthplace National Monument (GWBNM) is unusually long and complex and has been interpreted and reinterpreted throughout the past century, based on conflicting assumptions and on the collective memory of many different groups and individuals with diverse interests and goals. Civic-minded patriots, government agents, and concerned citizens alike have utilized or ignored in varying combinations archaeological investigation, historical research, and oral history, depending upon the meaning they intended to attach to the landscape there. Here, I critically examine and evaluate the development of the memorialization of space at GWBNM, and its subsequent interpretation and reinterpretation, focusing on the physical location and appearance of the house in which George Washington was born that was destroyed by fire during the latter part of the eighteenth century.

After the destruction of the original house, its exact location faded from local and family oral history traditions. As a result, "a location containing the foundations of an outbuilding was mistakenly commemorated for more than 120 years as the site" of the birthplace of George Washington

(Jones et al. 1999:2). This mistake was compounded when initial archaeological investigations aimed at preserving and commemorating the site focused on this erroneously memorialized location, known today as the Memorial House. Archaeological research contributed greatly to the debunking of the myth of the birthplace of George Washington, and to its current interpretation as well. The meaning of the site to the many groups that competed for control of its interpretation informed the history of its memorialization, as well as the subsequent controversy and debate surrounding its eventual reinterpretation.

Background History

In February of 1718, Augustine Washington, Sr., purchased 150 acres along Popes Creek in Virginia, including "houses, edifices, buildings, tobacco houses, fences, orchards, and garden" (Hudson 1956:12) from Joseph Abbington. The Washington family is thought to have occupied the Abbington cottage until the house Augustine commissioned carpenter David Jones to build was completed around 1726 (Hatch 1979:32–33; Olson 1974:2; Powell 1968:3–4); the Washington family may simply have added onto the existing Abbington cottage rather than building an entirely new structure (Barka 1978:3). George Washington was born in this house on February 22, 1732.

The appearance of the house built by Augustine Washington, Sr., is unknown, as no drawings or contemporary word descriptions of it survive (Hatch 1979:37; U.S. Department of the Interior n.d.:2). However, the 1762 inventory of Augustine Washington, Jr.'s personal property suggests a fairly large residence. Accommodations on the farm included a kitchen, pantry, laundry, storerooms, dairy, stable, barns, tobacco houses, and quarters for enslaved laborers (Barka 1978:4–5; Hudson 1956:13).

Over the years, Augustine Washington, Sr., purchased land from John Pope and others, expanding the plantation to a total of 590 acres (U.S. Department of the Interior 1941:6). Popes Creek Plantation was primarily centered on tobacco cultivation, but like most plantations, food and other commodities were also produced there, allowing it to be essentially self-sufficient (Barka 1978: 4). George Washington spent the first three years of his life at Popes Creek, until the family moved to Little Hunting Creek in 1735, known today as Mount Vernon (Hudson 1956:17; Powell 1968:4; Hatch 1979:34, 48). In 1738, Augustine Washington, Sr., purchased a 288 acre farm called Ferry Farm on the Rappahannock River near Fredericksburg, where he died on April 12, 1743.

Augustine Washington, Jr., inherited Popes Creek plantation in 1743. Orphaned at age eleven, George Washington visited his elder half-sibling at Popes Creek plantation from time to time and even surveyed the area in 1747 at age fifteen (Hatch 1979:51, 53; Hudson 1956:19). Augustine Washington, Jr., died in 1762, giving William Augustine Washington full title to the plantation after the death of his mother, Ann, in 1774 (Powell 1968:41).

By the 1770s, the property was known as Wakefield, apparently named for Oliver Goldsmith's 1766 poem, "The Vicar of Wakefield" (U.S. Department of the Interior 1941:7). The house accidentally caught fire on Christmas Day, 1779, and was never rebuilt (Powell 1968:62). The old mansion, dependencies, and outbuildings at the "Burnt House Plantation" (Barka 1978:4; U.S. Department of the Interior 1941:7–9) "stood empty, slowly melting, perhaps even aided by brick and building hardware salvagers" (Hatch 1979:64). Upon the death of William Augustine Washington in 1810, Wakefield passed to George Corbin Washington, who sold its 1,300 acres to John Gray in 1813, reserving for the Washington family the ownership of the family burial plot at Bridges Creek and "sixty feet square of ground on which the house stood in which General Washington was born" (U.S. Department of the Interior 1941:10; Powell 1968:63; Rodnick 1941:10).

In June 1815, George Washington Parke Custis, the adopted grandson of George and Martha Washington, visited Popes Creek expressly to mark the site of the original birth house with a stone slab inscribed with the date of George Washington's birth (Rodnick 1941:11). This first effort at commemorating the site is an event of utmost importance, as its placement became the basis for the interpretation of the site for nearly 150 years. Recalling the event some 36 years later, Custis reported that his party was "escorted to the spot, where a few bricks alone marked the birthplace of a chief. . . . We gathered together the bricks of an ancient chimney that once formed the hearth around which Washington in his infancy had played, and constructed a rude kind of pedestal, on which we reverently placed the FIRST STONE, commending it to the respect and protection of the American people" (Rodnick 1941:11; emphasis in original).

George Washington Parke Custis originally placed the stone in a location he determined to be "just inside the window of the room in which George Washington was born" (Hoppin 1930a:158). How he made this determination is not known, nor is it clear exactly what foundations or structures were visible at the site. This confusion is important because the placement of the Custis stone became the basis for much of the interpretation of the original birthplace site thereafter. For example, an anonymous newspaper account from the Washington, D.C., *Daily National Intelligencer* for November 11, 1857, reported that the substantial foundations and "filled-up cellar of the birth mansion" were visible at the site near the small chimney of a separate structure; from Custis's account, it appears that he placed the stone near this small standing chimney. However, Custis's description can also be interpreted to indicate that he placed the stone on a random scatter of bricks not associated with a visible foundation or chimney. Other local oral history accounts reported that he placed the stone within a larger group of foundations near, but not associated with, the chimney (Hatch 1979:66–69). David Rodnick (1941:12–13) adds to the confusion by observing that, "in the first place, no mention is made of any foundations existent at the spot . . . . Custis' description makes it seem that the stone was placed well outside any foundations. . . . The only structure evidently existing at the site was the chimney, later called the Ancient Chimney. . . . It seems quite evident, too, that Custis assumed that the kitchen chimney was part of the Washington Mansion."

Thus, the small standing chimney apparently represented the only surface remains at the time of Custis's visit, and its presence may have influenced his recollection of the site of the original birth house. Rodnick (1941:12–13) concludes "that Custis assumed the Washington mansion to be around this chimney as a base. We can rightly assume that perhaps even in 1815 no one knew where the . . . Mansion had been." To complicate things further, the Custis stone was vandalized and moved around shortly after its placement (Hatch 1979:68).

Other accounts from the 1850s clearly indicate that the small standing chimney was part of a separate smaller structure, and they also note the existence of another larger set of foundations nearby, which were believed to represent the birthplace of George Washington. For example, in his description of the visit of Virginia Commonwealth governor Henry A. Wise to the site in 1858, J. A. Weinberger (1858) reported that "an aged person present remarked that he distinctly remembered when a house occupied the spot where the chimney now stands and that it was used for a kitchen and laundry. Near this place [near the chimney] is plainly visible a filled-up cellar, having chimney marks at each end, about sixty feet apart. This is supposed to be the identical locality where the house stood in which George Washington was born. It was either burnt or pulled down previous to the Revolutionary War." This account seems to indicate that the Custis stone was originally placed within the larger foundations, and that the small standing chimney was part of a separate structure.

Even as late as 1873, a Westmoreland County correspondent for the *Alexandria Gazette* reported:

There is a chimney standing at the spot, but it [is] almost certain both from tradition and from unmistakable circumstances and local indications, that this chimney was not attached to the house in which Washington was born. It was no doubt a part of an outbuilding within the curtilage. The dwelling house stood nearer the margin of Pope's Creek for whilst every vestige of a building has long since perished, there are yet quite distinct traces of the foundation of a house, marked by indications of the bottom walls, and a perceptible sink, denoting the place of a cellar. (Keim 1873:42–45)

In short, no one knows where the Custis stone was originally placed or what foundations or structures were visible at the site in the early nineteenth century. Over the years the Custis stone was broken into three pieces, was moved to a grove of fig trees nearby, and finally disappeared completely by 1870, but popular memory gave it "the preciseness of valid, explicit gospel" (Hatch 1979:66). In spite of its rather complicated history, the Custis stone formed the basis for the tradition surrounding the location of the original birth site of George Washington, giving it the "enduring truth of first interpretation" (Linenthal 1999).

Memorialization and Public Ownership

Contemporary nineteenth-century accounts reflect the growing movement to memorialize the birthplace of George Washington. An 1835 *Gazetteer* report stated: "On Pope's Creek the scarcely distinguished remains of a house are discovered, which tradition designates as the spot on which the illustrious WASHINGTON was born. In a few years these will have become obliterated, as they are now barely perceptible, and not a stone be left to point the inquisitive patriot to the place that gave birth to the 'Father of his Country'" (Martin 1835; emphasis in original). According to an anonymous 1851 Richmond *Whig and Public Advertiser* reporter, "The neglected condition of the spot bears record of shame against his country for neglecting to lift up a monument there, to his memory" (Rodnick 1941:15).

As public interest in the site increased, contemporary accounts appealed to the patriotic sensibilities of Americans. The Fredericksburg *Virginia Herald* reported on March 17, 1832, that "nothing remains of the edifice . . . but a pile of ruins, and all around it has run to waste" and called for the erection "of some suitable memorial" to preserve the site "for the visitors who may make a pilgrimage to the Mecca of American patriotism."

Public ownership at the Washington house site began in 1858 when Lewis W. Washington, son of George Corbin Washington, deeded the family burial ground and a sixty-foot-square plot popularly believed to be the original site marked by the Custis stone to the Commonwealth of Virginia, with a stipulation that a "suitable and modest (though substantial)" memorial be erected "to commemorate to rising generations these notable spots" (Hatch 1979:69). However, the Commonwealth of Virginia did not erect a monument, "due in part to the upheaval of the Civil War" (U.S. Department of the Interior 1999:1.4), and in 1882, Virginia transferred its Popes Creek holdings to the United States, under the jurisdiction of the State Department (Hatch 1979:72; Powell 1968:6).

In 1881, Congress authorized the construction of a granite obelisk to mark the traditional birth site. In preparation for its erection, F. O. St. Clair, a civil engineer for the U.S. Department of State, conducted the first official excavation at the site between 1881 and 1882 "with the view of determining the character of the substrata" (Hatch 1979:71). Artifacts including "pieces of china, hinges and a candle . . . a silver teaspoon . . . [and] a bunch of keys" (Rodnick 1941:40) are mentioned in correspondence records, but no other documentation of the excavation exists.

Even as early as 1881, there was some dispute as to the actual location of the birth site. J. E. Wilson, the former owner of the land that included Wakefield, wrote to Secretary of State James G. Blaine on May 5 of that year asking that he reconsider the site to be marked (Rodnick 1941:26). Wilson had learned from newspaper accounts that the monument was to be built near the remains of an old chimney, and he thought this was a mistake, since "this chimney was never a part of the original building; and is forty-five to fifty feet from the nearest point of the foundations of the old mansion" (quoted in Hatch 1979:72; and see Rodnick 1941:26). However, the federal government simply assumed that the sixty-foot-square plot "was accurately situated over the foundation remains of the manor house in which George Washington was born" (Jones et al. 1999:3). Wilson's request was ignored and plans for the construction of the monument continued.

In 1896, to prepare for the construction of the fifty-one-foot granite obelisk, War Department engineer John Stewart "commenced his digging at a spot where he was told the Custis stone had formerly lain" (Rodnick 1941:91). The site chosen for the monument was centered in what the

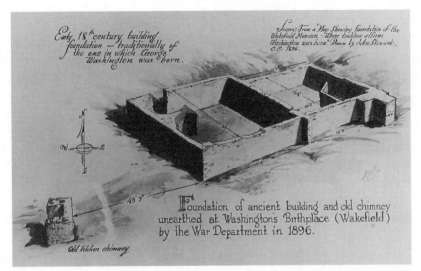

Early 18th century building foundation — traditionally of the one in which George Washington was born.

Source: From a Map Showing foundation of the Wakefield Monument - Where tradition affirms Washington was born. Drawn by John Stewart, C.E. 1896.

Foundation of ancient building and old chimney unearthed at Washington's Birthplace (Wakefield) by the War Department in 1896.

Old kitchen chimney

Figure 10.1. Perspective sketch of the foundations uncovered by John Stewart in 1896, where the Memorial House now stands, showing the "old kitchen chimney" foundation, lower left. (Courtesy National Park Service, George Washington Birthplace National Monument.)

federal government believed to be the sixty-foot-square plot originally deeded by Lewis Washington and revealed portions of a two-room brick structure about thirty feet long and twenty feet wide on an east-west orientation, which was interpreted as the birth site of George Washington (Barka 1978:7; Powell 1968:72). Stewart made only two maps of his excavations, with no mention of any associated artifacts (fig. 10.1).

The small size of the "rather slight structure" (Hatch 1979:73) engendered more controversy about the monument and prompted J. E. Wilson to protest once again, this time in an 1898 letter to the Army Corps of Engineers. Wilson did not appear to dispute the actual location of the structure, but simply its small size (Rodnick 1941:91). Stewart's findings "were disappointingly small and ultimately led to all kinds of apologies and explanations" (Hatch 1979:75) and also conflicted with the oral history of the area: "That the excavation in 1896 must have surprised many of the people in that neighborhood is evidenced by the rumors that rose later that the monument was placed on the wrong site" (Rodnick 1941:32–34). In spite of the small size of the foundations and numerous local protests, the fifty-one-foot-tall granite obelisk was erected on this site in 1896 (Jones et al. 1999:3; Powell 1968:20; Rodnick 1941:31).

Archaeology and the Construction of a Myth

In 1923, a group of "public spirited" citizens concerned with historical preservation organized the Wakefield National Memorial Association (WNMA) "to seek a more meaningful memorialization of the old Washington place where our first president was born" (Hatch 1979:83). The minutes of the WNMA's first meeting on June 11, 1923, stated that the main objective of the WNMA was "the preservation of the birthplace of George Washington . . . to build there a replica of the house in which Washington was born . . . [making] it a shrine to which Americans can go" (WNMA 1923). The date set for the completion of this most sacred patriotic task was February 22, 1932, the bicentennial anniversary of George Washington's birthday.

Led by Josephine Wheelright Rust, a collateral descendant of the Washington family, members of the WMNA raised funds to acquire land associated with the Wakefield plantation (Hudson 1956:27). Heirs of the Washington family and the Commonwealth of Virginia donated additional holdings as well (U.S. Department of the Interior n.d.: 2). Genealogist Charles Arthur Hoppin, WNMA historian, is credited with enlisting the support of John D. Rockefeller, Jr., who purchased 273 acres of the old Wakefield plantation and donated it to the WMNA in 1929 (Hatch 1979:83; Hudson 1956:27). On March 11, 1926, Virginia senator James W. Wadsworth, Jr., introduced a bill that gave the WNMA the authority to construct a replica at Wakefield "as nearly as may be practical, of the home in which George Washington was born," no small task as there was no surviving picture or description of the house (Rogers 1958:23).

The establishment of the WNMA was contemporary with a "wave of nationalism and nostalgia for the past" that overtook America in the late nineteenth and early twentieth centuries (Jones et al. 1999:8). The result of this nostalgia was "an era of historic preservation, archaeological investigation, and the reconstruction of America's Colonial past," which resulted in contemporary investigations at Williamsburg, Yorktown, and Jamestown, with the similarly patriotic goal of reconstructing an idealized colonial past (Jones et al. 1999:8). Like the investigations at GWBNM, much of the work was undertaken by historians, engineers, and architects seeking architectural data to oversee the reconstruction effort.

The WMNA's first task in the reconstruction of the birth home of George Washington was to plan the commemorative structure, which would then have to be approved by the Fine Arts Commission (FAC) and the Secretary of War, under whose jurisdiction the area fell (Hatch

1979:84). Questions once again surfaced regarding the accuracy of the granite memorial marking the location of the traditional birth site. Charles Moore, chairman of the FAC and vice president of the WNMA, noted in 1925 that "no picture of the house has come down to us, nor have excavations been made to locate it. . . . Unfortunately the location has never been investigated. . . . I have good reason to believe that the monument is not located on the site of the Washington House" (quoted in Rodnick 1941:37–38). Moore's misgivings were based "upon local rumor in Westmoreland County [and] . . . in 1925 the Wakefield Association knew no more of the site than that a monument had stood over it, and that ostensibly it was supposed to have been the house in which George Washington was born" (Rodnick 1941:38).

At Moore's insistence, the WNMA undertook excavations in 1926 to determine the extent and nature of the foundations under the granite obelisk. The excavations were supervised by engineer J. Arthur Hook, "with some direction from Mrs. Rust" (Hatch 1979:84). Hook published three short reports, one of which mentions the poor fit between the archaeological evidence and local oral history regarding the traditional birth site (Rodnick 1941:39).

Further opposition to the reconstruction plan was provided by landscape architect Frederick Law Olmsted, Jr., who visited the site in 1927 and recommended in a letter to Charles Moore, dated March 18, 1929, that the replica not be built on what were thought to be the original foundations, reasoning that the replica might eventually come to represent the "actual house in which that event took place" (Olmsted 1929). In spite of Olmsted's objections, Hook's inconclusive findings, and the conflicting oral history surrounding the site, the WNMA continued with reconstruction plans.

In 1927, Josephine Wheelright Rust submitted the reconstruction plans to Secretary of War Dwight Davis for his approval (U.S. Department of the Interior 1999:2.55). However, Davis did not agree to construct a memorial structure on the foundation ruins and announced in a letter to Rust on January 31, 1928, that the War Department would proceed with its own concept plan, which included a request for "an appropriation of funds for the employment of an architect and the preparation of plans for a proper development of . . . Wakefield. Accordingly, I do not wish to approve a definite location for the house until the studies . . . have been completed" (Davis 1928). These tentative plans for the improvement of Wakefield submitted by the War Department required a minimum of $450,000 for the cost of the reconstruction. As a result, Davis was forced to relinquish his resistance to the construction of the Memorial House, thus ending the influence of the War Department on the birthplace site (U.S. Department of the Interior 1999:2.57).

In 1929, the WNMA acquired additional land and two years later donated all its holdings at Wakefield to the U.S. government. By an act of Congress on January 23, 1930, George Washington Birthplace National Monument was designated to be administered by the National Park Service (NPS), U.S. Department of the Interior (Hudson 1956:29). The WNMA, however, continued to play a significant role in the development of the site (Hudson 1956:29; Olson 1974:4).

Archaeological exploration continued in advance of the relocation of the granite memorial and in preparation for the construction of the birth mansion. Excavating about fifty feet west of the traditional birth site foundations, NPS engineer O. G. Taylor uncovered a chimney foundation in 1930. Believed to be the remains of the small chimney still standing on the site at the time of the Custis visit, these remains were interpreted as an "ancient kitchen" and were incorporated into the reconstruction plan (Hudson 1956:40; Olson 1974:4–5).

It is worth noting, as discussed earlier, that the Custis stone's original location was purported to have been near a small standing chimney. The Custis stone, along with the elusive sixty-square-foot plot, formed the basis for the location of the reconstructed birth house. Thus, if Taylor had indeed unearthed the same chimney fifty feet away from the foundations under the granite memorial, its discovery should have alerted members of the WMNA and the NPS that the foundations under the granite memorial were not in the area originally marked by George Washington Parke Custis. This subtle discrepancy was apparently not noted by NPS or WNMA officials.

Obviously, archaeological excavation had failed to document the site of the birth home; indeed, it "clearly pointed [out] that the 'ancient mansion' did not occupy this site" at all (Hatch 1979:84). In the absence of archaeological evidence, the WNMA turned to historical research to plan for the outward appearance of the reconstructed birth home. As "the most painstaking research in this country and in England failed to produce any reliable evidence concerning the appearance, size, and shape of the house" (U.S. Department of the Interior 1941:13), the Memorial House that architect Edward Donn, Jr., designed was not intended to be a replica but rather an idealized "typical modest Virginia plantation [house] of the first half of the eighteenth century" (U.S. Department of the Interior 1941:13).

Using "knowledge inherited by the oldest and best-informed descen-

Figure 10.2. The Memorial House at George Washington Birthplace National Monument. (Courtesy National Park Service, George Washington Birthplace National Monument.)

dants," living members of the Washington family were also consulted (Hoppin 1930a:154). Mary Minor Lightfoot, a niece of George Washington Ball, remembered a picture of Wakefield shown to her by her uncle around 1850. Recalling its details some seventy-six years later, she reported that the house had "five dormers, ten in all. Four large double outside chimneys, and the house was built of native brick" (quoted in Hatch 1979:85). William Augustine Washington's great-great-grandson William Lanier Washington also recalled that "the bricks used in building this house at Wakefield were not imported . . . but were made in the brickyard at Wakefield . . . it was a house of probably a dozen or more rooms, on two floors" (quoted in Hoppin 1926:85). It was out of such "testimonial devices . . . that the Wakefield Association authenticated its plans, *after the drawings* [the Memorial House plans] *were made*" (Rodnick 1941:47; emphasis in original) (fig. 10.2).

Josephine Wheelright Rust exerted her own influence in the design of the Memorial House (U.S. Department of the Interior 1999:2.54). Edward Donn's design is reported to have drawn heavily on the manor houses of both Twiford, the childhood home of Rust, and Gunston Hall, the home of George Mason (Rodnick 1941:42–45). A 1937 memorandum on file at GWBNM notes that "current gossip advances the explanation that Mrs. Rust . . . believed so strongly that her childhood home (Twiford) had been designed after the original Washington birth house, that she prevailed upon the architect to pattern the restoration along the lines of Twiford" (Graham 1937). Gunston Hall was patterned after Wakefield (Rodnick 1941:44) (fig. 10.3). Regardless of the design's derivation, the WNMA applauded it, and under Rust's direction Donn's design plans were also exhibited to descendants of the Washington family, who gave their approval as well, further legitimizing the project (Hatch 1979:85).

Donn's design called for a structure fifty feet long and thirty-eight feet wide, *aligned north and south*. As noted here, the original foundations uncovered by Stewart in 1896 were about thirty-eight feet long and twenty feet wide, *oriented east and west*. This means that approximately "half of the Memorial House . . . [was] built where no foundations ever existed. . . . The Wakefield Association has built a Memorial House without any attention being paid to the original foundations in the ground" (Rodnick 1941:54–55). Furthermore, it was modeled after structures not proven to look anything like the original house built by Augustine Washington, Sr., in a location not demonstrated archaeologically to be the original site. All of this was based on the popular memory of the earliest loca-

Figure 10.3. Gunston Hall, home of George Mason, Fairfax County, Virginia. (Courtesy National Park Service, George Washington Birthplace National Monument.)

tion of the Custis stone, whose marking of the original birth site in the first place was still under debate.

The WNMA's logic, or illogic, in this rather glaring discrepancy was explained by Hoppin, who stated that "the excavations made in 1895 and 1926 reveal confirmation of what has been common knowledge for many years in the vicinity of Wakefield, i.e., that stone and brick have been removed from the old walls for use in other structures . . . consequently, the excavations and probings prove that the entire north wall of the foundation was removed many years ago" (Hoppin 1930a:154–62).

The WNMA chose to invoke the popular memory of local residents as well as "memories by descendants of the Washington family who never saw the original house" (Rodnick 1941:49) in an effort to legitimize Donn's building plan, whereas in regard to the location of the structure, such oral history had previously been ignored.

In spite of the fact that "the size of the building was most arbitrarily arrived at" and "completely inconsistent with the foundations" (Rodnick 1941:55), Hoppin's explanation was persuasive enough to allow FAC chairman Charles Moore to approve the design of the house. In fact, the FAC gave its approval not only to the architectural plan, but also to the destruction of the original foundations discovered by Stewart in 1896. These controversial foundations were indeed destroyed, without documentation, when construction on the Memorial House began in 1930. There was some objection; in a letter to the director of the Wakefield project, NPS landscape architect Charles Peterson referred to the excavation of the site of the Memorial House as "one of the most culpably destructive operations of which I have ever heard. To tear out the last remaining evidence of a structure of such important historical associations as these without first having made an accurate record of the findings is an inexcusable act of presumption by the architect . . . a great archaeological crime has been perpetrated" (Peterson 1930).

However, Edward Donn and Josephine Wheelright Rust defended the demolition on the grounds that "little value would be achieved by stopping the work of destruction" (Hatch 1979:95), particularly with the bicentennial of George Washington's birthday looming. In a brief memorandum to NPS director Horace Albright, NPS assistant director Arno Cammerer noted that "Peterson has a reaction similar to some others, who however have subordinated their opinions in the long run to the majority. I hope that Peterson will consider his opinions privately and not give voice to them publicly to our and his embarrassment" (Cammerer

1930). With the backing of the FAC and the construction plans on schedule, the NPS did not intervene.

Archaeology and the Deconstruction of a Myth

In September and October of 1930, with the reconstruction of the Memorial House and Ancient Kitchen about to begin, archaeological exploration led to additional discoveries of the utmost significance. Under the direction of Edward Donn, O. G. Taylor excavated trenches across a mound located about sixty feet south and west of the Memorial House site. Taylor excavated just enough to uncover the foundation of "a 'U' shaped building of considerable size . . . fifty-eight feet long and nineteen feet wide" on an east-west orientation (Taylor, quoted in Rodnick 1941:56), consisting of four units with a full cellar. Including both wings, the structure was nearly seventy feet long. By comparison with the "slight foundations at the old monument site, these new ones were massive" (Hatch 1979:88), and obviously not the remains of a dependency or outbuilding. Donn was "duly impressed and saw elements of a residence" (Hatch 1979:88). He drew a conjectural sketch of Building X, as he called it, and submitted it to WNMA historian Charles Arthur Hoppin for his opinion (fig. 10.4). Feeling that "any delay in building the house would prove rather embarrassing to the Wakefield Association" (Rodnick 1941:59), Hoppin responded that "it has never been possible for me to entertain a notion of any other site or house on any other part of the Wakefield estate, as the birthplace site and house, than the one where the monument was placed. I do not believe that there is anything whatever, or ever was anything, that can or ever could alter the site of the birthhouse" (Hoppin 1930b).

Even naming the structure Building X, rather than giving it a name that identifies its purpose, illustrates its controversial nature. Other sites encountered at GWBNM during this period were often identified and interpreted with minimal research or excavation and given names such as the Barn Site or the Ice House, based on the conjectural interpretation of the site's purpose. For example, a fourteen-foot-square brick foundation was discovered in 1935, and in spite of having no archaeological evidence to interpret the structure's purpose, based upon "its size and location," from that point on it was interpreted as a smokehouse (Worthington, quoted in Rodnick 1941:69–70). Even though archaeological excavation in 1936 failed to uphold the supposition that the structure was a smokehouse, it continued to be interpreted as such until the 1970s (Powell 1968:67–72).

Figure 10.4. Conjectural sketch of the Building X foundations. (Courtesy National Park Service, George Washington Birthplace National Monument.)

Hence, it was common during this period at GWBNM for structures to be named and interpreted in this manner. However, because of the size of Building X, it could not be interpreted as simply an outbuilding or dependency, but it could certainly not be interpreted by the WNMA or NPS as a residence, either.

Thus, although the discovery of Building X added to the controversy regarding "the true nature of the foundations located on the traditional birth site plot, construction of the Memorial House commenced a month later, according to schedule" (Jones et al. 1999:3–4). The full implication of the discovery of Building X "was imperfectly seen or recognized until it was too late," especially with the bicentennial of Washington's birth less than two years away (Hatch 1979:88). The foundations of Building X were backfilled, and its complete excavation postponed indefinitely.

Edward Donn apparently resolved his earlier doubts after construction began on the Memorial House and Ancient Kitchen. Donn's interpretation of Building X was that it could not have been a residence because at least three, if not all four, of the units had been built at different times, and because none of the four fireplaces were large enough to be kitchen fireplaces (Donn to Peterson 1932, in Rodnick 1941:60). The latter can be explained by the possibility of a separate cooking structure, and the former is simply irrelevant (Powell 1968:66). However, in spite of the fact that Donn gave no persuasive reasons, he supported the location of the Memorial House.

The Memorial House and Ancient Kitchen were completed in the spring of 1931 and opened to the public in July (Powell 1968:8). On February 22, 1932, a special open house was held to commemorate the bicentennial of George Washington's birthday, featuring a service to honor Josephine Wheelright Rust, who had died just before the completion of the Memorial House. In its final form, the Memorial House consisted of "a house of eight rooms, four downstairs and four in the half story upstairs, with a central hallway on each floor" (U.S. Department of the Interior 1941:13–14). An undated NPS pamphlet reports that "the present building has . . . been designed according to tradition about the old place and is typical of the period. . . . From its portals one beholds a beautiful view of Popes Creek and the Potomac River, and the house enjoys an environment which time has little changed" (U.S. Department of the Interior n.d.:2), an idyllic description that belies the turbulent history behind the construction of the traditional birth site.

In 1932, Phillip Hough became the first superintendent of GWBNM. Described as having "a keen appreciation of the value of archaeological research," he felt that archaeological investigation was "fundamental to the proper planning of this Monument" (Powell 1968:13). In December of 1935 Hough submitted a proposal for a comprehensive archaeological program that included research at Building X (Jones et al. 1999:4; Powell 1968:15). Excavation began in the spring of 1936 under the supervision of historian F. Northington, Jr., with labor furnished by the Civilian Conservation Corps (CCC).

Building X was carefully and systematically excavated, with attention to provenience, and extensive section drawings, photographs, plans, and detailed notes (Jones et al. 1999:4; Powell 1968:29–66). The results of this investigation exposed "a substantial multi-cellared brick foundation enclosing an ash and burned rubble layer . . . strongly suggest[ing] that Building X, rather than the foundation sealed beneath the Memorial House, was the true Wakefield" (Jones et al. 1999:4). Further support was provided by the more than 14,000 artifacts recovered from Building X, the types and time spans of which were consistent with the documented Washington family occupation (Jones et al. 1999:4; Powell 1968:41–66).

In spite of his interest in archaeological exploration, Superintendent Hough objected to the notion that Building X was the true birthplace. According to Hough, Building X "could not have been the principal structure—as it did not face the view afforded" (Hough, quoted in Rodnick

1941:78), or what he believed to be the most desirable panorama. Such a criticism is obviously neither valid nor relevant, as it only reflects Hough's opinion of what the birth home of George Washington should have been like. Furthermore, Rodnick (1941:78) has pointed out that "in terms of the eighteenth-century geometrical spacing of outbuildings around the mansion, House 'X' is the central building, since the other foundations are almost in line with it. On the other hand, if the Memorial House is assumed to be the central building, then there is no geometrical patterning."

Hough's archaeology program was terminated at the close of 1936 due to budget cutbacks. Nevertheless, another archaeological program was proposed and approved under the supervision of historian David Rodnick but was canceled due to wartime curtailment of the CCC (Jones et al. 1999:4; Powell 1968:14–18). Additional archaeological research at GWBNM was forestalled for nearly three decades.

In spite of Superintendent Hough's legitimization of the Memorial House site, the old questions regarding its authenticity still lingered. The information gathered from Northington's reexcavation of Building X was sufficient for Secretary of the Interior Harold Ickes to contact FAC chairman Charles Moore. Moore enlisted the help of historical architect Fiske Kimball to examine the data from Building X (Hatch 1979:93). In 1937, Kimball (quoted in Rodnick 1941:90–91) wrote that there was "no escape from the belief that these [Building X foundations] . . . were the foundations of the mansion house. They show a house of exceptional importance for the early 18th century—a house of four major rooms downstairs with four major chimneys, fully commensurate with the extent of Augustine Washington's inventory. This house of 'U' shape is a welcome instance of the survival of Jacobean types of plan. . . . It is too bad these foundations were not known in 1930."

Of course, the foundations of Building X were in fact "known" in 1930, as they were discovered *before* construction even began on the Memorial House. Kimball went on to say that the foundations under the Memorial House were "rightly regarded as inadequate for those of Washington's birthplace" and represented the remains of a large outbuilding, not the original birthplace of George Washington (Kimball, quoted in Rodnick 1941:90–91). Of course, at this point it was too late, and the official meaning of George Washington Birthplace National Monument was "authentically" sealed in handmade native brick.

The "confirmation, findings, and discussions (perhaps debates) in 1936 and 1937 did ultimately have an effect on interpretation" at GWBNM (Hatch 1979:97). The Memorial House was no longer "offered as a rep-

lica, a reproduction, or a likeness but rather as a period type, only suggestive of the times" (Rodnick 1941:86). This is confirmed by NPS publications that declare that the Memorial House is not "a replica" (Hudson
1956:29; U.S. Department of the Interior 1941:13) or "exact reproduction" (U.S. Department of the Interior n.d.:2). In spite of this concession,
the National Park Service was not quite ready to admit that Building X
was the structure built by Augustine Washington, Sr., and the actual birth
site of George Washington. Hudson's 1956 NPS historical handbook for
GWBNM cryptically mentions the possibility that Building X, "rather
than the smaller foundation on the memorial mansion site about 60 feet
away, was the exact spot where George Washington was born." This notion "cannot be ignored and will perhaps always remain an intriguing
question" (Hudson 1956:37).

New Directions

This "intriguing question" was addressed in due time. In 1967, GWBNM
administration submitted a master plan for cultural resource management
at the park, which called for continuing archaeological studies "to locate
dependencies and other physical features associated with the birthplace"
in advance of any further development at the site (U.S. Department of the
Interior 1967:20). Once again, this resurgence of archaeological research
at GWBNM was prompted by the patriotic social climate of the time, in
this case the upcoming bicentennial celebration of the Declaration of Independence (Jones et al. 1999:8).

In 1968, archaeologist B. Bruce Powell completed an evaluation of past
archaeological work at GWBNM as well as a reanalysis of previously
excavated materials. Powell's study resulted in "an informative synthetic
overview of archaeological information and potential that included a series of recommendations with implications for management and planning
with respect to cultural resources within the park" (Jones et al. 1999:4).
Powell called for a "fresh look at the underground remains at the National
Monument" and advised against any further reconstruction, but recommended a reinvestigation of previously developed areas (Powell 1968:
101–2). Based on his extensive overview and reanalysis of the remains of
Building X, he recommended "that Building X be re-excavated, stabilized,
and permanently exhibited to the public. . . . *I also recommend that it be
identified as the birth site of George Washington*" (Powell 1968:102;
emphasis in original). Powell was not the first researcher to make this
recommendation publicly, but it appears to be the first time that opposi-

tion to the location of the Memorial House was taken seriously by NPS administration.

Partly in an effort to address some of the issues raised by Powell, a series of archaeological projects supervised by Norman Barka were conducted in 1974 and 1975 by Southside Historical Sites, Inc., marking the first investigations at GWBNM to be "undertaken by trained archaeologists within the parameters of the established discipline of historical archaeology" (Jones et al. 1999:8). These excavations resulted in a number of important discoveries that presented a more complete picture of the history of the area (Barka 1978:1), including the location of a storage pit feature in association with an earth-fast structure in the Colonial Garden area. Originally identified as an outbuilding, the "location and orientation of the post structure, along with the presence of an apparent root cellar within it, have led to the reinterpretation that it was a dwelling, possibly a slave quarter" (Pogue and White 1994:32). This represents the first mention of the impact of African-Americans at GWBNM.

Three years after Southside Historical Sites, Inc., completed their excavations, site inventory forms were filed at the Virginia Research Center for Archaeology. Thus, "after almost a century of archaeological investigations, the resources [at GWBNM] were finally entered into the state's public record of archaeological sites" (Jones et al. 1999:5).

Archaeological research and interpretation continued at GWBNM during the 1970s and 1980s. Although archaeological research was still generally focused on sites directly associated with the Washington family and the colonial period, prehistoric American Indian sites were also recorded and tested (Blades 1979). Today, archaeological research and interpretation at GWBNM are centered on the identification of all "cultural resources, whether historic or prehistoric, so that a framework for a comprehensive interpretation of past lifeways at GWBNM can be developed to aid in planning and management efforts" (Jones et al. 1999:9). The 1999 cultural landscape report examines GWBNM as "a complex landscape composed of many layers of history" and includes recommendations for the understanding and interpretation of African-American and prehistoric American Indian sites (U.S. Department of the Interior 1999:1.6, 1.40–1.41).

A comprehensive archaeological survey carried out under a cooperative agreement between the National Park Service and the Colonial Williamsburg Foundation in 1997 and 1998 "reflects the expanded interests of contemporary archaeologists" and park management (Jones et al. 1999:9). Thus, while previous research and interpretation at GWBNM focused exclusively on the Washington family and on George Washington, more recently the focus has been on identifying *all* the cultural resources of the area, including those associated with American Indians and African-Americans.

Conclusion

Powell (1968:2) has noted that "the problems of understanding the historical remains at George Washington Birthplace National Monument are old problems. It seems, at this time and from this distance, that decisions in the past have sometimes been made on the basis of expediency, personal preference, incomplete evidence, or misunderstanding." Clearly, "at this time and at this distance," the current leadership at GWBNM is aware that there is more than one static meaning at the site. Today, GWBNM is concerned with the interpretation of the meaning of the site to all the groups represented in its history, and with the use of archaeological investigation to that end, in order to present a more complete picture of the area to the public.

Historical archaeologists have long declared that the past shapes the present as a means for legitimizing archaeological research at historic sites. However "a viewpoint archaeologists less often acknowledge is that the present shapes our rendering of the past" (Spector 1993:18). To groups such as the Wakefield National Memorial Association, the social and political context of the time demanded that the memorialized space at GWBNM represent an idealized patriotic past exemplified by the "Father of Our Country" who resided there. Today, visitors are able to explore the history of the site and its meaning to all the groups who have lived and worked there throughout history. The importance in historical archaeology of examining this "active relationship between the past and the present" (Shanks and Tilley 1987:2) is quite clear in the unusually long history of how memory and meaning have been inextricably intertwined at George Washington Birthplace National Monument.

References

Barka, Norman F.
  1978   Archaeology of George Washington Birthplace, Virginia. Southside Historical Sites, Inc. Department of Anthropology, College of William and Mary, Williamsburg, Virginia.
Blades, Brooke S.
  1979   Archaeological Excavations at the Henry Brooks and John Washington

Sites, George Washington Birthplace National Monument, Westmoreland County, Virginia. U.S. Department of the Interior, National Park Service, Mid-Atlantic Region, Office of Planning and Resource Preservation. Report on file at Colonial Williamsburg Foundation, Williamsburg, Virginia.

Cammerer, Arno
1930   Memorandum to NPS Director Horace Albright. George Washington Birthplace National Monument file, U.S. Deparment of the Interior, National Park Service, Washington, D.C.

Daily National Intelligencer, Washington, D.C.
1857   [description of the remains of the birthplace of George Washington] November 11. On file at George Washington Birthplace National Monument, Westmoreland County, Virginia.

1858   [report on Governor Wise's visit in response to the local movement to memorialize George Washington's birthplace] May 5. On file at George Washington Birthplace National Monument, Westmoreland County, Virginia.

Davis, Dwight
1928   Letter to Josephine Wheelright Rust, January 31, 1928. Record Group 66, Wakefield Association Files, Fine Arts Commission, National Archives, Washington, D.C.

Graham, Leona
1937   Memorandum from Leona Graham, Executive Assistant Secretary of the Interior, to Mr. Berlew, July 9, 1937. Research Correspondence file. George Washington Birthplace National Monument, Westmoreland County, Virginia

Handler, Richard, and Eric Gable
1997   The New History in an Old Museum: Creating the Past at Colonial Williamsburg. Duke University Press, Durham, North Carolina.

Hatch, Charles E., Jr.
1979   Chapters in the History of Popes Creek Plantation, published by the Wakefield National Memorial Association in cooperation with the U.S. Department of the Interior, National Park Service, Washington, D.C.

Hoppin, Charles A.
1926   The House in Which George Washington Was Born. Tyler's Quarterly Historical and Genealogical Magazine, VIII(2) October: 85–86.

1930a How the Size and Character of Washington's Birthplace Were Ascertained by the Wakefield National Memorial Association, Incorporated. Tyler's Quarterly Historical and Genealogical Magazine, 11(3) January: 146–62.

1930b Letter to Edward Donn. October 24. George Washington Birthplace National Monument files, Westmoreland County, Virginia.

Hudson, J. Paul
1956   George Washington Birthplace National Monument, Virginia. National

Park Service Historical Series Pamphlet #26. U.S. Department of the Interior, Washington, D.C.

Jones, Joe B., Julie Richter, Elizabeth Grzymala, and Paul Moyer
1999 Comprehensive Archaeological Survey of George Washington Birthplace National Monument. Colonial Williamsburg Foundation, College of William and Mary, Williamsburg, Virginia.

Keim, De B. Randolph
1873 A Guide to the Potomac River, Chesapeake Bay, and James River. *Alexandria [Virginia] Gazette,* June 11, 42–45.

Leslie, Linda, and Bill Choyke
1991 Westmoreland Washingtoniana. *Washington Post,* February 15, N68.

Linenthal, Edward Tabor
1999 The Problems and Promise of Public History. Paper presented at the "Commemoration, Conflict, and the American Landscape Conference," College Park, Maryland. Sponsored by the Department of Anthropology, University of Maryland, College Park.

Martin, Joseph
1835 *A New and Comprehensive Gazetteer of Virginia and the District of Columbia* vol. 291. Charlottesville, Virginia.

Olmsted, Frederick Law, Jr.
1929 Letter to Charles Moore, March 18. Record Group 66, Wakefield Files, Fine Arts Commission, National Archives.

Olson, Sarah
1974 Historic Furnishing Study: The Ancient Kitchen and Colonial Garden, George Washington Birthplace National Monument, Virginia. Typescript. Denver Service Center Historic Preservation Team, U.S. Department of the Interior, Denver.

Peterson, Charles
1930 Letter to the Director of the Wakefield Project, November 21. Record Group 79, National Park Service Records, National Archives. Washington, D.C.

Pogue, Dennis J., and Esther C. White
1994 Reanalysis of Features and Artifacts Excavated at George Washington's Birthplace, Virginia. *Quarterly Bulletin of the Archaeological Society of Virginia* 49(1): 32–45.

Powell, B. Bruce
1968 Archeology of the Popes Creek Area, George Washington Birthplace National Monument, Virginia. Typescript. U.S. Department of the Interior, National Park Service, Washington, D.C. On file at George Washington Birthplace National Monument, Westmoreland County, Virginia.

Rodnick, David
1941 Orientation Report on the George Washington Birthplace National Monument. Typescript. U.S. Department of the Interior, National Park

Service, Washington, D.C. On file at George Washington Birthplace National Monument, Westmoreland County, Virginia.

Rogers, Edmund B.

1958   George Washington Birthplace National Monument: History of Legislation through the 82nd Congress. U.S. Department of the Interior, National Park Service, Washington, D.C.

Shanks, Michael, and Christopher Tilley

1987   *Reconstructing Archaeology: Theory and Practice.* Cambridge University Press, New York.

Singleton, Teresa

1990   The Archaeology of the Plantation South: A Review of Approaches and Goals. *Historical Archaeology* 24(4): 70–77.

Spector, Janet D.

1993   *What This Awl Means: Feminist Archaeology at a Wahpeton Dakota Village.* Minnesota Historical Society Press, St. Paul.

U.S. Department of the Interior. National Park Service.

1941   *George Washington Birthplace National Monument.* Pamphlet. U.S. Government Printing Office, Washington, D.C.

1967   Master Plan for George Washington Birthplace National Monument. Typescript on file at George Washington Birthplace National Monument, Westmoreland County, Virginia.

1999   *George Washington Birthplace National Monument, Westmoreland County, Virginia, Cultural Landscape Report.* Volume 1, *Historical and Existing Conditions Documentation.* Northeast Region Philadelphia Support Office. Prepared by Oculus, Charlottesville, Virginia, in association with FPW Architects, Charlottesville, Virginia, and John Milner Associates, Alexandria, Virginia.

N.d.   *Wakefield: Washington's Birthplace.* Pamphlet. Published by George Washington Birthplace National Monument, Westmoreland County, Westmoreland, Virginia. On file at George Washington Birthplace National Monument.

Vosburgh, Frederick G.

1949   Shrines of Each Patriot's Devotion. *National Geographic,* January, 51–82.

Wakefield National Memorial Association (WNMA)

1923   Minutes of the First Meeting of the Wakefield National Memorial Association, June 11, 1923. Typescript copy. Record Group 66, Wakefield Files, Fine Arts Commission, National Archives, Washington, D.C.

Weinberger, J. A.

1858   The Home of Washington at Mount Vernon. *Williamsburg Virginia Gazette,* October.

Wells, Camille

1994   Social and Economic Aspects of Eighteenth-Century Housing on the

Northern Neck of Virginia. Ph.D. dissertation, College of William and Mary, Williamsburg, Virginia.

Wilbur, Ray Lyman

1932   Speech describing the Memorial Mansion on Dedication Day, May 14. Mimeograph. Colonial National Historical Park Library. George Washington Birthplace National Monument, Westmoreland County, Virginia.

Acknowledgments

My sincere appreciation goes to John Frye, James Laray, and the staff at George Washington Birthplace National Monument, Virginia, for their assistance and research contributions to this paper. Andrew Edwards, Matthew Reeves, and Stephen Potter also provided many useful comments and suggestions. Special thanks to Paul Shackel for inviting me to participate in this volume, and for his continuing mentorship and guidance.

11

Nostalgia and Tourism: Camden Yards in Baltimore

Erin Donovan

> The conservation, management, and exploitation of visible heritage in the landscape is now a flourishing "growth industry" in many countries.
> —Lily Kong and Brenda Yeoh

Introduction

Oriole Park and PSINet Stadium, the current homes of the Baltimore Orioles baseball and Ravens football teams, are collectively referred to as Camden Yards. The name, along with parts of two buildings that have been architecturally incorporated into the stadium complex, is all that remains of the central rail yard and station of the B & O Railroad. Virtually nothing in the landscape is reminiscent of the history of the area prior to the 1852 establishment of Camden Station, or of the industrial legacy of the site that followed the occupation of the railroad. Additionally, there is no interpretive signage to indicate to visitors the original use of the two buildings that are preserved, or the social history of the area as a whole (fig. 11.1).

Thus, as I began to research Camden Yards, I found myself wondering what R. Christopher Goodwin & Associates, Inc., the company that performed the cultural resource inventory of the area, meant by "Camden Yards, the new home of Oriole Park, now serves as a monument to those that lived and worked in that neighborhood and who laid the foundation for America's favorite pastime" (Goodwin 1992:296). Certainly it appears to be a modern monument, but rather than one dedicated to better understanding the struggles of working-class peoples in the past, it is committed to the present. Developed by urban planners and architects to enhance both the image and income of the City of Baltimore, Camden Yards

Figure 11.1. Camden Yards Sports Complex. November 1998. (Photo: Ron Acee.)

focuses not on educating Baltimoreans about bloody labor strikes but on reinventing the past to conjure feelings of nostalgia about the good old days and baseball and to promote an image of progress.

Although it has been the center of controversy, Camden Yards functions as an entertainment complex. Anthropological theory can certainly be applied to the understanding of this phenomenon, but where does it leave archaeologists, historians, museum professionals, and the like? Even in museum environments, postmodern theory has challenged these disciplines to question their own motives and to move toward representation of multiple perspectives in their interpretations of the past. The question of how the past can be accurately interpreted within nonmuseum environments is even more complicated. Does the act of preserving historic structures necessitate historic interpretation at all? Is history misrepresented through the lack of interpretation, or, since meaning changes through time anyway, is it legitimate to appropriate the past for use in the present?

Camden Yards: A Brief History

In 1783, the eighty-five-acre area now known as Camden Yards was annexed into the City of Baltimore. Prior to that, Rochambeau's forces camping in the area and some land speculation were the only activities that made the maps. The northern portion of the area was settled earliest (circa 1804), primarily by upper-class whites in rowhouses on main streets and lower-class whites and freed blacks in the alleys. Brickyards and clay pits were to the west through the 1820s. By the 1850s, the majority of the area was residential, with Irish and German immigrants replacing the more affluent populations of the past decades (Goodwin 1992).

In 1852, the B&O Railroad established Camden Station. The area became a mix of industrial and residential, with most southern expansion being for warehouses and the like, and housing becoming smaller and catering to unskilled laborers. During this time, one of the most violent strikes in labor history occurred at Camden Yards. Apparently, despite public statements of financial stability, B&O Railroad common stock fell dramatically early in 1877, bringing about a second 10 percent wage cut. As workers rebelled against the cut, B&O president John Work Garrett sought to keep the railroad operating. "The unhappy workers knew that Garrett would be quick to bring in strike breakers to man the trains and break the strike. They resolved to seize the trains and yards and to scare off the scabs with violence if necessary. On Monday, July 16, a hot and sticky day in Baltimore, the trouble started at Camden Junction" (Stover 1987:285). This strike was short-lived, but four days later, news of Governor John Lee Carroll's plans to send troops to stop workers from blocking trains in Cumberland brought the strike back to life. The Fifth and Sixth Regiments were instructed to meet at Camden Station and go by train to Cumberland. A mob of some 15,000 reacted to the order by assaulting troops, tearing up tracks, toppling passenger cars, and setting fires. The troops responded by firing into the crowd. Of 120 men in the Sixth Regiment, only 59 reached Camden Station. Ultimately, federal troops were called in to stop the violence (Stover 1987). The strike was one of the bloodiest in the history of the railroad.

Camden Station is also known for its use by the Underground Railroad and as the place where Lincoln secretly changed trains in his effort to travel safely from Pennsylvania to Washington, D.C., during the Civil War (*Commercial Renovation* 1993). After the war, the area became segregated, and ultimately primarily black. Residences were either replaced by industry, or combined with commercial establishments such as saloons. By the 1930s the area was completely industrial (Goodwin 1992).

Modern Development at Camden Yards

In 1987, the decision to build a new Orioles stadium at Camden Yards was made, and the area was again transformed (*Commercial Renovation* 1993). An overview of archival, archaeological, and architectural studies was produced by R. Christopher Goodwin & Associates, Inc., on behalf of the Maryland Stadium Authority and in compliance with Maryland Historic Preservation Legislation. In essence, according to Sue Sanders, Senior Project Manager at R. Christopher Goodwin & Associates, Inc., because state funding would be utilized in the construction of a ballpark on the site of the industrial Camden Yards, the Maryland Historical Trust required that an archaeological investigation of the eighty-five-acre project area be carried out prior to development (Goodwin 1992; Sue Sanders, personal communication, September 1998).

During the course of these investigations, the Ruth Saloon Site became the favorite of both the media and public programming. As Babe Ruth's father had once owned and operated a saloon where centerfield now is, there seemed good reason to celebrate this fact. However, none of the artifacts recovered from the excavation can be associated with the Ruth occupation of the site. Although it is not archaeologically significant, the Ruth Site was used for school days and press days and continues to be represented in the exhibits of the Babe Ruth Museum. Unfortunately, the curatorial staff at the museum is not aware of the artifacts' true affiliation and thus misrepresents them as belonging to the Ruth family (Goodwin 1990; Sanders, September 1998).

Through archival research and subsequent examination of material culture remains, only the James Pawley Pottery Kiln and J. S. Berry Pug Mill sites were determined to be significant enough to warrant more extensive excavations in the future (Goodwin 1992). Phase III excavations were subsequently conducted, and parts of both structures are currently "preserved" beneath the pavement of the Ravens' stadium (Goodwin 1998).

The architectural documentation of eight buildings within the project area was another component of the project. According to Peter Curtz, Administrator of Evaluation and Registration in the National Register Program of the Maryland Historical Trust, with the direction of the Trust the eight structures were documented according to Historic American Buildings Survey and Historic American Engineering Survey formats (Curtz 1998). These records, compiled prior to demolition and housed at the Maryland Historical Trust, are seen as permanent preservation. Structures include the Diggs-Johnson School, the B&O Office Building, Maryland Office Interiors, Baltimore Thermal Energy Corporation, the Monumental Hotel Supply Company, the W. B. Cassell Company Office and Warehouse, and the Inland-Leidy Chemical Company. The firm did not deem the B&O Railroad Warehouse, once attached to the B&O Railroad Office Building and now incorporated into the stadium complex, significant enough to preserve in situ and did not actively pursue nominating any sites or buildings to the National Register of Historic Places. Camden Station, the second building preserved on the site, was not addressed by the archaeological investigations since it would not be impacted (Goodwin 1992; Sue Sanders, personal communication, September 1998).

Although recommendations were made by the archaeologists for future public programming, these were primarily limited to discussions of the Babe Ruth Saloon, the James Pawley Pottery Kiln, and the J. S. Berry Pug Mill. To the archaeologists' credit, the Maryland Stadium Authority does currently have a small interpretive exhibit based on the latter two topics on view within the Ravens' stadium. Unfortunately, there is no legal component requiring this small exhibit to be permanent, and it is not accessible to the general public. There is no interpretive signage on the exteriors of the buildings nor was Camden Station documented as a site or recommended for the National Register of Historic Places. There was no mention in the archaeological reports of the labor strike of 1877. As a result, important elements of the history of the area continue to be overlooked.

Following the period of archaeological documentation, demolition and construction began. The Orioles' stadium opened for the 1992 baseball season (Rogers 1992) and the Ravens' stadium opened for football season in 1998 (Rogers 1998).

Politics at Play

The development of Camden Yards into a sports complex was the direct result of "political tussles between Orioles owner Edward Bennett Williams and Mayor-turned-Governor William Donald Schaefer that led to the building of the park to keep the team in Baltimore" (Richmond 1993: jacket). Seen in a larger context, the decision was but one of many made as part of a conscious effort of both the state and the city to revitalize the downtown area of Baltimore and thus increase revenues.

For example, in 1967, the Baltimore City Planning Commission printed a pamphlet entitled, "Baltimore: Preservation of the City's Character." It stated, "Herein are guidelines for a vigorous future built on a vigorous past, combining the best of both in a city being planned for people" (Baltimore Department of Planning 1967:1). Goals outlined in the publication included preserving sites identified with the history of Baltimore or the nation, buildings that were architecturally unique, whole neighborhoods, and sites considered symbolic of social or ethnic groups (Baltimore Department of Planning 1967:4).

In 1977, the same commission published "Baltimore's Development Program." The plan emphasized "preserving and rehabilitating the existing stock" (Baltimore Department of Planning 1977a:7). An appendix to this general plan, the "Historic Preservation Impact Assessment" (Baltimore Department of Planning 1977b) was prepared in compliance with federal regulations. The assessment determined that the largest threat to National Register properties in Baltimore was neglect and deterioration caused by their vacant and socioeconomically depressed status. The development plan, with its intent to encourage rehabilitation of existing structures, was viewed as primarily a positive change agent for historic properties (Baltimore Department of Planning 1977b).

By preserving the 1898 B&O Railroad Warehouse and Camden Station, preservation decisions at Camden Yards embodied these ideas of development by preserving the existing stock and by rehabilitating deteriorating structures. They further fit with Baltimore's city planning by extending the development area referred to as the Inner Harbor and advancing economic development goals, including increasing revenue through tourism.

In spite of the commitment of the state, however, the public was not initially anxious to embrace the idea. Reluctant to think that a new facility was needed or worth the inconvenience or expense, Baltimoreans opposed the project. They treasured Thirty-third Street's Memorial Stadium, a gathering place since 1922, and saw no need for change (Bagli 1992).

Partially in response to this opposition, the Maryland Stadium Authority, the organization responsible for the project, enlisted the assistance of the architectural firm Hellmuth, Obata & Kassabaum (HOK) Sports to work with them and the Baltimore Orioles in the creation of a stadium that would appeal to Baltimoreans' attachment to their history (Gunts 1992). A headline in the September 21, 1991 issue of the *Baltimore Sun* ran, "Stadium Agency Oks $11 Million for B&O Building." The article reported that the money would go toward the renovation of Camden Station, a structure dear to Baltimoreans' hearts. One of the B&O Railroad Warehouses was also saved and incorporated into Oriole Park as part of these efforts. True to the intentions of its designers, "this new ballpark is accepted because it fits," it is "unobtrusive as it blends with Camden Station and Warehouse, local hotels and neighborhood residences, [and] it has slipped into the area as comfortably as if it had been there for generations" (Bagli 1992). Joseph E. Spear, AIA, senior vice president of HOK, verifies this notion by explaining that key preservation decisions were made intentionally to make the park responsive to the place of Baltimore and to seem familiar (Spear 1992). Not only by incorporating historic architecture but by assuring "spectacular, picture-postcard views of the downtown skyline" as well, the stadium "celebrates Baltimore" (Gunts 1992:67).

Ironically, the same preservation efforts that placated Baltimore's citizens and planners by maintaining pieces of the city's history serve to obscure the other histories of the area. Don Fowler, in "Uses of the Past: Archaeology in the Service of the State" (1987:229), writes that "nation states, or partisans thereof, control and allocate symbolic resources as one means of legitimizing power and authority . . . a major symbolic resource is the past." Lily Kong (1993) addresses how new meanings are ascribed to previously "innocent" landscapes often to promote the politics and local structures of power and authority. In essence, by physically preserving part of Baltimore's history, developers were able to change the public meaning of the site without overt conflict.

Meaning and Symbolism at Camden Yards

"Amid the construction on Russell Street in Baltimore City, a symbol for the future is being built alongside a symbol for the past" (Preservation Maryland 1991:1). Camden Yards was intended by its creators to symbolize progress and prosperity to the city's own citizens as well as to visitors, an image Baltimore has often achieved through architectural endeavors. "Baltimore," the writer H. L. Mencken once observed, "is the one genuine cathedral city of our fair republic" (Gunts 1992:65). John Quincy Adams, in an 1827 toast, went so far as to label Baltimore the "Monumental City" (Hurry and Leone 1998:48). The cathedrals and monuments to which they refer were erected not only to commemorate people or events, but to promote the well-being of the City of Baltimore. These structures, generally visible from many angles, give the impression of prosperity and architectural superiority. In addition, they celebrate such figures as George Washington and war heroes and thus help to remind citizens of the greatness of their nation (Hurry and Leone 1998:31). Finally, they remind people of the ideals of the past.

Like these cathedrals and monuments, Camden Yards is a monumental structure, erected to promote the well-being of the City of Baltimore. Positioned at the convergence of I-95 and I-295, it is visible from afar and from many angles. It serves to remind people of the ideals of the past and it even celebrates such figures as Babe Ruth. Unfortunately, these images misrepresent and obscure much of the site's history.

"The model for ultimate glory is in the past. The classic corvette, the New York Yankees in their heyday . . . nostalgia for lost worlds spurs us onward to an imagined future that is really an idealized past" (Comer 1996:39–40). This concept of nostalgia, even more than the urban planning and development that helped to shape the Inner Harbor as a whole, can be seen as the driving force in "to preserve or not to preserve" at Camden Yards. Made by architects and planners, rather than historians or archaeologists, decisions regarding preservation were based on aesthetics rather than historical significance. The warehouse now incorporated into the structure of the baseball stadium proves an ideal example of this rationale. The original structure, constructed in 1898 as part of the B&O Railroad's Camden Yards, was initially intended to function as a warehouse (Goodwin 1992). Perhaps, too, it served as a symbol of the railroad's success or as a large, dominant structure in the lives of its workers. However, prior to incorporation into the stadium, it served instead as an abandoned reminder of the working-class American people who resided in small houses in the vicinity of the warehouse and worked for the railroad; it represented a bygone day of industrialization in the inner cities.

Regardless of these earlier associations, the building now functions as offices for the Maryland Stadium Authority and the Baltimore Orioles, and as home to a variety of merchandising and refreshment establishments. Symbolically, it serves to remind fans of the good old days, of baseball, the American dream. In this setting, the actual historical significance of the B&O Railroad Warehouse becomes insignificant. The building is not even listed on the National Register of Historic Places and no plaques or signs tell visitors about the building's original function.

Publicity surrounding the opening of Camden Yards provides evidence of this transformation of meaning. Oriole player Cal Ripken, Jr., for example, exclaimed on opening day, "This may be the first game, but it feels like baseball has been played here before" (Spear 1992). Another source states: "Saving the B&O Warehouse was a key decision that reinforced a number of objectives. It is a unique and instantly recognizable backdrop for television broadcasts and it creates a very warm and nostalgic sense" (Spear 1992). Yet another article discussed how the new park was to have its own identity and detail. This detail included dark-green slatted seats bearing the 1890s Baltimore Baseball Club logo and was part of a conscious decision by designers to include elements that triggered memories of older ballparks (Gunts 1992). Finally, from Peter Richmond in the book *Ballpark*: "Located on the site of an old railroad yard, the park turned back the clock from the days of sterile, round, cookie-cutter stadiums to the old-time charms of parks that were literally shaped by the cities they inhabited" (1992: jacket).

Thus, nostalgia and the idea of creating a setting that reflects what is considered to be American values contributed to the design of Oriole Park at Camden Yards. The deliberate manipulation of a historic structure to accomplish these ends is not unusual in the scheme of urban planning. "Heritage," states David Lowenthal at a 1998 lecture at the National Museum of American History, "is a malleable body of historical text subject to reinterpretation and easily twisted into myth." Many anthropologists and historians point to the reality that conservation of any structure makes it subject to reinterpretation in the context of modern society. Particularly in the case of urban conservation, the problem of changing meanings and symbolism is intensified by the fact that structures are often saved to promote economic development or to create nostalgia. Buildings are frequently preserved merely for aesthetic reasons, and original meanings and contexts are never even considered, let alone interpreted (Bower 1995; Ernstein 1998; Kong 1993; Kong and Yeoh 1994; Leone 1981; Lowenthal 1985).

The National Register of Historic Places (U.S. Department of the Interior 1969:1) states in its introduction: "If the past is the foundation of the present, then historic preservation is a cornerstone upon which efforts to improve present America can be built. Improvement of the old and familiar may be a better choice than destruction for the reward unknown. By this approach we choose not to impede progress, but to support it." As I review this statement, I see a major problem for historical archaeologists, historians, and museum professionals. Preservation tends to focus on structures themselves, on material culture as a physical entity, without interpreting the symbolic and cultural contexts from which the structures emerged or even those to which the structures become assigned. As structures are preserved within modern complexes, the resulting changes in meaning and symbolism can mislead the public as consumer. In essence, the public comes to identify the structure within its new context, perceiving a one-sided meaning promoted by the developers, and other meanings and functions can be forgotten.

Controversy and the Realities of Interpretation at Camden Yards

In 1996, the Cultural Cryptanalysts Collective (CCC) of Baltimore, an anonymous group describing itself as "a collective of individuals dedicated to revealing the secret messages found in our institutions, the media and our daily lives" (Lerner 1997:45), launched a project called Nine New Museums. According to Peter Walsh, an active member of Baltimore's arts

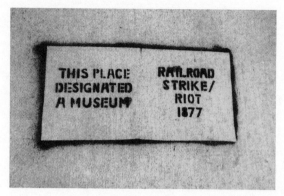

Figure 11.2. Stencil commemorating the Baltimore & Ohio Railroad labor strike of 1877. (Courtesy Cultural Cryptanalysts Collective, 1996.)

community and member of the CCC (Walsh 1999), the project was designed as a media hoax, pretending to be sponsored by the City of Baltimore. Nine sites were identified in the city that "possess a great deal of historic and cultural weight" (Lerner 1997:46). During July and August of 1996, a series of stencils reading "THIS PLACE DESIGNATED A MUSEUM" was created in an effort to alert Baltimoreans to their hidden past. Press releases, *ArtScape '96,* and the Internet were other ways in which the project manifested itself. One of the nine stencils was placed at Camden Yards and read, "THIS PLACE DESIGNATED A MUSEUM: RAILROAD STRIKE/ RIOT 1877" (Lerner 1997). That which the archaeologists had overlooked was, at least for a time, a designated site (fig. 11.2).

Curious about why I hadn't stumbled upon this labor strike before, I set out to look for answers. Under the mistaken impression that the plaque was permanent (rather than a stencil), I first scouted out Camden Yards. I found no signage indicating that a major labor strike had occurred at the site. In conversations in November 1998 with Ann Steel at the Museum of Industry, Eddie Leon at the Baltimore Commission for Historic and Architectural Preservation (CHAP), and Peter Curtz at the Maryland Historical Trust, I learned that none of them was aware of the project. The archivist at the B&O Railroad Museum, Anne Calhoun, told me in May 1999 that she had not heard of the project but was aware of the strike. She thought it would be interesting to know more about the strike from the railroad's perspective, but she did not have the appropriate documents in her collection and had never pursued the issue of interpreting the event. When I inquired about the content of guided tours at the stadium, Nolan Rogers, historian at Camden Yards, responded to inquiries about whether this event was in any way interpreted at Camden Yards by asking me why anyone would want to bring up such an embarrassing event in the history of the railroad (personal communication, November 1998).

Disturbed that the event was not in any way interpreted, I telephoned Bob Reynolds at the George Meaney Labor Archives in March 1999. He was well aware of the strike and its place in labor history and knew that the event was not interpreted to the public at Camden Yards. Interestingly, he pointed out that the omission and manipulation of labor uprisings are not unique to modern times but, rather, are the ways in which strikes are traditionally depicted. In the case of the strike at Camden Yards, for example, the event was immediately manipulated by the press (apparently serving the interests of the railroad) to seem unwarranted and irrational. Allan Pinkerton's *Strikers, Communists, Tramps, and Detectives* (1878) depicts the strikers in a negative light. Using such terms as "the bestial crowd," he praises the militia for holding their fire until "savagely attacked" (Pinkerton 1878:187). According to Pinkerton, "the soldiers were rudely beaten [by the] hordes of the strikers rushing in, like infuriated beasts of prey, scenting the blood of their torn victims" (Pinkerton 1878:188). He criticizes workers for striking, blaming them for not working their way to the top in this land of opportunity, and holding them directly responsible for both business failures and depressions. In the August 11, 1877, edition of *Harper's Weekly*, the labor strike was again reinterpreted to serve the interests of big business. The image in the publication shows the Sixth Regiment "fighting its way through Baltimore," glorifying the military rather than the workers (fig. 11.3). This biased rendition of the strike, following eighteenth-century military battle illustration conventions, is cited as a photograph. According to *Labor's Heritage*, the George Meaney Labor Archives' publication, this was not uncommon at the end of the nineteenth century. Publishers would obtain backdrop photographs of areas where events occurred, then hire artists to draw in the events themselves. In this way, photographs of strikes could be cited as real while actually reinterpreting events (Peterson 1997). Thus, the interpretation of Baltimore's 1877 strike denied the workers legitimacy from the onset. Today, Camden Yards continues to portray a sterile and peaceful image to the public, one that serves to enforce the authority of the dominant class.

Much as the original controversy over building the sports complex did, the controversy created over Camden Yards by the Cultural Cryptanalysts Collective eventually lost momentum, and there continues to be no interpretation of the event. Similarly, criticism about the fact that Camden

Figure 11.3. Biased depiction of the Baltimore & Ohio Railroad labor strike. *Harper's Weekly*, August 11, 1877. (Courtesy Maryland Historical Society.)

Station is not on the National Register of Historic Places has continued to be ignored. According to Eddie Leon of CHAP, letters have been received by their office regarding interpretation issues. In these instances, citizens requested that Camden Station be listed on the National Register of Historic Places and as a local landmark. The first letter, sent in 1973, received no response, as Camden Station was privately owned at the time. Another letter, received more recently, was passed along to the Maryland Stadium Authority. The station is still not on the National Register.

As for the future of interpretation, the George Meaney Labor Archives is producing a guide to labor history for the State of Maryland that will discuss the strike at Camden Yards. Nevertheless, Nolan Rogers is not likely to include the event in Camden Yards tours, and there is no organization currently working toward having the site commemorated. The Babe Ruth Museum will soon be opening up in the old Camden Station. The museum's curator, Greg Schwalenberg, once he was made aware of the fact that the building was not on the National Register of Historic Places, told me that he felt that it would be a good project for someone to pursue (June 1999). During the same conversation, however, he remarked that he understood why the "negative tales" of the past are not of interest to visitors, indicating that he will not work toward interpreting the event either.

Regarding other histories that will continue to be told at Camden Yards, there will always be the Babe Ruth connection. Commemorated by a statue within the complex, he lives on inside the walls of the stadium. Visitors to the Babe Ruth Museum can also view artifacts from the Ruth Saloon. Unfortunately, the artifacts predate the occupation of the Ruth Family and are thus misrepresented in the interest of perpetuating nostalgia.

As it stands today, preservation through incorporation of the B&O Railroad Warehouse and the restoration of Camden Station serves to provide the only historic material culture remains at Camden Yards (with the exception of the small exhibit in the Ravens' football stadium). There are no plaques or signs anywhere within the complex that indicate the original identities of the buildings (fig. 11.4). Patrons attend games at the football and baseball stadiums and enjoy the nostalgia of baseball and days gone by, only perhaps dimly aware of the industrial history of the site by the presence of the warehouse.

If visitors do choose to take a tour, Nolan Rogers is their best bet. He has written articles for the openings of both stadiums and is considered the house historian (Rogers 1992, 1998). Rogers sees no need to dredge up the

Figure 11.4. The Baltimore & Ohio Railroad Warehouse today. (Photo: Ron Acee.)

horrors of the B&O Railroad Strike and is not sure if Camden Station is on the National Register of Historic Places. He does see the value in letting people know that Lincoln was smuggled through Baltimore via Camden Station during the Civil War, and he would even like to see the building be a stop on the Civil War Trail, but he does not seem particularly interested in commemorating its use by the Underground Railroad. As he told me in November 1998, Rogers does, however, give context beyond the baseball and railroad history and lets tourists know about the firebrick and pottery kilns that predated the railroad. Other guides, since they are self-taught about the park's history, often focus their tours exclusively on baseball, centering on history only in the context of Babe Ruth and his family's saloon.

Conclusions

Museums are alive with talk of how to interpret preserved sites, attempting to tell the many sides of history (Gable and Handler 1997; Shanks and Tilley 1987). They are asking how to balance entertainment and education. This is enough of a challenge. But what of those many structures that have been preserved not for what can be learned from them about the past, but for reasons of aesthetics, urban planning and tourism? As we see with

Camden Yards, such preservation has led to a change in meaning and symbolism and to a lack of interpretation about the site's past.

It is impossible to define, let alone interpret, the original meaning of structures (Shanks and Tilley 1987). Symbolism—what material culture represents—is subject to context and to those who interpret its meaning. Thus, even sites preserved for the sake of interpretation are subject to changes in meaning. Sites such as Camden Yards, apparently, will suffer even more from this phenomenon as they are reinterpreted in a new context. These drastic changes in meaning are subject to criticism and cause conflict between those who view architecture merely as aesthetic and those who desire acknowledgment of original function and meaning through interpretation.

At Camden Yards, as is the case in much contract archaeology, archaeologists could have played a more active role in the preservation efforts and perhaps been effective in establishing a more balanced interpretation of the past. They could have worked to have Camden Station placed on the National Register of Historic Places, insuring that the building would have some interpretive signage. Additionally, they might have opted not to focus on the Ruth Saloon in their programming, working instead to interpret the industrial history of the area. Finally, they could have participated more actively in the preservation of the warehouse, at least gaining an interpretive plaque, perhaps even a permanent exhibition. Instead, virtually everything was mitigated and the opportunity was lost.

Organizations such as the Cultural Cryptanalysts Collective have shown that the public, too, can work toward a more balanced representation of history. Through their efforts, at least some of the population is now aware of the strike of 1877. Unfortunately, the dominant class has been continually successful in squelching the struggles of the working class. As we have seen, by appropriating the past for modern use, the dominant class continues to oppress the heritage of others. In the case of Camden Yards, the use of railroad buildings to perpetuate an image of nostalgia and a glorified past robs those laborers who fought there and deprives laborers who might identify with a history that they consider theirs. Similarly, the sterile image of the good old days continues to enforce dominant ideologies and leaves no room for those visitors who might want to know about other histories related to the site.

It is the responsibility of archaeologists, public historians, and museum professionals to work toward eliminating the biases of preservation, ridding our policies of their emphasis on merely the physical preservation of structures. Events may prove more significant than structures, and the original meaning of structures is significant enough to warrant interpretation. If meaning is derived from the perceptions of the observer, we must strive to make what is observed more inclusive of multiple perspectives and more representative of reality. We must not only participate as mitigators, but must also demand the authority to expand our investigations to include interpretation of buildings that may not be directly impacted (such as Camden Station) and to participate in ongoing preservation and interpretation activities. Only when archaeologists and museum professionals are able to work within the political realms of decision making will they be able to help multiple voices find their way into interpretation.

References

Bagli, Vince
    1992   Foreword to *The Baltimore Ballpark Project: The Creation of a Baseball Stadium,* by Janis Rettaliata. Self-published, Baltimore.
Baltimore Department of Planning
    1967   Baltimore: Preservation of the City's Character. On file, University of Maryland, Baltimore County Library, Catonsville, Maryland.
    1977a   Baltimore's Development Program. On file, University of Maryland, Baltimore County Library, Catonsville, Maryland.
    1977b   Historic Preservation Impact Assessment. On file, University of Maryland, Baltimore County Library, Catonsville, Maryland.
Baltimore Sun
    1973   Plans for Stadium Would Require Demolition of Old Camden Station. February 23, 6.
    1985   Homeowner Sees Irony in Stadium. December 6, B3.
    1989a   Camden Buildings Get Close Strutiny Before Demolition. August 28, 6B.
    1989b   Diggers at Orioles' New Digs Aiming for the Ruth's Saloon. December 12, A6.
    1990   Dig Seeks Secrets Buried under New Stadium Site. January 2, 5D.
    1991   Stadium Agency OKs $11 Million for B&O Building. September 21, 1B.
Belgrad, Herbert J.
    1990   Letter to Public, January 17. Addendum to Archaeological and Architectural Investigations at Camden Yards, 1992. On file, Maryland Stadium Authority, Baltimore.
Bower, Mim
    1995   Marketing Nostalgia: An Exploration of Heritage Management and Its Relation to the Human Consciousness. In *Managing Archaeology,* edited by Malcolm A. Cooper, Antony Firth, John Carmen, and David Wheatley, 33–39. Routledge, New York.
Cohen, Andrew
    1995   Birds in Paradise. *Athletic Business* 19(1): 51–55.

Comer, Douglas C.
1996   Ritual Ground. University of California Press, Berkeley.
Commercial Renovation
1993   Camden Station. Commercial Renovation, August, pp. 46–51.
Crosby, Theo
1970   The Necessary Monument: Its Future in the Civilized City. New York
        Graphics Society, New York.
Curtz, Peter
1998   Personal communication with the author. November.
Eco, Umberto
1973   Function and Sign: Semiotics of Architecture. Via 1:131–53.
Ernstein, Julie H.
1998   Nostalgia and the Perpetuation of an Historic Ideal: Two Views from a
        Twentieth-Century Maryland Suburb. Paper presented at the meeting of
        the Council for Northeast Historical Archaeology, Montreal, October 17.
Fagan, Brian M., and Charles E. Orser, Jr.
1995   Historical Archaeology. HarperCollins, New York.
Fowler, Don D.
1987   Uses of the Past: Archaeology in the Service of the State. American Antiq-
        uity 52(2): 229–48.
Fowler, Peter J.
1992   The Past in Contemporary Society: Then, Now. Routledge, London.
Goodwin, R. Christopher, and Associates, Inc.
1990   Archaeology and History at Camden Yards: The George Herman Ruth
        Saloon Site. Press packet. On file, Maryland Stadium Authority, Balti-
        more.
1992   Archaeological and Architectural Investigations at Camden Yards. On
        file, Maryland Stadium Authority, Baltimore.
1998   Phase III Investigations of the J. S. Berry Brick Mill and Architectural
        Mitigation of the Pawley Stoneware Kiln. On file, Maryland Stadium
        Authority, Baltimore.
Gunts, Edward
1983   Landmark Eyed for Factory Outlets. New American, September 23, 1A.
1992   Grand Stand. Architecture 81(7): 64–71.
Handler, Richard, and Eric Gable
1997   The New History in an Old Museum: Creating the Past at Colonial Wil-
        liamsburg. Duke University Press, Durham, North Carolina.
Hodder, Ian
1987   The Archaeology of Contextual Meanings. Cambridge University Press,
        London.
Hurry, Silas D., and Mark P. Leone
1998   Seeing: The Power of Town Planning in the Chesapeake. Historical Ar-
        chaeology 32(4): 31–59.

Inner Harbor Committee of the Citizen's Planning and Housing Association
1978   Planning for the Inner Harbor. On file, University of Maryland, Baltimore County Library, Catonsville, Maryland.
Kong, Lily
1993   Ideological Hegemony and the Political Symbolism of Religious Buildings in Singapore. *Environment and Planning: Society and Space* 11:23–45.
Kong, Lily, and Brenda S. A. Yeoh
1994   Urban Conservation in Singapore: A Survey of State Policies and Popular Attitudes. *Urban Studies* 31(2): 247–65.
Leone, Mark
1981   Archaeology's Relationship to the Present and the Past. In *Modern Material Culture and the Archaeology of Us,* edited by Richard A. Gould and Michael B. Schiffer, 5–14. Academic Press, New York.
Lerner, Adam J.
1997   Black Aggie, Cultural Cryptanalysts, and the Politics of Locality. *LINK* 2:41–51.
Linenthal, Edward T.
1993   *Sacred Ground: Americans and Their Battlefields.* University of Illinois Press, Urbana.
Little, Barbara J.
1994   People with History: An Update on Historical Archaeology in the United States. *Journal of Archaeological Method and Theory* 1(1): 5–40.
Little, Barbara J., and Paul A. Shackel
1992   Post-Processual Approaches to Meanings and Uses of Material Culture. *Historical Archaeology* 26(3): 5–11.
Lowenthal, David
1975   Past Time, Present Place: Landscape and Memory. *Geographical Review* 65(1): 1–36.
1985   *The Past Is a Foreign Country.* Cambridge University Press, New York.
Marquet, Jacques
1993   Objects as Instruments, Objects as Signs. In *History from Things: Essays on Material Culture,* edited by Steven Lubar and W. David Kingery, 30–40. Smithsonian Institution Press, Washington, D.C.
McGill, Greg
1995   *Building on the Past: A Guide to Archaeology and the Development Process.* Cambridge University Press, Cambridge.
National Trust for Historic Preservation
1975   *Economic Benefits of Preserving Old Buildings.* Preservation Press, Washington, D.C.
Notter, Finegold, and Alexander, Inc.
1988   *Baltimore Waterfront Study.* Charles Center Inner Harbor Management, Baltimore.
Patrell, Dan
1997   Making Yesterdays Matter Today. *Frederick Magazine,* May, 21–22.

Peterson, Larry
1997   Pullman Strike Pictures Molding Public Perceptions in the 1890s by New
        Visual Communication. *Labor's Heritage,* Spring, 14–36.
Pinkerton, Allen
1878   *Strikers, Communists, Tramps, and Detectives.* G. W. Carleton, New
        York.
Preservation Maryland
1991   Camden Yards: A Partnership for Preservation. *The Phoenix* [Newsletter
        of Preservation Maryland, Baltimore], March/April.
Rettaliata, Janis
1992   *The Baltimore Ballpark Project: The Creation of a Baseball Stadium.*
        Self-published, Baltimore.
Richardson, Miles
1989   The Artifact as Abbreviated Act: A Social Interpretation of Material
        Culture. In *The Meaning of Things: Material Culture and Symbolic Ex-
        pression,* edited by Ian Hodder, 172–77. Unwin Hyman, London.
Richmond, Peter
1993   *Ballpark: Camden Yards and the Building of an American Dream.* Simon
        and Schuster, New York.
Rogers, Nolan
1992   From B&O Railroad to Ballpark. Docent training handout. On file,
        Maryland Stadium Authority, Baltimore.
1998   From Bricks and Pianos to Football. *Baltimore Ravens Insider* 3(3): 5–7.
Sanders, Sue
1998   Personal communication with the author. November.
Shackel, Paul A.
1996   *Culture Change and the New Technology: An Archaeology of the Early
        American Industrial Era.* Plenum Press, New York.
Shanks, Michael, and Christopher Tilley
1987   *Re-Constructing Archaeology Theory and Practice.* Routledge, New
        York.
Smith, Curt
1997   The Return of Old Style Ballparks. *American Enterprise* 8(2): 52–57.
Spear, Joseph E.
1992   Oriole Park at Camden Yards. Foreword to *The Baltimore Ballpark
        Project: The Creation of a Baseball Stadium,* by Janis Rettaliata. Self-
        published, Baltimore.
Stover, John F.
1987   *History of the Baltimore and Ohio Railroad.* Purdue University Press,
        West Lafayette, Indiana.
U.S. Department of the Interior
1969   *The National Register of Historic Places.* U.S. Department of the Inte-
        rior, National Park Service, Washington, D.C.
Walsh, Peter
1999   Personal communication with the author. May.

12

Abraham Lincoln's Birthplace Cabin: The Making of an American Icon

Dwight T. Pitcaithley

Introduction

Abraham Lincoln became a national idol during the Progressive Era, a period roughly bounded by 1900 and 1920. It was during this period that the Lincoln we know today developed in the public mind. Lincoln transcended time because, according to Merrill Peterson, he, and his image, followed the time-honored virtues of honesty, kindness, temperance, industry, and pluck (Peterson 1994). But that Horatio Alger analogy does not fully explain his permanence in pubic memory. Barry Schwartz argues compellingly that while the nineteenth-century Lincoln was characterized by plainness, familiarity, and homeliness, twentieth-century Americans needed a more assertive image. During the Progressive Era, the United States became a world power, and it needed strong, powerful heroes with personal traits equal to the task of nation building, both international and domestic. "Great and powerful nations cannot be represented by common, weak men" (Schwartz 1990:95–104). So, over the course of the first two decades of the twentieth century, the virtues of stateliness, authority, and dignity were added to the list of Lincoln's singular qualities. By the time of the dedication of the Lincoln Memorial in 1922, Lincoln's memory had an egalitarian as well as an authoritarian dimension.

It was no accident then, that the development of Thomas Lincoln's farm near Hodgenville, Kentucky, as a shrine to the birth of Abraham Lincoln represented both the traditional Lincoln with simplicity, plainness, and intimacy, and the emerging progressive Lincoln with stateliness and remoteness. Historic sites, particularly those that tend to idealize the past rather than preserve a place, reflect the collective memories of the commemorators much more than they present historical reality. They are products of a contemporary time, quite distinct in form and meaning from the original place and time. As Michael Kammen (1991:9) recently observed, "We arouse and arrange our memories to suit our psychic needs." What is today the Abraham Lincoln Birthplace National Historic Site was once an abandoned farm, overgrown with weeds and brambles, suggesting nothing of its organic connection with the martyred president. The story of the transformation of the Sinking Spring farm from neglected woodlot to national shrine reveals how successive generations perceive the past and how historic sites evolve. For many years, however, the farm and the birthplace cabin took separate paths and developed separate stories.

The Birthplace Cabin

Thomas Lincoln purchased the Sinking Spring farm in December 1808. It is not known whether he had moved there and built a cabin before then or if he erected his cabin after purchasing the farm. In any event, Abraham Lincoln was born in a small cabin on the farm on February 12 of the following year. The Lincolns lived on the Sinking Spring farm for only two and a half years before moving on to Knob Creek, about ten miles away. Successive owners lived on the farm, and by 1860 the cabin had either fallen into ruin or been moved to an adjacent farm. There is no definitive evidence on the fate of the cabin. In 1906, several Hodgenville residents recalled that the Lincoln farm contained the ruins of a small round-log cabin in 1860, but they identified a more recent cabin as the one in which Lincoln was born. The conflicting recollections of these individuals, however, makes definitive conclusions impossible (Wilson 1906; Goff 1906; Creal 1906; Davenport 1906).

During the summer of 1860, a local delegate to the state Republican convention visited the farm, cut several walking canes from trees on the property (including one "from the very place in the house where the bed stood when he [Lincoln] was born," and noted that the cabin was no longer there (Wintersmith, quoted in Warren 1950:12). John B. Rowbotham visited the farm shortly after Lincoln's assassination with the intention of sketching the birthplace for a Cincinnati publishing firm. He likewise found no cabin on the site (Rowbotham 1865). A second correspondent visited the site in 1865 and found "no vestiges of the Lincoln cabin remaining," as the Philadelphia *Press* reported on its front page, September 1, 1865.

In 1894, a Major S. P. Gross acquired an option to buy the farm and create a historic site not unlike those already underway at Mount Vernon and Andrew Jackson's Hermitage. Gross's plan never materialized, but it is clear that the birthplace cabin was not a part of his grand design for the farm, which strongly suggests that the original cabin no longer existed ([Louisville] *Times* February 2, 1894. See also *LaRue County Herald* February 8, 1894). Due to the later esteem with which a reconstituted Lincoln cabin was afforded, it is noteworthy that during the visits of these men, local residents were unaware of any Lincoln cabin either in the immediate surrounding area or on the farm itself. On the basis of this evidence, it seems plausible that the original birthplace cabin had deteriorated by the time of Lincoln's election in 1860. The log cabin that eventually made its way into the memorial building near Hodgenville was, in fact, not identified as the Lincoln birthplace cabin until 1895, eighty-six years after his birth. A story in the *Louisville Courier-Journal* for March 26, 1894, reported that Alfred W. Dennett, a New York–based entrepreneur, had purchased Thomas Lincoln's farm with plans to develop it into a tourist attraction complete with a large hotel. Dennett announced to the press that he wanted to attract large numbers of Civil War veterans who would be assembling in Louisville (fifty miles to the north) for a Grand Army of the Republic encampment in the fall of 1895.

The *Louisville Courier-Journal* article significantly made no mention of a birthplace cabin nor did it suggest that the Lincoln cabin existed elsewhere in the vicinity. With the original cabin long since gone, Dennett apparently presumed that some kind of rude cabin would ensure a higher rate of return on his investment, and he instructed his agent in Kentucky, the Reverend James W. Bigham, to build a log cabin on the Lincoln farm on the exact spot as the original and with "identical logs that were in the original cabin" (*Larue County Herald,* August 29, 1895). Bigham quickly purchased a two-story cabin from a neighboring farm and had the best of its logs reerected on the Lincoln farm. At Bigham's request, a local photographer named Russell T. Evans made a photograph of the structure, which was widely published (fig. 12.1). Significantly, the photograph became accepted by the public as a picture of the actual cabin in which Lincoln was born.

Reverend Bigham's exorbitant admission charge and his "amateur promotional ineptitude," however, prompted few veterans to make the journey from Louisville to Hodgenville (Davis 1949: 3). Disappointed—but not deterred—Dennett and Bigham next laid plans to exhibit what they were now calling the "Lincoln Birthplace Cabin" at the Tennessee Centennial Exposition in Nashville in 1897. To enhance the exhibit, the two

Figure 12.1. "Abraham Lincoln's Birthplace Cabin," re-erected on the Thomas Lincoln farm in 1895. (Photo: Russell T. Evans. Courtesy Library of Congress.)

opportunists purchased another old log cabin claimed to be the birthplace of Jefferson Davis, who was born in 1811 near Fairview, Kentucky, roughly 150 miles southwest of Hodgenville (*Official Catalogue, Tennessee Centennial* 1897:183). When the exposition opened, the two cabins were found in the "Vanity Fair" section, which devoted itself not to dignified commemoration and displays, but to amusements such as the Giant See Saw, Chinese Village, Phantom Swing, Wild Animal Arena, and the Colorado Gold Mine. The official catalog of the exposition admonished all visitors to see these two "really" historic houses of the West, which for the occasion had been furnished by Dennett with several "authentic" Lincoln chairs (*Official Catalogue, Tennessee Centennial* 1897:183).

Although the *Nashville Banner* expressed a small degree of disbelief, the catalogue assured the visitor that Dennett had proof that both cabins were the "genuine and original homes of the two great men" (May 1, 1897).

Many years later, a newspaper reporter remembered asking Reverend Bigham about the authenticity of the Hodgenville cabin. Bigham's disingenuous reply was, "Lincoln was born in a log cabin, weren't he? Well, one cabin is as good as another" (Barbee 1948:8). Following the fair, Dennett shipped the logs of both cabins to New York City and stored them in the Bowery.

Before his departure from Nashville, Dennett met Frederick Thompson, who had built and later managed many of the attractions for the Nashville exposition. (Thompson, in partnership with Elmer Dundy, was to become one of the leading showmen and theatrical producers in the country and is remembered largely for designing, constructing, and operating Luna Park at Coney Island in 1903—at the time, the largest amusement park in the world [*National Cyclopaedia* 1967]). Thompson agreed to lease both cabins for the 1901 Pan-American Exposition in Buffalo.

Designed to foster visions of Pan-American harmony and illustrate U.S. cultural progress during the nineteenth century, the exposition's midway contained ethnographic displays in the form of living "villages" from Africa, Mexico, the Philippines, Alaska, Hawaii, and Japan. Amid its carnival rides of the giant see-saw and the rotating aero-cycle, and sandwiched between "Bonner—The Educated Horse" and Esau, a well-trained chimpanzee who was promoted as the "Missing Link," was the Old Plantation. Representing the "South be'fo de Wah," this exhibit dissolutely featured "150 . . . Old Uncles and Aunties, formerly slaves, living in the genuine cabins in which Abraham Lincoln and Jefferson Davis were born" (*Official Catalogue* 1901) (fig. 12.2). The meager furnishings added by Dennett for the Nashville fair were dramatically expanded by Thompson and Dundy into complete furnishings for both cabins.

A privately written, privately published guide to the Midway declared the Lincoln cabin authentic because the sign next to the door plainly announced that it was. The guide's author was reminded, however, of Mark Twain confronting myriad pieces of the "true cross" in European cathedrals. "He did not question the authenticity of the relics, for each plainly bore the announcement that it was a part of the real cross from Calvary, but Twain said that after awhile he wondered a little how Christ was able to carry all those pieces in one cross" (Barry 1901: 125–28).

Sometime following William McKinley's assassination at the Pan-American and the closing of the exposition, Thompson shipped the two cabins to Coney Island, where he and Dundy planned on incorporating at least the Lincoln cabin into their Luna Park enterprise. But alas, during the journey to Coney Island the logs of the cabins became intermingled, and when the Lincoln cabin was erected in 1903 for a local benefit it was revealed that the structure contained logs from both the Lincoln *and* the Davis cabins (*New York Times* March 23, 1903). While the "Lincoln and Davis Cabin" (as it briefly became known) temporarily resided in a shed at Luna Park, Thompson and Dundy apparently decided against its public

Figure 12.2. Runway clown Phoebe, posing in front of the Lincoln cabin at the Pan-American Exposition in Buffalo, New York. 1901. (Courtesy Library of Congress.)

display. At some point before 1906, all 142 pieces (from both cabins) were moved to College Point, Long Island (*Long Island Star*, February 1931).

The Farm Preserved

By this time, the Lincoln farm in Hodgenville had passed into the hands of Robert Collier, publisher of *Collier's Weekly*. Collier, more concerned with honoring the slain president's memory than with making money, created the Lincoln Farm Association to honor and perpetuate the memory of Abraham Lincoln by inculcating a spirit of patriotism, developing the farm into a national park, erecting monuments and buildings, and through the "purchase of historical relics to be placed on the grounds" (Certificate of Incorporation, April 18, 1906). To provide for the preservation and protection of the birthplace cabin, the Lincoln Farm Association (having among its Board of Directors Augustus Saint-Gaudens, Joseph H. Choate, Samuel L. Clemens, Ida Tarbell, and Clarence H. McKay) selected

John Russell Pope to design a memorial building in which the cabin would be enshrined (Peterson 1968:24–30). As one of the premier architects in Washington, D.C., Pope later designed the Jefferson Memorial, National Archives building, and National Gallery of Art.

Having purchased the farm, Collier tracked the Lincoln logs to Long Island, acquired them for $1,000, and had them hauled by wagon to New York City (fig. 12.3). (By this time, any connection between the logs and Jefferson Davis had been long forgotten.) There they were loaded on a flatcar decorated with red, white, and blue bunting and a portrait of Lincoln. Guarded by a contingent of the Kentucky militia—made necessary because of souvenir collectors—the 142 logs began a triumphant return to Kentucky with stops in major cities (*New York Daily Tribune* June 7, 1906).

As the logs were being readied for their return to Kentucky, the Lincoln Farm Association engaged a Hodgenville law firm to determine the authenticity of the cabin. The firm took affidavits from twelve local residents, but only four related to the cabin—and they contradicted one another. (The remaining eight dealt with the farm only.) The testimony of three residents supported the story that a cabin on the former Lincoln farm had been moved to a neighboring farm in 1860 and used there for various purposes until purchased in 1895 by Dennett and returned to its original site. All three testified that at the time of its removal in 1860, the cabin was well-known locally as the Lincoln birthplace (Wilson 1906; Goff 1906; Davenport 1906). The lawyers disregarded the testimony of a local judge, who, in addition to being born on a portion of the Lincoln farm in 1836 and selling it to Dennett in 1894, argued that the cabin was relatively new when moved in 1860 and therefore had no association with Abraham Lincoln (Creal 1906). The law firm transmitted its findings to Collier laden more with patriotism and reverence than with dispassionate analysis: "Many more witnesses could be had testifying substantially to the facts, but this would be merely cumulative and we close the testimony with the submission of the facts to the public, believing that the American people will not be so unreasonable or critical as to demand more conclusive evidence of the birthplace of this great American" (Williams and Handley n.d.).

The three affidavits constitute the best (and only) evidence linking Dennett and Bigham's 1895 cabin to Abraham Lincoln's birth. But the local residents disagreed not only on the origin of the cabin, but also on its location on the Lincoln farm. And their testimony is not supported by any other piece of evidence. As a whole, with their conflicting stories, second-

Figure 12.3. The transfer of the Lincoln logs from storage on Long Island, New York, to Kentucky. 1906. (Courtesy Library of Congress.)

hand knowledge, and elusive plausibility, the affidavits are justly suspect. If the Lincoln cabin had been removed in 1860, it surely would have been widely known in such a small place as Hodgenville and at least one of those looking for the cabin would have noted its relocation to a neighboring farm.

Arriving in Louisville in June 1906, the logs were erected in a local park. But because the Farm Association had unknowingly purchased the logs to two cabins, the structure put up in Louisville's Central Park was oversized. It now had a front *and* a back door, and two windows instead of the usual one—but the windows were on the rear of the cabin instead of the front. Nevertheless, the cabin was again so popular that an armed guard had to prevent visitors from chipping off pieces (*Louisville Courier-Journal* June 15, 1906). After a week, the cabin was dismantled and placed in storage. Three years later, its supporters moved the logs to Hodgenville for the laying of the memorial building's cornerstone.

The centennial of Lincoln's birth, February 12, 1909, was marked by celebrations including everything from twenty-six-mile marathon races to the release of the Lincoln penny. With less than a month left in his presidency, Theodore Roosevelt braved raw Kentucky weather to praise Lincoln at the laying of the cornerstone for the memorial building. The president spoke of Lincoln's personal strengths, his lofty ideals, and his "indomitable" resolve. The large crowd, braving occasional wind-driven drizzle, stood patiently throughout the one and three-quarter hour ceremony (*New York Times* February 11, 1909; February 13, 1909). Robert Todd Lincoln, by then a successful railroad executive in his midsixties, chose not to attend the Hodgenville observance. Instead he joined William Jennings Bryan and the French and British ambassadors at a tribute in Springfield, Illinois, site of his father's home and tomb (*New York Times* February 13, 1909) (fig. 12.4).

Following the 1909 ceremony, the cabin was yet again dismantled and returned to Louisville to await the completion of John Russell Pope's monument (fig. 12.5). But the ordeal of the Lincoln logs was not over. When the memorial building was finished in 1911 and the logs returned to Hodgenville, the cabin proved to be too large to allow visitors ease of movement within the monument. Pope's solution was to alter the cabin to fit the memorial. He simply trimmed the logs and reduced the cabin three

Figure 12.4. The "Lincoln Birthplace Cabin," reassembled by the Lincoln Farm Association on the Lincoln Farm for the cornerstone laying of the Memorial Building. 1909. (Courtesy Library of Congress.)

Figure 12.5. The Memorial Building designed by John Russell Pope to house the Lincoln cabin after its nine moves. 1911. (Courtesy Illinois State Historical Library.)

or four feet in width and one or two feet in length. Thus miniaturized, the cabin was in proper proportion to the monument's interior dimensions (Appleman 1939:4). It was in this reduced state that the cabin passed into the hands of the governor of Kentucky, then to the War Department, and finally to the National Park Service. Today, the cabin is visited annually by several hundred thousand respectful visitors.

The Controversy

Although the National Park Service questioned the authenticity of the cabin shortly after it began administering the site (Stauffer 1936), no one publicly challenged the cabin's origins until Lincoln scholar Roy Hays (1948) published an article titled "Is the Lincoln Birthplace Cabin Authentic?" in *The Abraham Lincoln Quarterly*. The article, which questioned the authenticity of the cabin, prompted, as might be imagined, a flurry of research activity within the National Park Service. In 1949, the park's historian, Benjamin Davis, produced a detailed study titled "Report of Research on the Traditional Abraham Lincoln Birthplace Cabin." Through deed research that carefully dismantled the local tradition linking the cabin to the Sinking Spring farm, Davis concluded that any connection between the cabin and Lincoln would have to be completely "accidental" (Davis 1949:38–39). To ensure that every avenue had been explored, the director of the National Park Service, Newton Drury, asked three Lincoln scholars, Paul Angle, J. G. Randall, and Louis A. Warren, to examine the evidence and offer their opinion on the cabin's authenticity. Angle, of the Chicago Historical Society, and Randall, from the University of Illinois, strongly argued that the enshrined cabin possessed no Lincoln antecedents. Angle wrote the director, "If the case against the cabin consisted only of inadequate and conflicting evidence I wouldn't be so much impressed by it, but when the connivings of a couple of scamps like Dennett and Bigham are added, then I become highly skeptical, to say the least" (Angle 1949).

Louis Warren, director of the Lincoln National Life Foundation, thought otherwise. But then, the local tradition for the cabin's authenticity had found its fullest expression in Warren's own 1926 book, *Lincoln's Parentage & Childhood: A History of the Kentucky Lincolns Supported by Documentary Evidence*. Warren, a Lincoln authority and long-time editor of "Lincoln Lore," a weekly newsletter of the Lincoln National Life Insurance Company, passionately wanted the logs to be original, but in fact, based his argument on the patriotic and romantic symbolism of the cabin. "For nearly thirty years," he wrote, "the cabin has made a positive inspirational contribution to an ever increasing number of pilgrims who pay homage at this American shrine. . . . It does not appear to this reviewer that additional evidence of sufficient importance has been presented to prove that no logs in the present structure can be associated with the original birthplace of Abraham Lincoln" (Warren 1950:2, 10–11). Summarizing the issue for director Drury, Charles Porter, a Washington-based National Park Service historian, discounted Warren's argument, the Lincoln Farm Association's ambiguous affidavits, *and* the exaggerated claims of the "charlatans" Dennett and Bigham. He concluded with what became the Service's official position: "There simply isn't any trustworthy recorded evidence for the authenticity of the cabin. In view of the mountebank character of Dennett and Bigham, the traditions springing from them are certainly not to be trusted" (Porter 1950).

The Cabin Memorialized

From the early 1950s, the National Park Service attempted to clarify the issue for visitors by posting several signs within the memorial and referred to the cabin as the "traditional birthplace." The distinction between authentic and traditional, however, was largely lost on a worshipful public

Figure 12.6. After nine moves and the replacement of over half the logs identified in 1895, the "Lincoln Birthplace Cabin" was finally placed within the Memorial Building. (Courtesy National Park Service.)

eager for a glimpse of the deified president's humble origins. Interpretation at the site in recent years has been more forthright. But in spite of the cabin's amusement park beginnings, it remains a powerful symbol of Abraham Lincoln and a popular shrine to his memory. The small National Park Service site in rural Kentucky is visited by 300,000 tourists annually (fig. 12.6).

To ensure that the log cabin tradition continued, several full-scale replicas of the cabin have been constructed. A story in the *Fort Wayne Journal-Gazette* for July 5, 1936, reported that in 1920, Louis A. Warren, who championed the cabin long after all other Lincoln students had given up on its legitimacy, arranged for the Lincoln National Life Insurance Company to erect and donate to the city of Fort Wayne, Indiana, a copy of the cabin that still stands in Foster Park. Four years later, Mary Bowditch Forbes, descendant of Robert Bennet Forbes of China trade fame and fortune, had a replica constructed in her back yard in Milton, Massachusetts (Scaife 1926). And for many years a replica cabin graced the interior of the Chicago Historical Society. These structures were replicas of the miniaturized cabin in the memorial building and not of the larger 1895 version or the later Lincoln/Davis cabin.

A product of the "Midway Age," Alfred Dennett's 1895 cabin outlived its amusement park origins and with the passage of time has become one of the nation's most venerable relics. Although most certainly not a genuine Lincoln artifact, the cabin is nonetheless significant for its role in perpetuating the image of Lincoln as the martyred president and of his dramatic rise from poverty to the White House. The shrine, as reverently conceived by the Lincoln Farm Association, presents a provoking interplay between the humble and the majestic. The crude cabin, reduced to almost playhouse size, evokes thoughts of Lincoln the rail splitter, the frontier populist. The surrounding John Russell Pope "tomb" with its grand approach of fifty-six steps, six-column Doric portico, and large bronze doors represents a more reserved and stately Lincoln.

Our collective heritage is as much memory as fact, as much myth as reality, as much perception as preservation. The public's perception of the Lincoln cabin is important to the nation's image and an indispensable part of the nation's ritualistic public tribute to its own humble origins. It is symbolic of a need for an accessible past and a willingness to embrace myths that are too popular, too powerful, to be diminished by the truth.

References

Angle, Paul M.
   1949   Letter to Newton B. Drury, May 26. Box 3, "Correspondence Re Abraham Lincoln Birthplace Cabin." History Division Files, National Park Service, Washington, D.C.
Appleman, Roy Edgar
   1939   Report on Conference with Dr. Louis A. Warren and Recommendations Relative to Future Development Program, Abraham Lincoln National Park. On file, Abraham Lincoln Birthplace National Historic Site, Hodgenville, Kentucky.
Barbee, David Rankin
   1948   Lincoln Cabin Hoax. *Washington Post,* October 11, 8.
Barry, Richard H.
   1901   *Snap Shots on the Midway of the Pan-Am Expo: Including Characteristic Scenes and Pastimes of Every Country There Represented* . . . Robert Allan Reid, Buffalo, New York.

Certificate of Incorporation of the Lincoln Farm Association
  1906   April 18. On file, Abraham Lincoln Birthplace National Historic Site,
          Hodgenville, Kentucky.
Creal, John C.
  1906   Affidavit. May 28. On file, Abraham Lincoln Birthplace National His-
          toric Site, Hodgenville, Kentucky.
Davenport, John A.
  1906   Affidavit. May 30. On file, Abraham Lincoln Birthplace National His-
          toric Site, Hodgenville, Kentucky.
Davis, Benjamin H.
  1949   Report of Research on the Traditional Abraham Lincoln Birthplace
          Cabin. On file, Abraham Lincoln Birthplace National Historic Site,
          Hodgenville, Kentucky.
Goff, Zerelda Jane
  1906   Affidavit. May 30. On file, Abraham Lincoln Birthplace National His-
          toric Site, Hodgenville, Kentucky.
Hays, Roy
  1948   Is the Lincoln Birthplace Cabin Authentic? *The Abraham Lincoln Quar-
          terly* 5(3): 127–63.
Kammen, Michael
  1991   *Mystic Chords of Memory: The Transformation of Tradition in Ameri-
          can Culture.* Knopf, New York.
LaRue County Herald, Hodgenville, Kentucky
  1894   Untitled article. February 8:1.
  1895   Untitled article. August 29:3.
Long Island Star
  1931   Untitled article. February. Reprinted in the *North Shore News,* Flushing,
          N.Y., October 10, 1963, p. 5.
Louisville Courier-Journal
  1894   Untitled article. March 26:5.
  1906   Lincoln's Cabin Attracts Visitors to Central Park. June 15:1.
Louisville Times
  1894   Lincoln and Davis Cabin. February 2.
Nashville Banner
  1897   Untitled article. May1: 14.
The National Cyclopaedia of American Biography . . .
  1967   Volume 19. University Microfilms, Ann Arbor, Michigan.
New York Daily Tribune
  1906   Lincoln Cabin Goes, Started to Kentucky. June 7.
New York Times
  1903   Lincoln and Davis Cabin. March 23:14.
  1909   President at Lincoln Farm. February 11:5.
  1909   Roosevelt Praises Lincoln as Fighter. February 13:3.
  1919   Untitled article. June 7:13.
Official Catalogue, Tennessee Centennial
  1897   *Official Catalogue, Tennessee Centennial.* Knoxville, Tennessee.

Official Catalogue and Guide Book to the Pan-American Exposition, with Maps of Exposition and Illustrations
1901   *Official Catalogue and Guide Book to the Pan-American Exposition, with Maps of Exposition and Illustrations.* Charles Ahrhart, Buffalo, New York.

Peterson, Gloria
1968   *An Administrative History of Abraham Lincoln Birthplace National Historic Site.* U.S. Department of the Interior, National Park Service, Washington, D.C.

Peterson, Merrill D.
1994   *Lincoln in American Memory.* Oxford University Press, New York.

Porter, Charles
1950   The Lincoln Log Cabin Question. Box 3, "Correspondence Re Abraham Lincoln Birthplace Cabin." History Division Files, National Park Service, Washington, D.C.

The Press, Philadelphia
1865   Untitled article. September 1:1.

Rowbotham, John B.
1865   Letter to William H. Herndon, June 24. Herndon-Weik Collection. Library of Congress.

Rydell, Robert W.
1984   *All the World's a Fair: Visions of Empire at American International Expositions, 1876–1916.* University of Chicago Press, Chicago.

Scaife, Lauriston L.
1926   *The Lincoln Cabin.* Reprinted from Stone and Webster Journal; original in files of the Captain Robert Bennet Forbes Museum and Library, Milton, Massachusetts.

Schwartz, Barry
1990   The Reconstruction of Abraham Lincoln. In *Collective Remembering,* edited by David Middleton and Derek Edwards, 95–104. Sage, London.

Stauffer, A. P.
1936   Letter to Verne Chatelain, February 26. On file, Abraham Lincoln Birthplace National Historic Site, Hodgenville, Kentucky.

Times, Louisville
1894   Lincoln and Davis Cabin. February 2:7.

Warren, Louis A.
1950   The Traditional Birthplace Cabin. On file, Abraham Lincoln Birthplace National Historic Site, Hodgenville, Kentucky.

Williams and Handley
N.d.   Submission of Evidence, Attorneys for the Lincoln Memorial Farm Association, copy of signed transcript. On file, Abraham Lincoln Birthplace National Historic Site, Hodgenville, Kentucky.

Wilson, Lafayette
1906   Affidavit. June 5. On file, Abraham Lincoln Birthplace National Historic Site, Hodgenville, Kentucky.

Selected References

Aaron, Daniel
1973   *The Unwritten War: American Writers and the Civil War.* Knopf, New York.

Abbey, Edward
1968   *Desert Solitaire: A Season in the Wilderness.* Ballantine Books, New York.

Akwesasne Notes
1974   *Voices from Wounded Knee 1973.* Akwesasne Notes, Rooseveltown, New York.

Ames, Kenneth
1981   Ideologies in Stone: Meanings in Victorian Gravestones. *Journal of Popular Culture* 14(4): 641–56.

Andrews, Peter
1966   *In Honored Glory: The Story of Arlington.* Putnam, New York.
1985   *Arlington House: The Robert E. Lee Memorial, Official National Park Handbook.* U.S. Department of the Interior, National Park Service, Washington, D.C.

Archibald, Robert R.
1997   Memory and the Process of Public History. *Public Historian* 19(2): 61–64.

Armstrong, D. V.
1990   *The Old Village and the Great Hall: An Archaeological and Historical Examination of Drax Hall Plantation, St. Anns Bay, Jamaica.* University of Illinois Press, Urbana.

Baker, L.
1981   *The Concentration Camp Conspiracy: A Second Pearl Harbor.* AFHA, Lawndale, California.

Barbee, David Rankin
1948   Lincoln Cabin Hoax. *Washington Post,* October 11:8.

Barnett, Steve, and Martin G. Silverman
1979   *Ideology and Everyday Life.* University of Michigan Press, Ann Arbor.

Barry, Richard H.
1901   *Snap Shots on the Midway of the Pan-Am Expo: Including Characteristic Scenes and Pastimes of Every Country There Represented . . .* Robert Allan Reid, Buffalo, New York.

Batteau, A. W.
1990   *The Invention of Appalachia.* University of Arizona Press, Tucson.
Beasley, Conger, Jr.
1995   *We Are a People in This World: The Lakota and the Massacre at Wounded Knee.* University of Arkansas Press, Fayatteville.
Bender, Thomas
1974   The "Rural" Cemetery Movement: Urban Travail and the Appeal of Nature. *New England Quarterly* 47:196–211.
Benson, Richard, and Lincoln Kirstein
1973   *Lay This Laurel: An Album on the Saint-Gaudens Memorial . . .* Eakins Press, New York.
Birnbaum, Charles A., ed.
1996   *The Secretary of the Interior's Standards for the Treatment of Historic Properties with Guidelines for the Treatment of Cultural Landscapes.* U.S. Department of the Interior, National Park Service, Washington D.C.
Blanton, Dennis, and Patricia Kandle
1997   *The Archaeological Survey of Jamestown Island.* Jamestown Archaeological Assessment Technical Report Series 2, submitted to Colonial National Historical Park, Jamestown, Virginia.
Blatti, Jo
1997   Public History as Contested Terrain: A Museums Perspective. *Public Historian* 19(2): 57–60.
Blight, David W.
1989   "For Something beyond the Battlefield": Frederick Douglass and the Struggle for the Memory of the Civil War. *Journal of American History* 75(4): 1156–78.
Bodner, John
1992   *Remaking America: Public Memory, Commemoration, and Patriotism in the Twentieth Century.* Princeton University Press, Princeton, New Jersey.
Boime, Albert
1990   *The Art of Exclusion: Representing Blacks in the Nineteenth Century.* Smithsonian Institution Press, Washington, D.C.
Booth, W.
1997   A Lonely Patch of History: Japanese Americans Were Forced to Live Here. They Don't Want It to Be Forgotten. *Washington Post,* April 15:D1.
Bower, Mim
1995   Marketing Nostalgia: An Exploration of Heritage Management and Its Relation to the Human Consciousness. In *Managing Archaeology,* edited by Malcolm A. Cooper, Antony Firth, John Carmen, and David Wheatley, 33–39. Routledge, New York.

Breene, Timothy H.
1989   *Imagining the Past: East Hampton Histories*. Addison-Wesley, Reading, Massachusetts.

Brooke, James
1996   3 Suffragists (in Marble) to Move Up in the Capitol. *New York Times*, September 27:A18.

Brown, Dee
1970   *Bury My Heart at Wounded Knee: An Indian History of the American West*. Holt, New York.

Brown, K. L., and D. C. Cooper
1990   Structural Continuity in an African-American Slave and Tenant Community. In Historical Archaeology on Southern Plantations and Farms, edited by C. E. Orser, Jr. *Historical Archaeology* 24(4):7–19.

Bunce, Michael
1994   *The Countryside Ideal: Anglo-American Images of Landscape*. Routledge, New York.

Burchard, Peter
1965   *One Gallant Rush: Robert Gould Shaw and His Brave Black Regiment*. St. Martin's Press, New York.

Burnette, Robert, and John Koster
1974   *The Road to Wounded Knee*. Bantam Books, New York.

Caffin, Charles H.
1913   *American Masters of Sculpture: Being Brief Appreciations of Some American Sculptors and of Some Phase of Sculpture in America*. Doubleday, Page, New York.

Campbell, Edward D. C., ed.
1987   Shadows of an Era. *Virginia Cavalcade* 36(3):128–43.

Carmichael, David L., Brian Reeves, Jane Hubert, and Audhild Schanche
1994   *Sacred Sites, Sacred Places*. Routledge, New York.

Casteñeda, Quetzil E.
1996   *In the Museum of Maya Culture: Touring Chichén Itzá*. University of Minnesota Press, Minneapolis.

Chidester, David, and Edward T. Linenthal, eds.
1995   *American Sacred Space*. Indiana University Press, Bloomington.

Churchill, Ward
1994   The Bloody Wake of Alcatraz: Political Repression of the American Indian Movement during the 1970s. *American Indian Culture and Research Journal* 18(4):253–300.

Cohen, Andrew
1995   Birds in Paradise. *Athletic Business* 19(1):51–55.

Collier, Sylvia
1991   *Whitehaven, 1660–1800*. Royal Commission on the Historical Monuments of England, London.

Comer, Douglas C.
1996   *Ritual Ground*. University of California Press, Berkeley.

Conrat, M., and R. Conrat
1972   *Executive Order 9066: The Internment of 110,000 Japanese Americans*. Anderson, Ritchie, and Simon, Los Angeles.

Cornell, J. T.
1994   War Stories at Air and Space: At Smithsonian, History Grapples with Cultural Angst. *Air Force Magazine*, April 24.

Cotter, John L.
1957a   Excavations at Jamestown, Virginia, Site of the First Permanent English Settlement in America. *Antiquity*. March:19–24.
1957b   Jamestown: Treasure in the Earth. *Antiques* (46)1: 44–46.
1957c   Rediscovering Jamestown. *Archaeology* 10 (1): 25–30.
1958   *Archaeological Excavations at Jamestown, Virginia*. No. 4, National Park Service Archaeological Research Series. U.S. Department of the Interior, National Park Service, Washington, D.C.

Cotter, John L., and Edward B. Jelks
1957   Historic Site Archaeology at Jamestown. *American Antiquity* 22(4): 25–30.

Crosby, Theo
1970   *The Necessary Monument: Its Future in the Civilized City*. New York Graphics Society, New York.

Crow Dog, Leonard, and Richard Erdoes
1995   *Crow Dog: Four Generations of Sioux Medicine Men*. HarperCollins, New York.

Crow Dog, Mary, and Richard Erdoes
1990   *Lakota Women*. HarperCollins, New York.

Daily National Intelligencier, Washington, D.C.
1857–1958 issues.

Daniels, R.
1971   *Concentration Camps USA: Japanese-Americans and World War II*. Holt, Rinehart, and Winston, New York.

Davies, Stephen
1982   Empty Eyes, Marble Hand: The Confederate Monument and the South. *Journal of Popular Culture* 16(3):2–21.

de Beauvoir, Simone
1953   Introduction to *The Second Sex*. In *The Second Wave*, edited by Linda Nicholson, 11–18. Routledge, New York.

Deitz, Paula
1997   "Open to All Real Plant Lovers": Beatrix Farrand's Invitation to Reef Point Gardens. In *The Bulletins of Reef Point Gardens*, by Beatrix Farrand. Island Foundation, Bar Harbor, Maine. Sagapress, Sagaponack, New York.

Dewing, Rolland
1985 *Wounded Knee: The Meaning and Significance of the Second Incident.* Irvington Publishers, New York.

Dryfhout, John H
1982 *The Works of Augustus Saint-Gaudens.* University Press of New England, Hanover, New Hampshire.

Du Bois, W.E.B.
1994 [1903] *The Souls of Black Folk.* Gramercy Books, New York.

Duncan, Russell, ed.
1992 *Blue-Eyed Child of Fortune: The Civil War Letters of Colonel Robert Gould Shaw.* University of Georgia Press, Athens.

Dunford, Penny
1989 *A Biographical Dictionary of Women Artists in Europe and America since 1850.* University of Pennsylvania Press, Philadelphia.

Eco, Umberto
1973 Function and Sign: Semiotics of Architecture. *Via* 1:131–53.
1986 Function and Sign: Semiotics of Architecture. In *The City and the Sign: An Introduction to Urban Semiotics,* edited by Mark Gottdiener and Alexandros Lagopolous, 55–86. Columbia University Press, New York.

Eliot, Charles W.
1928 *The Future of Mount Desert Island; A Report to the Plan Committee, Bar Harbor Village Improvement Association.* Bar Harbor Village Improvement Association, Bar Harbor, Maine.

Embrey, S. K., A. A. Hansen, and B. K. Mitson
1986 *Manzanar Martyr: An Interview with Harry Y. Ueno.* California State University Oral History Program, Fullerton.

Emerson, Edward W.
1907 *Life and Letters of Charles Russell Lowell, Captain Sixth United States Cavalry, Colonel 2nd Massachusetts Cavalry, Brigadier General United States Volunteers.* Houghton Mifflin, Boston.

Emilio, Luis F.
1969 [1894] *A Brave Black Regiment: History of the Fifty-Fourth Regiment of Massachusetts Volunteer Infantry, 1863–1865.* Arno Press and New York Times, New York.

Engle, R.
1998 Shenandoah National Park: Historical Overview. *CRM* 21(1):7–10.

Epperson, T. W.
1991 Race and the Disciplines of the Plantation. In Historical Archaeology on Southern Plantations and Farms, edited by C. E. Orser, Jr. *Historical Archaeology* 24(4):7–19.

Ernst, Joseph W.
1991 *Worthwhile Places: Correspondence of John D. Rockefeller, Jr., and*

Horace M. Albright. Published for the Rockefeller Archive Center by Fordham University Press, New York.

Evans, Sara M.
1997   *Born for Liberty*. Free Press, New York.

Everett, Edward
1879   *Orations and Speeches on Various Occasions*. Little, Brown, Boston.

Fagan, Brian M., and Charles E. Orser, Jr.
1995   *Historical Archaeology*. HarperCollins, New York.

Faragasso, Frank, and Doug Stover
1997   Adelaide Johnson: A Marriage of Art and Politics: Placing Women in the Past. *CRM* 20(3):54–55.

Farrand, Beatrix
1997   *The Bulletins of Reef Point Gardens*. Island Foundation, Bar Harbor, Maine. Sagapress, Sagaponack, New York.

Farrell, James J.
1980   *Inventing the American Way of Death*. Temple University Press, Philadelphia.

Fernandez, Josie
1998   Practicing History in the Public Interest. *CRM, Understanding the Past* 21(11):3.

Foner, Eric
1997   Changing Interpretation at Gettysburg National Military Park. *CRM* 21(4):17.

Foote, Kenneth E.
1997   *Shadowed Ground: American Landscapes of Violence and Tragedy*. University of Texas Press, Austin.

Foresta, Ronald A.
1984   *America's National Parks and Their Keepers*. Resources for the Future, Washington, D.C.

Forman, H. Chandlee
1938   *Jamestown and St. Mary's: Buried Cities of Romance*. Johns Hopkins University Press, Baltimore.
1957   *Virginia Architecture in the Seventeenth Century*. 350th Anniversary Celebration Corporation, Richmond.

Forstenzer, M.
1996a   Bitter Feelings Still Run Deep at Camp. *Los Angeles Times*, April 4:A3.
1996b   Manzanar: A Place That Still Divides Americans: Federal Plan to Preserve California Internment Site Is Raising Some Hostility. *Seattle Times*, May 7:A5.

Fosdick, Raymond B.
1956   *John D. Rockefeller, Jr.: A Portrait*. Harper, New York.

Foster, Gaines M.
1987   *Ghosts of the Confederacy: Defeat, the Lost Cause, and the Emergence of the New South, 1865–1913*. Oxford University Press, New York.

Foulds, H. Eliot
  1996   *Cultural Landscape Report for Blackwoods and Seawall Campgrounds,*
          Acadia National Park. Cultural Landscape Publication No. 11. Olm-
          stead Center for Landscape Preservation. U.S. Department of the Inte-
          rior, National Park Service, Boston.
Fowler, Don D.
  1987   Uses of the Past: Archaeology in Service of the State. *American Antiquity*
          53(2):229–48.
Fowler, Peter J.
  1992   *The Past in Contemporary Society: Then, Now.* Routledge, London.
Fox, J., Jr.
  1901   The Southern Mountaineer. *Scribner's Magazine* 29: 387–99, 556–70.
Fox, S.
  1990   *The Unknown Internment: An Oral History of the Relocation of Italian*
          Americans during World War II. Twayne, Boston.
Franco, Barbara
  1997   Public History and Memory: A Museum Perspective. *Public Historian*
          19(2):65–67.
Frassanito, William A.
  1978   *Antietam: The Photographic Legacy of America's Bloodiest Day.* Scrib-
          ner, New York.
Fremon, D. K.
  1996   *Japanese-American Internment in American History.* Enslow, Spring-
          field, New Jersey.
French, Stanley
  1974   The Cemetery as Cultural Institution: The Establishment of Mount Au-
          burn and the Rural Cemetery Movement. *American Quarterly* 26(1):
          37–59.
Frisch, Michael
  1989   American History and the Structure of Collective Memory: A Modest
          Exercise in Empirical Iconography. *Journal of American History* 75(4):
          1131–55.
  1990   *A Shared Authority: Essays on the Craft and Meaning of Oral and Public*
          History. State University of New York Press, Albany.
  1997   What Public History Offers, and Why It Matters. *Public Historian*
          19(2):41–43.
Frost, W. G.
  1899   Our Contemporary Ancestors in the Southern Mountains. *Atlantic*
          Monthly (March) 83:311.
Galke, Laura, ed.
  1992   *Cultural Resource Survey and Inventory of a War-Torn Landscape: The*
          Stuart's Hill Tract, Manassas National Battlefield Park, Virginia. Occa-
          sional Report 7, Regional Archeology Program, National Capital Region,
          U.S. Department of the Interior, National Park Service, Washington, D.C.

Garrett, J. A., and R. C. Larson, eds.

1977 *Camp and Community: Manzanar and the Owens Valley.* California State University Oral History Program, Fullerton.

Gillis, John

1994 Introduction to *Commemorations: The Politics of National Identity,* edited by John Gillis, 3–24. Princeton University Press, Princeton, New Jersey.

Glassberg, David

1990 *American Historical Pageantry: The Uses of Tradition in the Early Twentieth Century.* University of North Carolina Press, Chapel Hill.

1996 Public History and the Study of Memory. *Public Historian* 18(2):7–23.

1998 Presenting History to the Public: The Study of Memory and the Uses of the Past. Understanding the Past. *CRM* 21(11): 4–8.

Goldstein, Judith S.

1992 *Tragedies and Triumphs: Charles W. Eliot, George B. Dorr, John D. Rockefeller, Jr., The Founding of Acadia National Park.* Port-in-a-Storm Bookstore, Somesville, Maine.

Gonzalez, Mario, and Elizabeth Cook-Lynn

1999 *The Politics of Hallowed Ground: Wounded Knee and the Struggle for Indian Sovereignty.* University of Illinois Press, Chicago.

Green, George N.

1991 The Felix Longoria Affair. *Journal of Ethnic Studies* 19(3):23–49.

Green, Jerry

1994 Medals of Wounded Knee. *Nebraska History* 75(2):200–8.

1996 *After Wounded Knee.* Michigan State University Press, East Lansing.

Griffith, Elizabeth

1984 *In Her Own Right: The Life of Elizabeth Cady Stanton.* Oxford University Press, New York.

Gunts, Edward

1983 Landmark Eyed for Factory Outlets. *New American,* September 23: 1A.

1992 Grand Stand. *Architecture* 81(7):64–71.

Hainsworth, D. R.

1983 *The Correspondence of Sir John Lowther of Whitehaven, 1693–1698.* British Academy, London.

Hampton, Joan

1932 The Primitive Life in Modern Virginia: A Crisis for the Hill Folk. *Baltimore Sun,* May 1, magazine section.

Handler, Richard

1991 Who Owns the Past. In *The Politics of Culture,* edited by Bret Williams, 66–74. Smithsonian Institution Press, Washington, D.C.

Handler, Richard, and Eric Gable

1997 *The New History in an Old Museum: Creating the Past at Colonial Williamsburg.* Duke University Press, Durham, North Carolina.

Harney, Will Wallace
  1873   A Strange Land and a Peculiar People. *Lippincott's Magazine,* October:429–38.
Harrington, J. C.
  1943   *Historic Site Archaeology in the United States.* University of Chicago Press, Chicago.
  1954   Dating Stem Fragments of Seventeenth and Eighteenth Century Clay Tobacco Pipes. *Quarterly Bulletin of the Archaeological Society of Virginia* 9(1):10–14.
  1984   Jamestown Archaeology in Retrospect. In *The Scope of Historical Archaeology,* edited by David Orr and Daniel G. Crozier, 294–310. Temple University Press, Philadelphia.
Harris, Neil, Martin Harwit, Richard H. Kohn, Edward T. Linenthal, Martin J. Sherwin, David Thelen, and Thomas A. Woods
  1995   History and the Public: What Can We Handle? A Round Table about History after the *Enola Gay* Controversy. *Journal of American History* 82 (3):1029–1114.
Hartwig, D. Scott
  1990   *The Battle of Antietam and the Maryland Campaign of 1862: A Bibliography.* Heckler, Westport, Connecticut.
Harwit, M.
  1996   *An Exhibit Denied: Lobbying the History of the* Enola Gay. Copernicus, New York.
Hatamiya, L. T.
  1993   *Righting a Wrong: Japanese-Americans and the Passage of the Civil Liberties Act of 1988.* Stanford University Press, Stanford.
Hay, D.
  1977   *Whitehaven: An Illustrated History.* Michael Moon's Book Shop, Whitehaven, Cumbria, England.
Hays, Roy
  1948   Is the Lincoln Birthplace Cabin Authentic? *Abraham Lincoln Quarterly* 5 (3):127–63.
Henry, Thomas D.
  1936   200 Years of Calm in Blue Ridge Hollow Broken as Resettlement Workmen Erect New Village. *Washington Post.* (Clipping on file in Shenandoah National Park Archives, Luray, Virginia, n.d.)
Heysinger, Isaac W.
  1912   *Antietam and the Maryland and Virginia Campaigns of 1862: From the Government Records . . .* Heale, New York.
Higginson, Thomas Wentworth
  1971   [1870] *Army Life in a Black Regiment.* Corner House, Williamstown, Massachusetts.
Hitch, M.
  1931   Life in a Blue Ridge Hollow. *Journal of Geography* 30(8):309–22.

Hodder, Ian
1987   *The Archaeology of Contextual Meanings.* Cambridge University Press, London.
Horning, Audrey J.
1995   "A Verie Fit Place for the Erecting of a Great Cittie": Comparative Contextual Analysis of Archaeological Jamestown. Ph.D. dissertation, American Civilization, University of Pennsylvania. UMI microfilm, Ann Arbor, Michigan.
1996   Myth Versus Reality: Agricultural Adaptation and Innovation in the Nicholson Hollow District, Shenandoah National Park. In *Upland Archaeology in the East,* compiled by Michael B. Barber, Eugene B. Barfield, Harry A. Jaeger, and William Jack Hranicky, 17–115. U.S. Department of Agriculture, Forest Service Special Publication (38)5, Archaeological Society of Virginia, Richmond.
1997   Connections: An Archaeological Perspective on Becoming Americans. *Colonial Williamsburg Research Review* 7(1): 25–29.
1998   "Almost Untouched": Recognizing, Recording, and Preserving the Archeological Heritage of a Natural Park. *CRM* 21(1):31–33.
1999a   Finding the Town in Jamestown: Archaeology of the Seventeenth-Century Capitol *CRM* (22)1:7–9.
1999b   In Search of a "Hollow Ethnicity": Archaeological Explorations of Rural Mountain Settlement. In *Current Perspectives on Ethnicity in Historical Archaeology,* edited by M. Franklin and G. Fesler, 121–38. Research Publications Series, Colonial Williamsburg Foundation, Williamsburg, Virginia.
2000a   Archaeological Considerations of Appalachian Identity: Community-Based Archaeology in the Blue Ridge Mountains. In *The Archaeology of Communities: A New World Perspective,* edited by Marcello Canuto and Jason Yaeger, 210–30. Routledge, New York.
2000b   Beyond the Valley: Interaction, Image, and Identity in the Virginia Blue Ridge. In *After the Backcountry: Nineteenth-Century Life in the Valley of Virginia,* edited by W. Hofstra and K. Koons. 145–66. Knoxville, University of Tennessee Press.
2000c   Urbanism in the Colonial South: The Development of Seventeenth-Century Jamestown. In *Archaeology of Southern Urban Landscapes,* edited by Amy Young, 52–68. Tuscaloosa, University of Alabama Press.
Horton, James Oliver
1998   Confronting Slavery and Revealing the "Lost Cause." In Slavery and Resistance, *CRM,* 21 (4): 14–16.
Houston, J. W., and J. D. Houston
1973   *Farewell to Manzanar.* Bantam Books, New York.
Hudson, J. Paul
1957   Jamestown Artisans and Craftsmen. *Antiques* 46(1): 47–50.

Hurry, Silas D., and Mark P. Leone
1998   Seeing: The Power of Town Planning in the Chesapeake. *Historical Archaeology* 32(4):31–59.
Jackson, Kenneth T., and Camilio Jose Vergura
1989   *Silent Cities: The Evolution of the American Cemetery.* Princeton Architectural Press, New York.
James, T.
1987   *Exile Within: The Schooling of Japanese Americans, 1942–1945.* Harvard University Press, Cambridge.
Jensen, Richard, R. Eli Paul, and John Carter
1991   *Eyewitness at Wounded Knee.* University of Nebraska Press, Lincoln.
Johnson, Sam
1995   Prepared Statement of Congressman Sam Johnson before the Senate Committee on Rules and Administration Hearing on the Smithsonian Institution: Management Guidelines for the Future. *Federal News Service: Federal Information System Corp.* May 18 In the News.
Jones, Lynn
1999   Crystals and Conjuring in an Annapolis Household. *Maryland Archaeology,* 35(2): 1–8.
Jones, R. A.
1996   Whitewashing Manzanar. *Los Angeles Times* April 10:B2.
Josephy, Alvin, Jr.
1993   Wounded Knee: A History. In *Wounded Knee: Lest We Forget,* by Alvin Josephy, Jr., Trudy Thomas, and Jeanne Eder. Buffalo Bill Historical Center, Cody, Wyoming.
Josephy, Alvin, Jr., Trudy Thomas, and Jeanne Eder
1993   *Wounded Knee: Lest We Forget.* Buffalo Bill Historical Center, Cody, Wyoming.
Kammen, Michael
1991   *Mystic Chords of Memory: The Transformation of Tradition in American Culture.* Knopf, New York.
1997a *In the Past Lane: Historical Perspectives on American Culture.* Oxford University Press, New York.
1997b Public History and the Uses of Memory. *Public Historian* 19(2):49–52.
Katz, William Loren, ed.
1969   [1940] *The Negro in Virginia.* Compiled by the Writers Program of the Work Projects Administration. Arno Press and New York Times, New York. Hampton Institute, Hastings House Publishers, New York.
Kehoe, Alice Beck
1989   *The Ghost Dance: Ethnohistory and Revitalization.* Holt, Rinehart, and Winston, Chicago.
Keim, De B. Randolph
1873   A Guide to the Potomac River, Chesapeake Bay, and James River. *Alexandria [Virginia] Gazette,* June 11:42–45.

Kelso, Gerald K., Stephen Mrozowski, Andrew C. Edwards, Marley R. Brown III, Audrey J. Horning, Gregory J. Brown, and Jeremiah Dandoy

1995 Differential Pollen Preservation in a Seventeenth-Century Refuse Pit, Jamestown Island, Virginia. *Historical Archaeology* 29(2):43–54.

Kelso, William M.

1986 Mulberry Row: Slave Life at Thomas Jefferson's Monticello. *Archaeology* 39(5):28–35.

Kipp, Woody

1994 "The Eagles I Fed Who Did Not Love Me." *American Indian Culture and Research Journal* 18(4):213–32.

Klingelhofer, E.

1987 Aspects of Early Afro-American Material Culture: Artifacts from the Slave Quarters at Garrison Plantation, Maryland. *Historical Archaeology* 21 (2):112–19.

Kong, Lily

1993 Ideological Hegemony and the Political Symbolism of Religious Buildings in Singapore. *Environment and Planning: Society and Space* 11:23–45.

Kong, Lily, and Brenda S. A. Yeoh

1994 Urban Conservation in Singapore: A Survey of State Policies and Popular Attitudes. *Urban Studies* 31 (2):247–65.

Larrabee, John

1997 Blacks Claim Share of Civil War Glory: The Growing Number of Blacks in Reenactment Groups Recalls the Sacrifices of Thousands Who Fought and Died. *USA Today* June 2:3A.

Lauerhass, Ludwig

1997 *The Shaw Memorial: A Celebration of an American Masterpiece.* Eastern National, Conshohocken, Pennsylvania.

Lazarus, Edward

1991 *Black Hills, White Justice: The Sioux Nation Versus the United States, 1775 to the Present.* HarperCollins, New York.

Leff, Mark H.

1995 Revisioning United States Political History. *American Historical Review* 100:833.

Leone, Mark P.

1981 Archaeology's Relationship to the Present and the Past. In *Modern Material Culture and the Archaeology of Us,* edited by Richard A. Gould and Michael B. Schiffer, 5–14. Academic Press, New York.

1984 Interpreting Ideology in Historical Archaeology: Using the Rules of Perspective in the William Paca Gardens in Annapolis, Maryland. In *Ideology, Power, and Prehistory,* edited by Daniel Miller and Christopher Tilley, 25–36. Cambridge University Press, New York.

1992   Epilogue: The Productive Nature of Material Culture and Archaeology. In *Meanings and Uses of Material Culture,* edited by Barbara J. Little and Paul A. Shackel. *Historical Archaeology* 26(3):130–33.

Leone, Mark P., Parker B. Potter, Jr., and Paul A. Shackel
1987   Toward a Critical Archaeology. *Current Anthropology* 28(3):283–302.

Lerner, Adam J.
1997   Black Aggie, Cultural Cryptanalysts, and the Politics of Locality. *LINK* 2:41–51.

Leslie, Linda, and Bill Choyke
1991   Westmoreland Washingtoniana. *Washington Post,* February 15:N68.

Lewis, Kenneth E., Jr.
1975   The Jamestown Frontier: An Archaeological Study of Colonization. Ph.D. dissertation, University of Oklahoma, Norman.

Lewis, Stephen Johnson
1994   [1942] *Undaunted Faith: The Life Story of Jennie Dean, Missionary, Teacher, Crusader, Builder. Founder of the Manassas Industrial School.* Manassas Museum, Manassas, Virginia. Circuit Press, Catlett, Virginia.

Lifton, R. J., and G. Mitchell
1995   *Hiroshima in America: Fifty Years of Denial.* Putnam, New York.

Lindgren, James M.
1993   *Preserving the Old Dominion: Historic Preservation and Virginia Traditionalism.* University Press of Virginia, Charlottesville.

Linenthal, Edward T.
1993   *Sacred Ground: Americans and Their Battlefields.* University of Illinois Press, Urbana.
1997   Problems and Promises in Public History. *Public Historian* 19(2):45–47.

Linenthal, Edward, and Tom Engelhardt
1996   *History Wars: The Enola Gay and Other Battles for the American Past.* Holt, New York.

Little, Barbara J.
1994   People with History: An Update on Historical Archaeology in the United States. *Journal of Archaeological Method and Theory* 1(1):5–40.

Little, Barbara J., and Paul A. Shackel
1992   Post-Processual Approaches to Meanings and Uses of Material Culture. *Historical Archaeology* 26(3):5–11.

Loose, Cindy
1995   They Got the Vote, but Not the Rotunda. *Washington Post,* August 19:A1.

Love, Alice A.
1995   Latest Round in War of the Statue Pits Warner against GOP Women. *Roll Call,* October 5:3.
1996   Women's Groups to Raise $75,000 to Move the Statue. *Roll Call* February 19:6.

Lowenthal, David
  1968   The American Scene. *Geographical Review* 58(1):61–88.
  1975   Past Time, Present Place: Landscape and Memory. *Geographical Review* 65(1):1–36.
  1985   *The Past Is a Foreign Country.* Cambridge University Press, Cambridge, England.
  1996   *Possessed by the Past: The Heritage Crusade and the Spoils of History.* Free Press, New York.
  1997   History and Memory. *Public Historian* 19(2):31–39.
  1998   *The Heritage Crusade and the Spoils of History.* Cambridge University Press, London.
Luvass, Jay, and Harold Nelson, eds.
  1996   *Guide to the Battle of Antietam: The Maryland Campaign.* University Press of Kansas, Lawrence.
Lyman, Stanley David
  1991   *Wounded Knee 1973.* Edited by June Lyman, Floyd O'Neil, and Susan Mckay. University of Nebraska Press, Lincoln.
Lynch, Kevin
  1972   *What Time Is This Place?* MIT Press, Cambridge.
MacCannell, Dean
  1976   *The Tourist: A New Theory of the Leisure Class.* Schocken Books, New York.
Maier, Charles
  1993   A Surfeit of Memory? Reflections on History, Melancholy, and Denial. *History and Memory* 5 (Fall/Winter):136–52.
Marquet, Jacques
  1993   Objects as Instruments, Objects as Signs. In *History from Things: Essays on Material Culture,* edited by Steven Lubar and W. David Kingery, 30–40. Smithsonian Institution Press, Washington, D.C.
Martin-Perdue, N.
  1983   Case Study—On Eaton's Trail: A Genealogical Study of Virginia Basketmakers. In *Traditional Craftsmanship in America: A Diagnostic Report,* edited by J. C. Camp, 79–101. National Council for the Traditional Arts, Washington, D.C.
Martin Seibert, Erika K.
  2001   Exploring the Consumerism of a Free African-American Family: From the Civil War through the Jim Crow Eras, A Minimum Vessel Analysis from Manassas National Battlefield Park. In M. Parsons, *Archeological Investigation of the Robinson House, Site 44PW288: A Free African-American Domestic Site Occupied from the 1840s to the 1930s.* Regional Archeology Program, National Capital Region, U.S. Department of the Interior, National Park Service, Washington, D.C., and Harpers Ferry National Historical Parks.

Marx, Leo
1964   *The Machine in the Garden.* Oxford University Press, New York.

Masumoto, D. M.
1991   The Ghosts of Dec. 7 Still Haunt Thousands. *USA Today,* December 3:13A.

Mattes, M. J.
1952   *Report on the Historical Investigations of the Wounded Knee Battlefield Site, South Dakota.* U.S. Department of the Interior, Region 2, National Park Service, Omaha, Nebraska.

Matturi, John
1993   Windows in the Garden: Italian-American Memorialization and the American Cemetery. In *Ethnicity and the American Cemetery,* edited by Richard E. Meyer, 14–34. Bowling Green State University Popular Press, Bowling Green, Ohio.

May, Nina
1997   A Renaissance of Womanhood: The Founding Mothers Fought for More Than Equality. *Paradigm,* Spring:4–7.

Mayo, Edith
1980   Adelaide Johnson. In *Notable American Women,* volume 4, *The Modern Period,* edited by Carol Hurd Green and Barbara Sicherman, 380–81. Harvard University Press, Cambridge.

McClelland, L. F.
1998   Skyline Drive Historic District: A Meeting Place of Culture and Nature. *CRM* 21(1):13–15.

McGill, Greg
1995   *Building on the Past: A Guide to Archaeology and the Development Process.* Harvard University Press, Cambridge.

McGuire, Randall
1988   Dialogues with the Dead: Ideology and the Cemetery. In *The Recovery of Meaning,* edited by Mark P. Leone and Parker Potter, 435–80. Smithsonian Institution Press, Washington, D.C.

1997   *The Memorial: Women in Military Service for America Memorial Brochure.* Arlington National Cemetery, National Park Service, U.S. Department of the Interior, Washington, D.C.

McPherson, James M.
1969   Foreword to *A Brave Black Regiment: History of the Fifty-Fourth Regiment of Massachusetts Volunteer Infantry, 1863–1865,* by Luis F. Emilio. Arno Press and New York Times, New York.

1988   *Battle Cry of Freedom: The Civil War Era.* Oxford University Press, New York.

1999   A Debatable Picture of the Confederacy: Tenn. Museum Says Many Blacks Fought for South; Scholars Call Claim Bogus. *Washington Post,* December 27:A16.

Means, Russell
    1995   Where White Men Fear to Tread. St. Martin's Press, New York.
Meltzer, Milton, and Patricia Holland, eds.
    1982   Lydia Maria Child: Selected Letters, 1817–1880. University of Massachusetts Press, Amherst.
Merida, Kevin
    1997   A Vote against Suffrage Statue. Washington Post, April 4:A1.
Meyer, Richard
    1993   Strangers in a Strange Land: Ethnic Cemeteries in America. In Ethnicity and the American Cemetery, edited by Richard E. Meyer, 1–13. Bowling Green State University Popular Press, Bowling Green, Ohio.
Michaud, K.
    1998   Shenandoah National Park: Laboratory for Change. CRM 21(1):11–12.
Mill, John Stuart
    1869   The Subjection of Women. In Feminism: The Essential Historical Writings, edited by Miriam Schneir, 163–78. Vintage Books, New York.
Miller, Perry
    1953   The New England Mind: From Colony to Province. Harvard University Press, Cambridge.
Mitchell, Reid
    1995   A Northern Volunteer. In Divided Houses: Gender and the Civil War, edited by Catherine Clinton and Nina Silber, 43–54. Oxford University Press, Oxford.
Mondics, Chris
    1997   Black Women's Groups Fight Plan for Prominent Placement of Suffragist Statue Depicting Only White Women. Knight-Ridder/Tribune News Service, April 24:424–25.
Morris, Douglas K.
    1998   Foreword: Shenandoah-Managing Cultural Resources in a Natural Park. CRM 21(1):3.
Mullins, Paul Raymond
    1996   The Contradictions of Consumption: An Archaeology of African America and Consumer Culture, 1850–1930. Ph.D. dissertation, University of Massachusetts, Amherst.
    1999   Race and Affluence: An Archeology of African America and Consumer Culture. Kluwer Academic/Plenum Publishers.
Mungen, Donna
    1997   Let's Get the History and Our Statue Right. USA Today, April 25, A15 [cited October 3, 1997]. [Found at http://www.umi.com.]
Murfin, James V.
    1982   The Gleam of Bayonets, The Battle of Antietam and Robert E. Lee's Maryland Campaign, September, 1862. Louisiana State University Press, Baton Rouge.

Murry, Freeman H. M.
1916   *Emancipation and the Freed in American Sculpture: A Study in Interpretation.* Freeman Murry, Washington, D.C.

Nagata, D. K.
1993   *Legacy of Injustice: Exploring the Cross-Generational Impact of the Japanese American Internment.* Plenum Press, New York.

Nakashima, Ellen
1996   Plan to Expand Cemetery Angers Preservationists. *Washington Post,* June 22:B3, 5).

Nash, Gary B., Charlotte Crabtree, and Ross E. Dunn
1998   *History on Trial: Culture Wars and the Teaching of the Past.* Knopf, New York.

Nash, Roderick
1973   *Wilderness and the American Mind.* Yale University Press, New Haven.
1967   *The National Cyclopaedia of American Biography . . .* Vol. 19. University Microfilms, Ann Arbor, Michigan.

National Trust for Historic Preservation
1975   *Economic Benefits of Preserving Old Buildings.* Preservation Press, Washington, D.C.

Neihardt, John G.
1961   *Black Elk Speaks: Being the Life Story of a Holy Man of the Oglala Sioux.* University of Nebraska Press, Lincoln.

Nelligan, Murray
1953   *Old Arlington: The Story of the Lee Mansion National Memorial.* U.S. Department of the Interior, National Park Service, Washington, D.C.
1961   *Custis-Lee Mansion: The Robert E. Lee Memorial, Handbook Series No. Six.* U.S. Department of the Interior, National Park Service, Washington, D.C.

Neustadt, Richard, and Ernst May
1986   *Thinking in Time: The Uses of History for Decision-makers.* Free Press, New York.

Newcomb, Robert M.
1979   *Planning the Past: Historical Landscape Resources and Recreation.* Archon Books, Hamden, Connecticut.

Newhall, Nancy
1957   *A Contribution to the Heritage of Every American: The Conservation Activities of John D. Rockefeller, Jr.* Knopf, New York.

New York Daily Tribune
1906   Lincoln Cabin Goes, Started to Kentucky. June 7.

New York Times
1903   Lincoln and Davis Cabin. March 23:14.
1909   President at Lincoln Farm. February 11:5.
1909   Roosevelt Praises Lincoln as Fighter. February 13:3.

Nishimoto, R. S.
1995 *Inside an American Concentration Camp: Japanese American Resistance at Poston, Arizona.* Edited by L. R. Hirabayashi. University of Arizona Press, Tucson.

Noble, P.
1995 *Judgement at the Smithsonian.* Marlowe and Company, New York.

Notter, Finegold and Alexander, Inc.
1988 *Baltimore Waterfront Study.* Charles Center Inner Harbor Management, Baltimore, Maryland.

Nye, David E.
1997 *Narratives and Spaces: Technology and the Construction of American Culture.* Columbia University Press, New York.

Official Catalogue, Tennessee Centennial
1897 Knoxville, Tennessee.

Official Catalogue and Guide Book to the Pan-American Exposition, with Maps of Exposition and Illustrations
1901 Charles Ahrhart, Buffalo, New York.

Okihiro, G. Y.
1996 *Whispered Silences: Japanese Americans and World War II.* University of Washington Press, Seattle.

Park Service Handbook: Lee Mansion National Memorial
1941 U.S. Department of the Interior, National Park Service, Washington, D.C.

Parker Pearson, Michael
1982 Mortuary Practices, Society, and Ideology: An Ethnoarchaeological Study. In *Symbolic Structural Archaeology,* edited by Ian Hodder, 99–114. Cambridge University Press, Cambridge.

Parman, Donald L.
1994 *Indians and the American West in the Twentieth Century.* Indiana University Press, Indianapolis.

Parsons, Mia T., ed.
2001 *Archeological Investigation of the Robinson House, Site 44PW288: A Free African-American Domestic Site Occupied from the 1840s to the 1930s.* Regional Archeology Program, National Capital Region, National Park Service, Washington, D.C., and Harpers Ferry National Historical Park.

Patrell, Dan
1997 Making Yesterdays Matter Today. *Frederick Magazine,* May:21–22.

Patten, Drake
1992 Mankala and Minkisi: Possible Evidence of African American Folk Beliefs and Practices. *African American Archaeology* 6:5–7.

Perdue, C., and N. J. Martin-Perdue
1979– Appalachian Fables and Facts: A Case Study of the Shenandoah National
1980 Park Removals. *Appalachian Journal* 7:84–104.

1991   To Build a Wall around These Mountains. *Magazine of Albemarle County History* 49:49–71.

Perusek, Anne M.
1997   Ground Swell of Support Raises Monument from Crypt to Rotunda. *Magazine of the Society of Women Engineers* July/August:10–12.

Peterson, Gloria
1968   *An Administrative History of Abraham Lincoln Birthplace National Historic Site.* U.S. Department of the Interior, National Park Service, Washington, D.C.

Peterson, Larry
1997   Pullman Strike Pictures Molding Public Perceptions in the 1890s by New Visual Communication. *Labor's Heritage,* Spring:14–36.

Peterson, Merrill D.
1994   *Lincoln in American Memory.* Oxford University Press, New York.

Pogue, Dennis J., and Esther C. White
1994   Reanalysis of Features and Artifacts Excavated at George Washington's Birthplace, Virginia. *Quarterly Bulletin of the Archaeological Society of Virginia* 49(1):32–45.

Pollock, G. F.
1960   *Skyland.* Chesapeake Book Company, Berryville, Virginia.

Potter, Parker B., Jr.
1994   *Public Archaeology in Annapolis: A Critical Approach to History in Maryland's Ancient City.* Smithsonian Institution Press. Washington, D.C.

Radford-Ruether, Rosemary
1996   Fight for Women's Vote Key to Nation's Identity. *National Catholic Reporter* 33(4):22.

Reeder, J., and C. Reeder
1991   *Shenandoah Secrets: The Story of the Park's Hidden Past.* Potomac Appalachian Trail Club, Washington, D.C.

Reeves, Matthew B.
1998   *Views of a Changing Landscape: An Archeological and Historical Investigation of Sudley Post Office (44PW294), Manassas National Battlefield Park Manassas, Virginia.* Occasional Report No. 14, Regional Archaeology Program, National Capital Region, National Park Service, U.S. Department of the Interior, Washington, D.C.

In   Generations of Conflict: African-Americans at Manassas National Battpress   tlefield Park. In Remembering Conflict on the American Landscape, edited by P. A. Shackel. *Historial Archaeology.*

Rettaliata, Janis
1992   *The Baltimore Ballpark Project: The Creation of a Baseball Stadium.* Self-published, Baltimore.

Rhodes, Diane Lee

1983 *Archaeological Investigations at Fabbri Memorial, Acadia National Park, Bar Harbor, Maine.* U.S. Department of the Interior, National Park Service, Denver Service Center, Northeast Team, Denver.

Richardson, Miles

1989 The Artifact as Abbreviated Act: A Social Interpretation of Material Culture. In *The Meaning of Things: Material Culture and Symbolic Expression,* edited by Ian Hodder, 172–77. Unwin Hyman, London.

Richmond, Peter

1993 *Ballpark: Camden Yards and the Building of an American Dream.* Simon and Schuster, New York.

Rieley, William D., and Roxanne S. Brouse

1989 *Historic Resource Study for the Carriage Road System, Acadia National Park, Mount Desert Island, Maine.* Prepared for the U.S. Department of the Interior, National Park Service, North Atlantic Regional Office. Rieley and Associates, Landscape Architects, Charlottesville, Virginia.

Rogers, P.

1997 W.W. II Internment Camp Survivors Upset by Lack of Progress on Memorial. *San Jose Mercury News,* March 10:A1.

Roosevelt, Franklin Delano

1938 *Public Papers and Addresses.* Random House, New York.

Ross, C.

1991 Return to Manzanar. *Americana* 19(1):55–58.

Ruffins, Faith Davis

1992 Mythos, Memory, and History: African-American Preservation Efforts, 1820–1990. In *Museums and Communities: The Politics of Public Culture,* edited by Ivan Karp, Christine Mullen Kreamer, and Steven D. Lavine, 506–611. Smithsonian Institution Press, Washington, D.C.

Rydell, Robert W.

1984 *All the World's a Fair: Visions of Empire at American International Expositions, 1876–1916.* University of Chicago Press, Chicago.

Saint-Gaudens, Homer

1913 *The Reminiscences of Augustus Saint-Gaudens.* 2 vols. Century, New York.

Sanchez, Carlos

1989 Another Unknown Soldier. *Washington Post,* May 28:B1.

Savage, Kirk

1997 *Standing Soldier, Kneeling Slaves: Race, War, and Monument in Nineteenth-Century America.* Princeton University Press, Princeton, New Jersey.

Sax, Joseph L.

1980 *Mountains Without Handrails: Reflections on the National Parks.* University of Michigan Press, Ann Arbor.

Scaife, Lauriston L.
1926   *The Lincoln Cabin.* Reprinted from Stone and Webster Journal; original in files of the Captain Robert Bennet Forbes Museum and Library, Milton, Massachusetts.

Schneir, Miriam, ed.
1992   *Feminism: The Essential Historical Writings.* Vintage Books, New York.

Schwartz, Barry
1982   The Social Context of Commemoration: A Study in Collective Memory. *Social Forces* 61:374–402.

1990   The Reconstruction of Abraham Lincoln. In *Collective Remembering,* edited by David Middleton and Derek Edwards, 95–104. Sage, London.

Sears, Stephen W.
1983   *Landscape Turned Red: The Battle of Antietam.* Popular Library, New York.

Seidman, Steven
1993   Identity and Politics in a "Postmodern" Gay Culture: Some Historical and Conceptual Notes. In *Fear of a Queer Planet: Queer Politics and Social Theory,* edited by Michael Warner, 105–42. University of Minnesota Press, Minneapolis.

Sellars, Richard West
1997   *Preserving Nature in the National Parks: A History.* Yale University Press, New Haven, Connecticut.

Shackel, Paul A.
1996   *Culture Change and the New Technology: An Archaeology of the Early American Industrial Era.* Plenum Press, New York.

1997   A Long-Overdue Salute: African-American Troops Who Fought in the Civil War Are Being Honored in a National Monument. *Atlanta Journal-Constitution,* November 2:C2.

2000   Craft to Wage Labor: Agency and Resistance in American Historical Archaeology. In *Agency Theory in Archaeology,* edited by John Robb and Marcia-Anne Dobres, 232–46. Routledge Press, London.

Shackel, Paul A., and Barbara J. Little
1992   Post-Processual Approaches to Meanings and Uses of Material Culture in Historical Archaeology. In Meanings and Uses of Material Culture, edited by Barbara J. Little and Paul A. Shackel. *Historical Archaeology* 26(3):5–11.

Shanks, Michael
1990   Reading the Signs: Responses to Archaeology after Structuralism. In *Archaeology after Structuralism,* edited by Ian Bapty and Tim Yates, 294–310. Routledge Press, London.

Shanks, Michael, and Christopher Tilley
1987   *Re-Constructing Archaeology: Theory and Practice.* Cambridge University Press, Cambridge.

Shapiro, H.

1966 A Strange Land and Peculiar People: The Discovery of Appalachia, 1870–1920. Ph.D. dissertation, Rutgers University, New Brunswick, New Jersey.

1978 *Appalachia on Our Mind.* University of North Carolina Press, Chapel Hill.

Shepard, Paul

1991 *Man in the Landscape: A Historic View of the Esthetics of Nature.* Texas A&M University Press, College Station.

Sherman, M., and T. R. Henry

1933 *Hollow Folk.* Virginia Book Company. Berryville, Virginia.

Shopes, Linda

1997 Building Bridges between Academic and Public History. *Public Historian* 19 (2):53–56.

Singleton, Theresa

1990 The Archaeology of the Plantation South: A Review of Approaches and Goals. *Historical Archaeology* 24 (4):70–77.

1991 The Archaeology of Slave Life. In *Before Freedom Came: African-American Life in the Antebellum South,* edited by Edward D. C. Campbell, Jr., and Kym S. Rice, 155–75. Museum of the Confederacy, Richmond.

Sloane, David Charles

1991 *The Last Great Necessity: Cemeteries in American History.* Johns Hopkins University Press, Baltimore.

Smith, Curt

1997 The Return of the Old Style Ballparks. *American Enterprise* 8 (2):52–57.

Smith, G. S.

1986 Racial Nativism and Origins of Japanese Ameican Relocation. In *Japanese Americans: From Relocation to Redress,* edited by R. Daniels, S. Taylor, and H. Kitano, 79–85. University of Utah Press, Salt Lake City.

Smith, Henry Nash

1950 *Virgin Land: The American West as Symbol and Myth.* Harvard University Press, Cambridge.

Snell, Charles W., and Sharon A. Brown

1986 *Antietam National Battlefield and National Cemetery: An Administrative History.* U.S. Department of the Interior, National Park Service, Washington, D.C.

Spear, Joseph E.

1992 Oriole Park at Camden Yards. Foreword to *The Baltimore Ballpark Project: The Creation of a Baseball Stadium,* by J. Rettaliata. Self-published. Baltimore.

Spector, Janet

1993 *What This Awl Means.* Minnesota Historical Press, St. Paul.

Stanley, J.
1994   *I Am an American: A True Story of Japanese Internment.* Crown, New York.

Stanton, Elizabeth Cady
1848   Declaration of Sentiments. In *Feminism: The Essential Historical Writings,* edited by Miriam Shneir, 77–82. Vintage Books, New York.

Stanton, Robert
1998   Foreword. *CRM, Slavery and Resistance* 21 (4):3.

Stover, John F.
1987   *History of the Baltimore and Ohio Railroad.* Purdue University Press, West Lafayette, Indiana.

Stringer, L.
1998   *Grand Central Winter: Stories from the Street.* Washington Square Press, New York.

Suter, S. H.
1995   Basketry and Invisible Skills: Gaps in the Archaeological Record. In *Upland Archaeology in the East,* compiled by Michael B. Barber, Eugene B. Barfield, Harry A. Jaeger, and William Jack Hranicky, 126–34. U.S. Department of Agriculture, Forest Service—Southern Division, Special Publications 38 (5). Archaeological Society of Virginia, Richmond.

Taft, Lorado
1969 [1924] *The History of American Sculputre.* Arno Press, New York.

Taylor, S. C.
1993   *Jewel of the Desert: Japanese American Internment at Topaz.* University of California Press, Berkeley.

Thomas, George E.
1996   Resolving the Past. *Los Angeles Times,* July 14:M1.

Thompson, Benjamin F.
1903   *An Authentic History of the Douglass Monument.* Rochester Herald Press, Rochester, New York.

Tilberg, Frederick
1960   *Antietam National Battlefield Site, Maryland.* U.S. Department of the Interior, National Park Service Series 31, Washington, D.C.

Trigger, Bruce
1989   *A History of Archaeological Thought.* Cambridge University Press, Cambridge.

Unrau, H. D.
1996   *The Evacuation and Relocations of Persons of Japanese Ancestry during World War II: A Historical Study of the Manzanar War Relocation Centery.* 2 volumes. U.S. Department of the Interior, National Park Service, Washington, D.C.

URS Greiner, Inc.
1998   *Management Summary: Archaeological Investigations at Antietan National Battlefield, Sharpsburg, Maryland.Prepared for: National Capital Area National Park Service.* URS Grenier, Florence, New Jersey.

U.S. Congress. House of Representatives
1929   Committee on Military Affairs. Transfer of National Military Parks: Hearings before the Committee of Military Affairs. 70th Congress, 2nd Session, January 31, S4173.

1991   Committee on Interior and Insular Affairs. Establishing the Manzanar Historic Cite in the State of California, and for Other Purposes. 102nd Congress 1st session, HR 593.

U.S. Congress. Senate
1990   Select Committee on Indian Affairs. Wounded Knee Memorial and Historic Site Little Big Horn National Monument Battlefield: Hearing before the Select Committee on Indian Affairs.

1993   Committee on Energy and Natural Resources. Truman Farm Home; Wounded Knee National Memorial; Bodie Bowl, Preservation of Taliesin Site; and Alaska Peninsula Subsurface Consolidation Act: Hearing before the Subcommittee on Public Lands, National Parks and Forests.

U.S. Department of the Interior, National Park Service (USDOI)
1941   *Antietam, National Battlefield Site, Maryland.* U.S. Government Printing Office, Washington, D.C.

1958   *Antietam National Battelfied Site, Maryland.* By Harry W. Doust, superintendent, and Robert L. Lagemann, historian, Antietam National Battlefield Site. Printed for the Civil War Round Table of the District of Columbia, Washington, D.C.

1977   *Proposed Antietam National Battlefield Site, Maryland. Submitted as an Accompanying Part of the Communication to the Secretary of the Interior.* U.S. Government Printing Office, Washington, D.C.

1988   *Antietam National Battlefield: Analysis of the Visible Landscape.* U.S. Government Printing Office, Denver.

1990   *Alternatives: Antietam National Battlefield.* U.S. Government Printing Office, Washington, D.C.

1991   *The Wounded Knee Update, Cankpe Opi Wonahuna.* Issue 1, September. U.S. Government Printing Office,Washington, D.C.

1992a   *General Management Plan, Acadia National Park, Maine.* North Atlantic Region. Boston.

1992b   *Summary General Management Plan and Final Environmental Impact Statement Antietam National Battlefield.* U.S. Government Printing Office, Denver.

1992c   *The Wounded Knee Update, Cankpe Opi Wonahuna.* Issue 2, March. U.S. Government Printing Office, Washington, D.C.

Unrau, H. D.
1996   *The Evacuation and Relocation of Persons of Japanese Ancestry during World War II: A Historical Study of the Manzanar War Relocation Center.* 2 vols. U.S. Department of the Interior, National Park Service, Washington, D.C.

Utley, Robert M.
1961   *The Last Days of the Sioux Nation.* Yale University Press, New Haven.
1993   Foreword to *Sacred Ground,* by Edward T. Linenthal, ix–xi. University of Illinois Press, Urbana.

Van Horn, Lawrence F., Allen R. Hagood, and Gregory J. Sorensen
1996   Wounded Knee: 1890 and Today: A Special Resource Study for Planning Alternatives. *Landscape and Urban Planning* 36:135–58.

Vosburgh, Frederick G.
1994   Shrines of Each Patriot's Devotion. *National Geographic,* January, 51–82.

Wachtel, Nathan
1986   Memory and History, Inrocution. *History and Anthropology* 2 (October):2–11.

Weinberger, J. A.
1858   The Home of Washington at Mount Vernon. *Williamsburg Virginia Gazette,* October 2:54.

Wells, Camille
1994   Social and Economic Aspects of Eighteenth-Century Housing on the Northern Neck of Virginia. Ph.D. dissertation, College of William and Mary, Williamsburg, Virginia.

Wheeler, Linda
1996   Remembering Forgotten Heroes. *Washington Post,* September 11:C1.

Will, George F.
1997   Ladies in the Rotunda. *Washington Post,* March 23.

Williams, George W.
1969   *A History of the Negro Troops in the War of the Rebellion, 1861–1865.* [Originally published in 1888.] Negro University Press, New York.

Wilson, Alexander
1992   *The Culture of Nature: North American Landscape from Disneyland to the Exxon Valdez.* Blackwell, Cambridge, Massachusetts.

Wilson, Chris
1997   *The Myth of Santa Fe: Creating a Modern Regional Tradition.* University of New Mexico Press, Albuquerque.

Wylie, A.
1993   Invented Lands/Discovered Pasts: The Westward Expansion of Myth and History. *Historical Archaeology* 27 (4):1–19.

Yonge, Samuel H.
1903   *The Site of Old Jamestown.* Association for the Preservation of Virginia Antiquities, Richmond.

Yowell, C. L.
  1926 *A History of Madison County, Virginia*. Virginia Publishing House, Strasbourg, Virginia.
Zenzen, Joan
  1995 *Battling for Manassas: The Fifty-Year Preservation Struggle at Manassas National Battlefield Park*. History Associates, Rockville, Maryland.

About the Contributors

Joy Beasley is the research archaeologist for the cooperative program between the University of Maryland and the National Park Service. She graduated from the MAA program in the Department of Anthropology, University of Maryland, and has published several articles on memory and archaeology.

Gail Brown received his undergraduate degree from Purdue University and a master's degree in applied anthropology from the University of Maryland. He is currently the director of the Veraestau Historic Center, Historic Landmarks Foundation of Indiana.

Laurie Burgess is a museum specialist in the Repatriation Office, National Museum of Natural History, Smithsonian Institution. Her research interests include historical archaeology, and she specializes in the material culture of the nineteenth century.

Janice Dubel has taught English as a second language on the island of Oahu as well as in Tokyo. She is active in human rights issues in Asia and is associated with the State Department.

Erin Donovan is an archaeologist and a museum consultant. She is responsible for creating exhibits related to tourism and the regional development of Maryland. She is the former registrar for the Baltimore Museum of Art.

Audrey J. Horning has directed archaeological excavations at Jamestown and in Shenandoah National Park with the Colonial Williamsburg Foundation for the National Park Service. She is currently in charge of the postgraduate program in historical archaeology at the School of Archaeology and Paleoecology at Queen's University of Belfast in Northern Ireland. She is pursuing the comparative archaeology of British expansion in North America and Ireland.

Edward T. Linenthal is Edward M. Penson Professor of Religion and American Culture at the University of Wisconsin, Oshkosh. He is the author of *Sacred Ground: Americans and Their Battlefields* and *Preserving Memory: The Struggle to Create America's Holocaust Museum* and the coeditor, with Tom Engelhardt, of *History Wars: The* Enola Gay *and Other Battles for the American Past.* His next book, forthcoming in 2001, is *The Unfinished Bombing: Oklahoma City in American Memory.*

Matthew Palus is working toward completing his doctoral degree in the Department of Anthropology, Columbia University. He acquired an interest in the meaning of road systems while working for the Arizona Department of Transportation as a consulting archaeologist. He has published several articles related to the industrialization of the United States.

Dwight Pitcaithley has been the chief historian for the National Park Service since 1995. He is former president of the National Council for Public History and has published primarily on issues related to historic preservation and the interpretation of historic sites.

Erika K. Martin Seibert is the archaeologist for the National Register of Historic Places. She is a Ph.D. candidate in the American Studies Department, University of Maryland. She has published several articles on the development of race and African-American archaeology.

Paul A. Shackel is an associate professor in the Department of Anthropology, University of Maryland. He is author of *Personal Discipline and Material Culture* (1993), *Culture Change and the New Technology* (1996), and *Archaeology and Created Memory: Public History in a National Park* (2000). He has also edited four volumes on the meanings and uses of material culture.

Martha Temkin is a historical archaeologist for the National Park Service's Cultural Landscape Program in the National Capital Region. Her research interests include historical archaeology, the history of vernacular landscapes, and geographical information system applications.

Courtney Workman serves as the program coordinator at the National Coalition for Cancer Survivorship, where she conducts program evaluation and coordinates outreach efforts for cancer survivors. She is currently pursuing a master's degree in public policy, focusing on gender and social policy.

Index

Abraham Lincoln National Birthplace Historic Site (Kentucky), 241; authenticity and, 249–52

Acadia National Park (Maine), xii, 12, 178, 179–93; automobile roads at, 186; Brown Mountain Gate Lodge in, 187–88; carriage roads building at, 180, 181–84; created landscape of, 186–87; General Management Plan for, 189–91; Jordan Pond Gate Lodge in, 187–88; Lafayette National Park (1919) and, 182; Mount Desert Island and, 182; nostalgia and, 185, 187; John D. Rockefeller, Jr., and, 179–93; Sierra Club and, 191; Sieur de Monts National Monument (1916) and, 182; tourism at, 179, 181–87, 190

African-Americans: archaeological assemblages related to, 72–80; —Brownsville, Va., 75; —Nash, Va., 74–76, 79; —Robinson House, Va., 72–74, 79; —Sudley Post Office, Va., 75; Civil War and the memory of, 146–56; Manassas National Battlefield Park and, 68–80

Air Force Association, 7

American Indian Movement (AIM), 108–12

American Legion, 7

Antietam National Battlefield (Maryland), xii, 8, 10, 120; Dunkard church at, 126; early commemoration at, 123–25; establishment of, 124–25; General Management Plan of 1982 for, 128–29; — of 1992 for, 129–30; impact of Mission 66 on, 126–28; national cemetery at, 124–25, 131; postwar National Park Service management of, 125–26; 1970s

and 1980s park management of, 128; Sierra Club and, 172

Antiquities Act of 1906, 10, 177

Anti-Slavery Convention, 49

Anthony's List, 57–58

Appalachia, 5, 18, 23–24, 29–37

Arlington Historical Society, 172

Arlington House. *See* Robert E. Lee Memorial

Arlington National Cemetery (Virginia), xii, 9, 120, 159–73; creation of, 160–62; early landscape of, 162–64; gendered space and, 169–71; marginalized groups and, 169–72; National Park Service interpretation of, 164–69; sacred space and, 166–69

Association for the Preservation of Virginia Antiquities, 31

authenticity, 179–93

Babe Ruth Museum, 224

Baltimore City Planning Commission, 225

Big Foot Memorial Ride, 112–13

Bull Run. *See* Manassas National Battlefield Park

Camden Station, Maryland, 222, 226

Camden Yards, Maryland, xii, 12, 178, 221–36; archaeology and interpretation at, 225; history of, 222–23; labor unrest at, 223, 225, 230; meaning and symbolism of, 227–35; modern development at 223–25; Ruth Saloon site at, 224, 234

Chickamauga National Military Park (Tennessee), 10

Civil Conservation Corps (CCC), 21, 25